Lecture Notes in Educational Technology

The series *Lecture Notes in Educational Technology* (LNET), has established itself as a medium for the publication of new developments in the research and practice of educational policy, pedagogy, learning science, learning environment, learning resources etc. in information and knowledge age, – quickly, informally, and at a high level.

More information about this series at http://www.springer.com/series/11777

J. Michael Spector · Vivekanandan Kumar
Alfred Essa · Yueh-Min Huang
Rob Koper · Richard A. W. Tortorella
Ting-Wen Chang · Yanyan Li
Zhizhen Zhang
Editors

Frontiers of Cyberlearning

Emerging Technologies for Teaching and Learning

Springer

Editors
J. Michael Spector
Department of Learning Technologies
University of North Texas
Denton, TX
USA

Vivekanandan Kumar
School of Computing and Information System
Athabasca University
Athabasca
Canada

Alfred Essa
Analytics and R&D
McGraw-Hill Education
Boston, MA
USA

Yueh-Min Huang
Department of Engineering Science
National Cheng Kung University
Tainan
Taiwan

Rob Koper
Open University in the Netherlands
Heerlen
The Netherlands

Richard A. W. Tortorella
School of Computing
University of Eastern Finland
Joensuu
Finland

Ting-Wen Chang
Smart Learning Institute
Beijing Normal University
Beijing
China

Yanyan Li
School of Educational Technology
Beijing Normal University
Beijing
China

Zhizhen Zhang
School of Educational Technology
Beijing Normal University
Beijing
China

ISSN 2196-4963 ISSN 2196-4971 (electronic)
Lecture Notes in Educational Technology
ISBN 978-981-13-0649-5 ISBN 978-981-13-0650-1 (eBook)
https://doi.org/10.1007/978-981-13-0650-1

Library of Congress Control Number: 2018943385

This Springer imprint is published by the registered company Springer Nature Singapore Pte Ltd.
The registered company address is: 152 Beach Road, #21-01/04 Gateway East, Singapore 189721, Singapore

Contents

Learning Any Time, Anywhere: Big Educational Data from Smart Devices

Mark A. Riedesel and Patrick Charles

Abstract For many people, especially young people, a smartphone is a constant companion. Mobile apps which allow individuals to use a smart device to enhance their learning have the potential to be very useful for mastering basic educational material. In order to evaluate and enhance the effectiveness of such applications when deployed at large scale, an infrastructure designed specifically for the collection of educational analytics data from such mobile apps is required. We detail here a set of applications and their associated infrastructure which was developed to allow students in courses using digital textbooks to enhance their knowledge of the basic course content anywhere and anytime by using their smart device to do spaced practice of the knowledge components of a course. The power of current smart devices allows the entire application, including content and adaptive algorithm to be hosted and run locally on the user's smart device, so it functions fully even when no network connection is available. The infrastructure for the collection and analysis of the educational analytics data is entirely cloud-based, using AWS S3 for data collection and storage, and the Apache Spark parallel computing framework for data analysis. Thus, the entire system requires only laptop computers for the mobile developers who create the applications and this is also sufficient for the learning scientists who analyze the data. Both the data collection system and the data analysis system can scale to handle the data from many millions of users with no modification to their architecture. Similar architectures are now used for the Internet of Things (IOT) but have not yet been widely used for educational applications. These applications have currently been deployed to thousands of users' smart devices and analytics data is being received from these users' smart devices from a wide range of locations on several continents. In our highly connected world, this type of application will become much more common. We describe here the type of infrastructure, security, and analytic methods needed to use these apps to advance learning and learning science.

M. A. Riedesel (✉) · P. Charles
McGraw-Hill Education, 281 Summer Street, Boston, MA 02210, USA
e-mail: mark.riedesel@gmail.com

P. Charles
e-mail: patrick.charles@mheducation.com

J. M. Spector et al. (eds.), *Frontiers of Cyberlearning*, Lecture Notes in Educational Technology, https://doi.org/10.1007/978-981-13-0650-1_1

Keywords Spaced practice · Adaptive flashcards · Mobile learning
Messaging systems · Parallel computing · Cloud computing

1 Introduction

For many subjects, memorizing basic facts is an important first step in learning and mastering content. In learning a foreign language, for example, basic vocabulary must be memorized as an essential part of learning syntax and grammar. In medicine, it is still considered essential for doctors, nurses, medical assistants, and EMTs to have basic knowledge of anatomy and physiology, pharmacology, and medical terminology memorized for immediate recall in critical situations. Even for subjects which involve higher levels of cognition, retention of basic knowledge is commonly the foundation upon which higher levels of abstraction are built (Bloom, Engelhart, Furst, Hill, & Krathwohl, 1956).

Applications designed for long-term memorization are often conceptually based on models for human memory which grew out of early work on how memories decay with time but can be reinforced by repetition spaced in time (Ebbinghaus, 1885). Further research, particularly in the past 20 years, has shown that three related methods can help optimize the memorization of material: spaced practice (Cepeda, Vul, Rohrer, Wixted, & Pashler, 2008), active retrieval (Roediger & Karpicke, 2006; Karpicke & Roediger, 2008), and interleaving (Brown, Roedinger, & McDaniel, 2014).

Spaced practice is a method where material one wants to learn is repeated on a schedule designed to reinforce decaying memories. Ideally, an item (an atomic piece of knowledge) would be repeated just before it would otherwise be forgotten. Using very specific models for the forgetting process allows mathematical optimization methods to be employed to produce optimal schedules for spaced practice (Pavlik & Anderson, 2005; Pavlik & Anderson, 2008; Mozer & Lindsey, 2016; Settles & Meeder, 2016).

Active retrieval is the principle that requiring a learner to recall material in response to a challenge is more effective than re-reading material. This is true even when there is some active involvement when reading, such as highlighting the most important parts of a passage. Thus, requiring a learner to respond to a question is significantly more effective than having the learner re-read a text containing the same basic piece of knowledge. Questions can be in several modes such as multiple-choice single-answer, multiple-choice multi-answer, fill-in-the-blank, or matching.

Interleaving is a method where questions on different topics or subtopics are intermixed. It has been shown in learning arithmetic problems, for example, that mixing up different types of problems in practice sessions is more effective than concentrated drill on just one type (Rohrer & Taylor, 2007).

A learning program which can easily incorporate all three of these methods is through the use of flashcards. Flashcards always require active retrieval and can also be timed and sequenced to incorporate spaced practice and interleaving. Manual methods of doing this have been used at least since the 1970s (Leitner, 1972) but to implement a system which can optimize the user experience, a computer program is an especially effective way to accomplish this. In a computer-based flashcard system, algorithms can be employed to create schedules for spaced practice which incorporate the user's record of correct and incorrect responses, the subject matter of each question, and the timing of the appearance of each item.

Several such systems have been deployed over the past 25 years or so. These are typically designed for learning hundreds or thousands of facts overtimes extending over weeks, months, or years. Such applications include SuperMemo, Anki, Duolingo, Brainscape, FireCracker, and Memorang (http://www.supermemo.com, http://ankisrs.net, http://www.duolingo.com, http://www.brainscape.com, http://www.firecracker.me, http://www.memorangapp.com). Most of these applications require a web browser with an active network connection. Those which have self-contained mobile versions which can operate offline do not allow a centralized collection of user interaction data. More academically based applications which do allow this have not yet been widely deployed (Kam, Kumar, Jain, Mathur, & Canny, 2009; Pavlik, Kelly, & Maass, 2016).

With the smart devices currently available, it is possible to develop self-contained mobile applications which include all of the educational content and which have the software needed to adaptively schedule spaced practice completely independent of a central computational service. Such applications can generate user interaction data messages which can be sent to a central collection point. Such data is needed for learning scientists to evaluate student performance and to further refine scheduling algorithms. This allows users to make optimal use of their time in learning the material with these applications. As large datasets accumulate, such data will also be very valuable for advancing basic understanding of the learning process.

2 Mobile Practice of Course Content

The Higher Education division of McGraw-Hill Education (MHE) was interested in a way for students in a course using one of MHEs online, interactive textbooks, called SmartBooks (http://www.mheducation.com/highered/platforms/smartbook.html), to be able to use their smartphones to memorize some of the declarative knowledge presented in a title. They quickly realized that a mobile phone application which had been developed to allow candidates in India to study for the U.S. Medical Licensing Exam (USMLE), called StudyWise, could be adapted for this purpose.

This application was developed to utilize the existing homework questions from medically related titles and present them as flashcards on a smart mobile device. The application was entirely self-contained, with the content, the user interface, and the scheduling algorithm all entirely contained on the smart device. This allowed the application to function even when a network connection was not available, a requirement for use in areas with spotty WiFi or cellular coverage.

It was recognized that this software could be re-targeted to provide optimized practice of course material within the time frame of a college semester by modifying the scheduling algorithm to optimize for practice of dozens to hundreds of items over a few weeks or months rather than the USMLE application which was designed for study of thousands of items over the course of 1 to 2 years. By leveraging published research on learning and memory, a new algorithm was successfully developed which fit this use case (Riedesel, Zimmerman, Baker, Titchener, & Cooper, 2017).

2.1 Smart Device Mobile Applications

As currently deployed, each of eight separate content titles has its own IOS and Android app. Each app presents the homework questions in a title as an electronic flashcard, grouped by topic. The questions, known as probes or items, come from MHE's existing SmartBook database of probes. There are currently about 1500 SmartBook titles on a wide range of subjects. For all of these titles combined, there are some 2,350,000 distinct probes with almost three billion recorded answers for them from the web-browser-based SmartBook system.

In SmartBook, each probe is associated with a knowledge component called a Learning Objective (LO). The LOs are organized by topic, which in turn are related to the title's subject. In a course that uses a SmartBook title, the instructor creates an assignment for a specified set of LOs. Students see only probes associated with the LOs for that assignment, which they do online through a web browser.

StudyWise was designed as a mobile application which would allow students to practice all of the LOs in a title, organized by topic. The mobile nature of the applications allows users to learn and master material whenever they have a few spare moments and wherever they happen to be. The algorithm is designed to allow the learner to master each LO by repeated practice. Once an LO's associated probes have been answered correctly three times, it is considered learned.

The fact that it is entirely self-contained on the mobile device means that it can be used whenever the user has a few spare minutes. The pattern of session durations suggests shows that these applications are indeed being used primarily for a few minutes at a time, as can be seen in Fig. 1. This is rather different from the originally envisioned usage model, which was for dedicated 30 min sessions each day.

At present, there are separate IOS and Android apps for each of eight titles in subjects including Anatomy and Physiology, Medical Terminology, Psychology, Human Resources Management, American History, Majors Biology, Human Anatomy, and Medical Assisting Certification Prep.

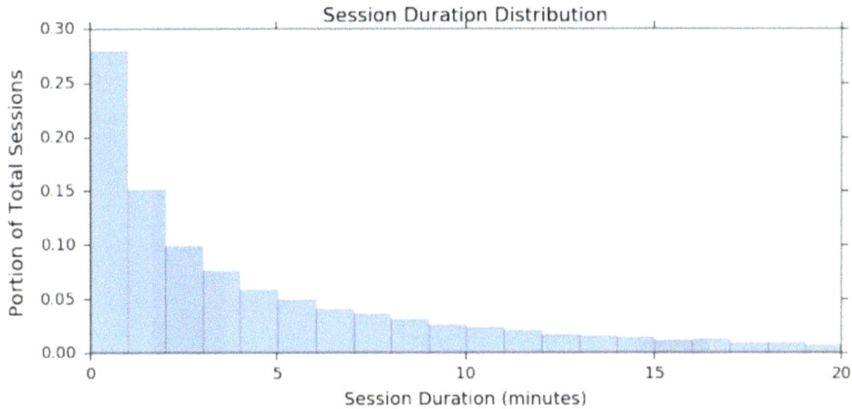

Fig. 1 A histogram of session duration times in minutes. More than one-fourth of all sessions are just one minute or less

2.2 *User Interface*

The StudyWise apps are all native applications specifically written for smartphones, with an IOS and an Android version available for each title. When a user opens an app for the first time, they are asked if they want to register with an email address. This information is used only to allow the synchronization of a user's progress in the app between two different devices, such as, for example, an iPhone and an iPad or between an Android phone and an iPhone. There is a hamburger menu in the upper left-hand corner of the screen which allows the user to (a) study, (b) get help, or (c) create an account for synching between devices and to also check for updates to the app's content.

To start a learning session, the user goes to the "Study" page, which gives the app's name at the top of the page and has two modes: "Targeted" which presents a list of Topics from which the user then chooses a topic from which questions will be drawn or "Review" which presents an overall measure of progress through the app and then will present questions from the set of Topics a user has previously studied (Fig. 2).

Once a topic is selected, the algorithm selects the first LO and one of that LO's probes is then chosen at random. This first probe is then displayed on the next screen. The question presented will be one of several types found in SmartBook: multiple-choice single-answer (as shown in Fig. 3), fill-in-the-blank, multiple-choice multi-answer, matching, matching-rank, or deconstruction (a special type for medical terminology).

At the bottom of the page, a question about the learner's confidence about their knowledge of the question appears: "Do you know the answer?", with the two possible choices "Yes, I know it" or "I'm unsure". The user must answer this question in

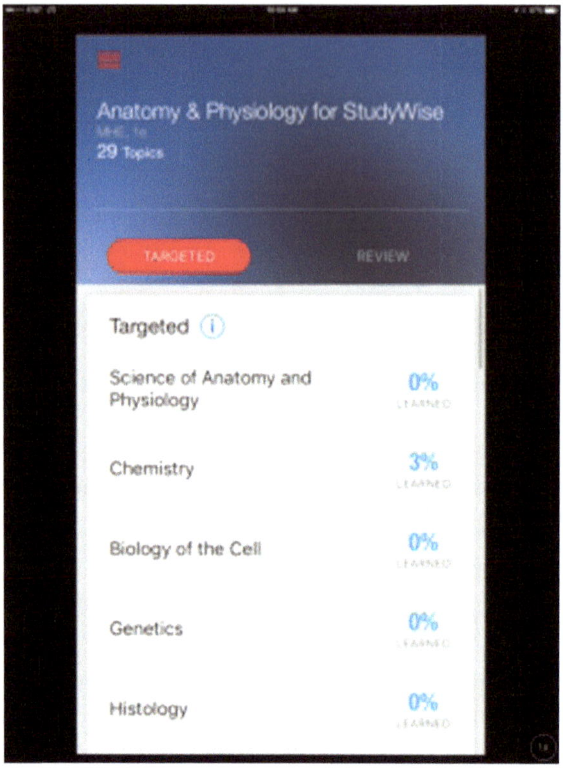

Fig. 2 The Topic selection page for the IOS anatomy and physiology for StudyWise app, with targeted mode selected

order to move on to the next page. For fill-in-the-blank, matching, matching-rank, and deconstruction questions, answering the confidence question submits the answer for grading.

For multiple-choice single-answer and multiple-choice multi-answer, the next page is the answer selection page (Fig. 4). For this case, the user can then either scroll back to the question page and update their confidence after seeing the possible answers (after which the answer page is again displayed) or simply select their answer(s) from those shown.

Once the user's answer is submitted, the answer is checked against the correct one and an answer response page is then shown (Fig. 5). This page reiterates the user's answer and indicated confidence, whether or not the answer was correct, and then gives additional background information on the question's content. The level of this additional information varies from question to question depending upon how much such background the author of the SmartBook probe included when it was originally created.

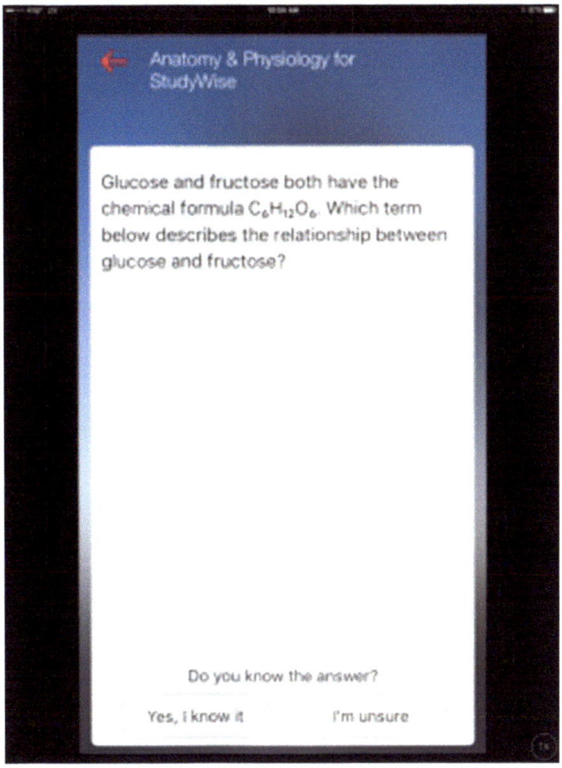

Fig. 3 The question presentation page

The user then can select the "NEXT" button at the bottom of the page to move on to a new LO's probe chosen by the algorithm or the user can hit the back arrow in the upper left-hand corner to return to the Topic selection page, ending that session. At that point, the user can again choose a Topic or can hit their device's "Home" button to exit the application.

2.3 Algorithm Self-contained Within the Smart Device

A key element of effective memorization is repeating an item often enough for it to be remembered. However, we do not want to waste the learner's time by repeating items already well learned. The algorithm used in StudyWise is a proprietary one that uses a mathematical algorithm which has adjustable parameters that vary the appearance time of the questions associated with each LO. This spacing also depends on whether or not an LO's previous question was answered correctly or not, if this was not the first appearance of that LO. For an LO to be considered learned, a total of three correct answers to that LO's associated questions is required.

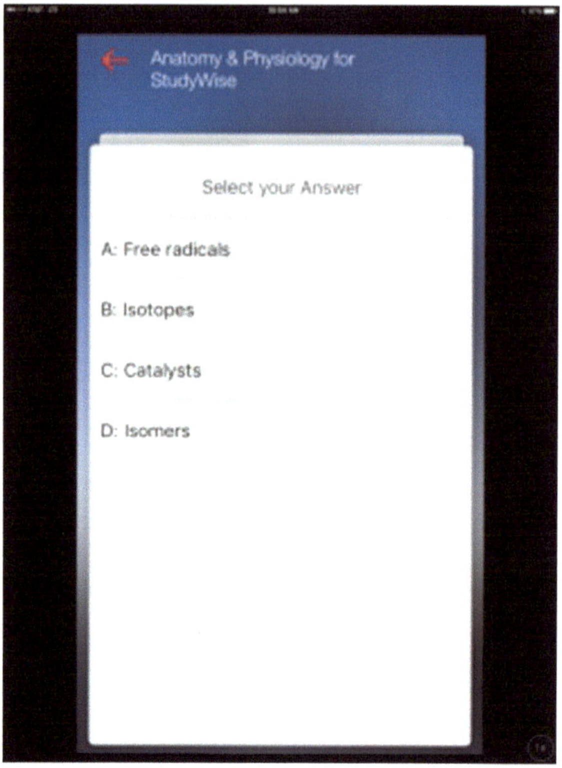

Fig. 4 The answer selection page for multiple-choice questions

When an LO first appears, it will be repeated frequently until the first correct answer is given. After this, the LO is repeated somewhat less frequency, and after a second correct answer, the repetition interval is lengthened even more. The spacing also depends on the number of LOs included in a given topic. The desired practice schedule was specified by subject matter experts, who wanted topics of a particular size to fit within a specified practice schedule. A sample pattern of LO appearances with time is shown in Fig. 6, for a Topic with 100 LOs (Riedesel et al. 2017).

This algorithm is compact in both size and computational complexity and is easily self-contained within a learner's smart device. The learner's complete record of progress through each topic within a title is also stored locally. This means that the full adaptive experience can be presented to the learner even when not connected to the Internet. A learner can practice for hours, days, weeks, or even months without a network connection. This was originally motivated by the desire for medical students in rural India to be able to use this application but it also means that it can be used seamlessly even on an airplane flight or other locations where cellular data service is not available.

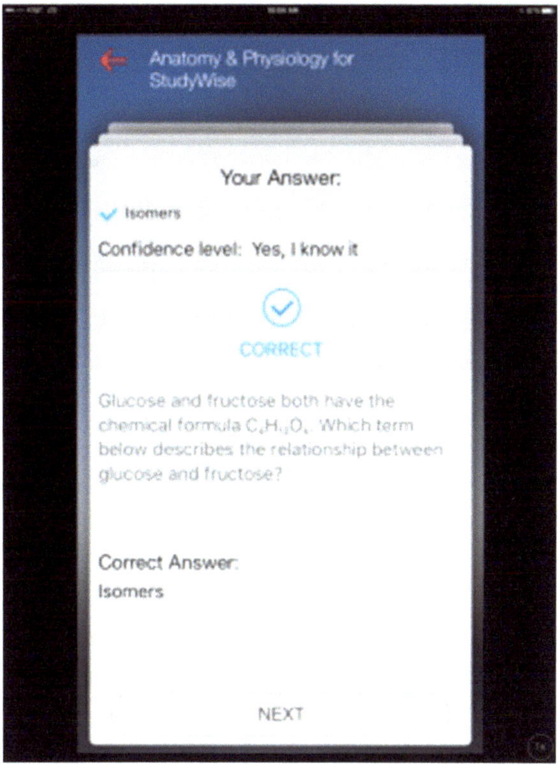

Fig. 5 The answer response page

3 Data Messaging System

The availability of cloud-based computing and storage allows a smart device to return information on user interactions with StudyWise apps without the need for a database to present the user interface or to store data messages produced by user interactions. In this way, smartphones hosting StudyWise operate in the same way as devices which are part of the Internet of Things (IOT). The particular architecture used for StudyWise is based on Amazon Web Service's "Serverless Computing" technology (http://aws.amazon.com/serverless/), which is frequently employed for IOT systems.

This architecture works very well for applications which are designed to stand alone on a user's smart device, and it is also at the heart of how Internet-connected sensors and devices which are part of IOT return the data used in machine learning and other predictive analytics. Using this type of architecture, as noted, there is no database behind the application. This means that the usual methods of doing both business and educational analytics by querying relevant data from an OLTP database are not available. All of the data that business analysts and learning scientists use must come from a custom-designed system of messages which are sent as learners interact with the system.

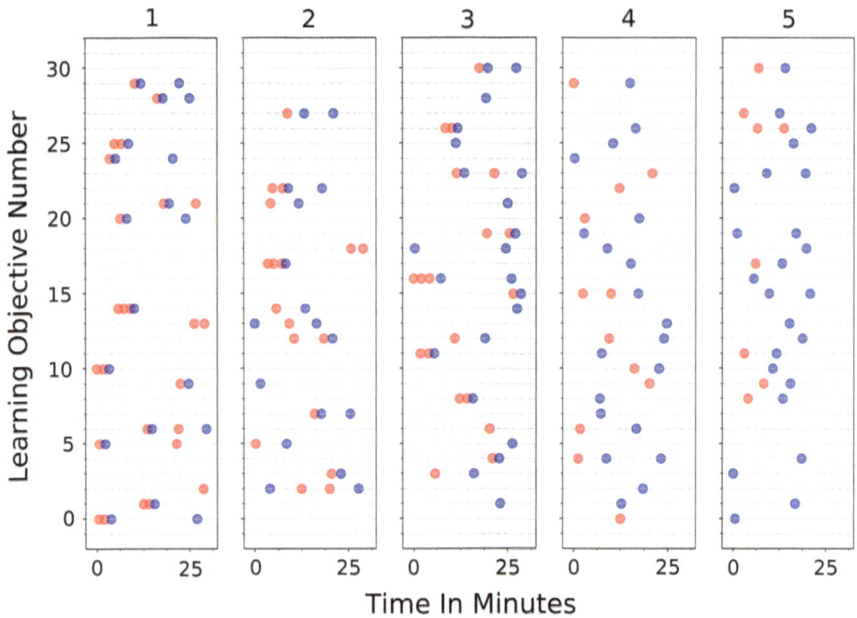

Fig. 6 Plots of the first 30 LOs from a 100 LO deck. Five 30-min sessions were needed to complete 100 LOs. Red dots indicate incorrect answers, as computed by the model, and blue dots are for correct answers. The start times for the sessions are separated by 24 h

When designing the messaging system, we solicited input from both the business owners of the application and learning scientists. We wanted to ensure the availability of the data needed for an understanding of the frequency and patterns of use needed for business analytics and for doing the Learning Science related to spaced practice and active retrieval. Both types of information can be used to improve the user experience and the educational effectiveness of this suite of applications.

By design, as little personally identifiable information (PII) is ever solicited from the users as possible and none is transmitted to the data collection system. The only PII information StudyWise is the email address used to synchronize a user's progress between devices. Even this information is contained in the JSON messaging data only as a non-reversible hash of the input email address.

3.1 *Questions for Business Analytics*

To determine what data might be needed for business analytics, we asked the Higher Education group for a list of the type of reports they might want to be able to construct from the messaging data. They provided a list which guided our design.

Here are some examples of the types of questions the business analysts wanted to be able to address:

- How much was each application used in terms of questions answered per unit of time (hour/day/week/month)?
- What is the pattern of usage in terms of time of day, in local time?
- How is usage correlated with the time of year, such as the start, middle, or end of a semester?
- How many learning objectives have been answered for each topic for each title?
- What is the average user progress through each topic?
- What is the usage of IOS versus Android for each title?

One field added specifically to address some of the business questions was the local time zone, in terms of offset from UCT.

3.2 Questions for Learning Science

In addition to data for business analysis, we also wanted to be able to measure the efficacy of the apps and to be able to gain insight into the learning science related to spaced practice and active retrieval. To be as comprehensive as possible, we consulted with the MHE Data Science team and with academic learning scientists while defining the messaging fields.

Among the types of questions we would like to be able to address in this area include:

- Which app (i.e., which Title) is the learner using?
- Which question (including its Topic and Learning Objective) has just been answered?
- Which answer was selected and was it the correct answer?
- How long did it take to answer the question?
- How long was spent looking at the explanation of the answer?
- What do the learning curves look like for each learning objective and or each student?
- What confidence level was chosen and how does it correlate with the correctness of the answer?
- How do performance and confidence vary as a given LO is repeated?
- How far through a given topic has the user progressed?

3.3 Data Fields and JSON Schema for the Messaging System

To be able to answer all of the above questions, the data fields in Table 1 were created. There are also several fields to identify the version of each app overall and the version of the adaptive algorithm which are not shown in this table. As the application is in

Table 1 Data messaging schema

Item	Type	Example	Source
IOS version number	String	9.0.1	Mobile OS
Device type	String	iPhone 6+	Mobile OS
IP address	String	10.10.10.10	Mobile OS
StudyWise application	String	A&P	App
Software version	String	1.0.0	App
Algorithm version	String	1.0.0	App
Topic IDs	String	[224562,135283,252034]	App
Topic titles	List string	["Countries and capitals", "Present tense irregular verbs", "Past tense of verbs"]	App
StudyWise topic size	Number	68	App
User ID	String	315352FD-44B1-406E-A785-B74100A0B2A9	App
Session ID	String	3B20792D-F46B-48B4-8F45-AA79AE620EA	App
Date/time session start	String	2015-08-01T06:00:00.000Z	App
Event type	String	One of "targeted" or "review"	App
Learning objective ID	String	CL323778e1-8d23-425f-8be4-996f20ae4933	App
Question identifier	Number	589823749	App
Question type	String	Multiple-choice/MCQ	App
Date/time presented	String	2015-08-01T06:00:00.000Z	Mobile OS
Date/time answered	String	015-08-01T06:00:00.000Z	Mobile OS
Answer selected	String	CL323778e1-8d23-425f-8be4:243565606:0	App
Success/failure	Number	0 for failure, 1 for success	App
Confidence	List	1 or 2 [1, 2]	App
User interrupted details	List or string	["phone", "other"]	Mobile OS
Session progress	Number	53%	App
Product title	String	Anatomy and physiology	App
Product Id	Number	151514	App
Local time zone	String	−5	Mobile OS
Date/time session end	String	2015-08-01T06:00:00.000Z	App

use, each time an answer to a question is submitted, information is sent. Fields which are directly linked to a user's practice session come from the StudyWise "App" and those which give information on the user's device, time zone, and other information on the session's context come from the mobile devices "Mobile OS" and hardware.

Although both IOS and Android mobile devices can transmit a user's location, the business owners were concerned that asking the user for permission to include their location would be seen as unnecessarily intrusive and might also raise student privacy issues, so this information is not collected. Local time zone information is collected for determining the time of day an app is being used.

3.4 JSON Schema

JSON was specified by MHE's data engineering group for encoding the messages in order to be compatible with a company-wide standard for data messaging systems for future educational software products. IMS Caliper was considered as the basis for this API, but at the time this API was designed (in mid-2016). Caliper lacked a number of fields needed to satisfy both the educational and business requirements, and MHE's data architects approved the schema shown here.

One great advantage of using JSON is the ability to query a collection of JSON documents using standard SQL query commands. This can be done either through systems such as Apache Spark (http://spark.apache.org), jQuery (https://jquery.com), or other similar tools. Even quite complex queries have worked successfully and an experienced database analyst can fully leverage their background in the SQL language while analyzing this type of data. In analyses done thus far, essentially all SQL queries attempted using Apache Spark SQL have worked on this dataset.

3.5 Online and Offline Modes

The first version of StudyWise was created to allow medical students overseas to study for the United States Medical Licensing Exam (USMLE). Such students could possibly be in areas where network coverage was spotty, so StudyWise was designed to be fully usable when the user's mobile device had no cellular data connection. This means that all of the logic and code needed for a fully adaptive experience needed to be contained in JavaScript code on the mobile device. Similarly, all of the questions, answers, explanations for incorrect answers, and ability to determine if an answer was correct or incorrect are included in the mobile app.

However, it was still desired to have a record of user interaction data, even for sessions done offline. In order to accommodate this, the JSON analytics data message for each interaction is either (1) buffered and then sent to the collection server in MHE's AWS virtual private cloud (see below) if the user is connected or (2) stored locally on the mobile device for later transmission if a network connection is not currently available. Stored data from offline sessions is later sent to the collection server when a user is running the StudyWise app and has a network connection. At present, this is the only widely available mobile educational application of which we know that has this capability.

3.6 Receiving System

As an app is in use, each time a learner answers a question and a JSON record is generated. This record is stored locally in a buffer and when this buffer is full or the session ends, the buffer of records is securely transmitted to a receiving service running on an AWS instance. The receiving service validates the data, as described below, and stores it in a flat file in a secure location in AWS S3 file storage.

The storage is a simple directory hierarchy organized by year, month, day, and hour. Many utilities exist to read JSON data stored in this way, including in Apache Spark. As noted above, this type of JSON file system can also be directly queried using SQL just as if it was a relational database.

This method of collecting and storing the data is limited in speed by the transmission time of the Internet but otherwise is capable of very high data throughput and can be set up in parallel to scale almost arbitrarily, if necessary. Total storage available is essentially limited only by the ability to pay for it.

This means that this data system could handle potentially millions of users daily by simply scaling out the receiving and storage systems, with no change in architecture. Using the capabilities of AWS means that no server or storage hardware need be purchased to set up such a system.

4 Security and Privacy

As a system which is used in education, it is very important to maintain the privacy of each user's data. This requires an architecture which protects the integrity and security of the data at each step of the collection and analysis. An important first step, as noted above, is to store no personally identifiable information in the analytics data stream.

4.1 Data Encryption

Data encryption is a critical element of security. Strong encryption of data both at rest and in transit prevents an attacker who might gain access to a storage system or communication channel from obtaining sensitive information. In StudyWise, this means that all communications between the mobile application, the data collection end point, and the processing pipeline are encrypted using HTTPS/SSL.

Data stored for analysis, and the derived datasets that comprise the output of those analyses, are encrypted in cloud storage. Amazon S3 supports multiple mechanisms including SSE-S3 (transparent server-side encryption), SSE-KMS (server-side encryption using AWS key management), and SSE-C (server-side encryption using customer-provided keys).

Furthermore, the pipeline runs in a virtual private cloud on infrastructure not directly accessible from public networks.

4.2 Access Policies and Controls

User authentication controls who can access the analytics environment. Integrated identity management can simplify user management by leveraging a service to authenticate users. Examples include SAML2.0 and Active Directory.

In order to ensure that only authorized users can access data stored and processed in the analytics pipeline, role-based access provides fine grain controls on storage (who can access data sources in the processing environment), on clusters (who/what is authorized to configure/launch/terminate/restart clusters), on processing jobs (who/what can attach and run processing on clusters) and the environment (configuration and settings).

Auditing and logging provide the ability to alert on, monitor, and review key events in the environment.

4.3 Data Integrity

In the compute layer, within Apache Spark, the RDD (see below) provides data immutability and fault tolerance by design. In the storage tier, AWS S3 provides not only an extremely high level of durability (99.999999999%) but also the ability, via the optional Content-MD5 request header, to verify the integrity of data stored there.

4.4 Certifications

An end-to-end data analytics pipeline, especially one reliant on third-party managed or cloud services, is a system based on the integration of many components. No matter how strong the data encryption and access policies in place, the system is only as secure as its weakest link. Managed service and cloud providers certify their platforms according to documented compliance standards.

The FERPA (Family Educational Rights and Privacy Act) standard governs access to educational information and records. Other standards, many originating in the financial and health industries, are also relevant in education.

AWS documents their compliance at (https://aws.amazon.com/compliance/). Certifications include FERPA, HIPPA, GLBA, FISMA, RFR, and PCI DSS.

Databricks, the computing environment used here for data analysis, documents their platform security and compliance at http://go.databricks.com/. Their security measures are based primarily on SOC2 Type-1 Certification. SOC2 Certification encompasses five key areas: security, availability, processing integrity, confidentiality, and privacy.

5 Data Processing and Analysis

In order to use the data collected for either educational or business insights, we need to set up a system to read, clean up, and analyze the JSON data produced originally on each user's device which has been sent to the AWS S3 collection system. It is possible to do all of this entirely in the cloud using AWS and other services, and this is the approach that we have taken with StudyWise.

In particular, we would like a system which has the following characteristics: (1) straightforward to access, use, and maintain and (2) powerful and scalable enough to handle increasing amounts of data as StudyWise is more widely deployed. In the past 10 to 15 years, several systems have been developed which have been designed to satisfy these types of needs. All are based on horizontally scalable clusters of servers to allow computing to be done in parallel.

Many high-performance computing systems in use by the academic and government research communities use the Message Passing Interface (MPI) to do parallel computing. This requires writing code in either C or Fortran. This is scalable to the very largest systems in existence and can be used for the most complex types of parallel computing but it requires a very high level of specialized knowledge and expertise to use. MPI can be used not just for processing large amounts of data in parallel but also for doing very large parallel theoretical calculations for such applications as global climate models and modeling the interiors of stars.

A system designed to make parallel computing more accessible to a wider range of users is the Apache Hadoop/MapReduce system of software developed for the parallel processing of large amounts of data. This system is simpler than MPI but still requires the use of the Java programming language and also requires writing intermediate results in its processing pipeline to disk, which can make it rather slow.

To overcome the limitations of MPI and Hadoop/MapReduce, a system called Apache Spark (http://spark.apache.org/) has been developed by the open-source community which allows all of the computation to be done in a compute node's memory and which also combines some of the steps in map/reduce processing, making the writing of code to process large amounts of data in parallel considerably easier than previous systems. Apache Spark has come into widespread use in just the last 3 to 4 years but is becoming the dominant method of processing very large amounts of data.

Spark also is available with APIs for programming in Scala, Python, R, and SQL, making it accessible to a much wider audience. On a practical level, a Spark program can be many, many times faster (x100, in some cases) than an equivalent Hadoop/MapReduce program, as long as all of a given subset of data in a parallel processing job can be fit into the memory of one of the servers in a Spark computing cluster.

In this section, we show how Apache/Spark can be used to process and analyze large-scale data with examples of its use in StudyWise.

5.1 Apache Spark

Apache Spark is both an engine and API for large-scale data processing, making very large-scale parallel computing accessible to a much wider range of users than previous parallel computing methods. Large organizations have deployed Apache Spark on clusters consisting of thousands of nodes, processing petabyte-sized datasets which grow on the order of terabytes per day (Tsai, 2017).

The main abstraction in Apache Spark is the "RDD", or resilient distributed dataset.

"Resilient" refers to redundancy of data across compute nodes, Apache Spark's fault tolerance and ability to continue processing when compute nodes fail.

"Distributed" refers to the fact that data is partitioned across many multiple cluster nodes. More importantly, computations are moved to the data, rather than the traditional approach of moving data to central location(s) for processing. This eliminates I/O bottlenecks and allows processing to scale in a linear fashion as the amount of data grows.

"Dataset" refers to large-scale collections of data. An important attribute of these datasets in Apache Spark is immutability. Immutability drastically simplifies the cost and complexity of coherently processing distributed data. Spark represents processing steps in a directed acyclic graph. This traversable graph, combined with the immutability of data at each intermediate step in the process, allows datasets to be easily reconstructed on failure, contributing both to the resiliency and distributed characteristics of the system.

More recently, Apache Spark has added an additional abstraction layer on top of the RDD called a dataframe. The dataframe makes the manipulation and processing of the data conceptually simpler than is the case for RDDs and it is very similar to dataframes found in Python Pandas and in R (where the concept was first developed).

Data streaming Apache Spark supports both batch-oriented and stream processing using a single unified API. The use of streaming allows essentially up to the second processing to be done on the analytics data as it arrives from the user's mobile devices, if desired.

The Apache Spark Structured Streaming API mimics the Apache Spark batch API, but behind the scenes it utilizes the SparkSQL engine to continuously update data as new information arrives. The same SparkSQL queries and operations that work on batch-loaded information can also be performed on streaming dataframes.

In the concrete examples below, Spark Structured Streaming is used to perform event-driven processing.

APIs and Analysis Tools Apache Spark's processing API supports multiple languages, including Scala/Java, Python, and R as well as a dialect of SQL. In the following example, data is ingested into a Spark dataframe. Here are brief examples of how to read JSON flat files into a Spark dataframe for the different Spark languages:

Table 5.1. Scala

```
val eventSampleDf = spark.read.json ("pathBatch / *. json")
```

Table 5.2. Pyspark (Python)

```
eventSampleDf = spark.read.json ("pathBatch / *. json")
```

Table 5.3. SparkR (R)

```
eventSampleDf = read.df (sqlContext, "pathBatch/* . json", "json")
```

The Apache/Spark API also allows SQL-like operations to be performed on dataframes.

A simple select/filter operation in Scala using the SparkSQL API:

Table 5.4. SQL query using Scala

```
val apDf = eventsBatchDf .
                    filter ($"session.studywiseApplication" === "A&P")
```

The same operation expressed in Spark SQL syntax:

Table 5.5. SQL query directly in Spark SQL

```
%sql select * from apDf where session.studywiseApplication = 'A&P'
```

5.2 Processing Pipeline

Pipelines typically have at least three layers: input, processing, and output. These are shown in Fig. 7.

In StudyWise, these layers coordinate with software components that facilitate user authentication, data collection, transmission, and persistence.

Layers of Processing

Ingestion via messaging system: The input layer is preceded by event hooks instrumented in the client mobile application. These event hooks trigger calls to REST APIs that authenticate the user and transmit events to an event collector and cloud-based storage.

Once these events are persisted (in AWS S3, for example), the Apache Spark datasources API can be used to ingest the events into a dataframe for processing.

The Apache Spark API supports both batch and streaming semantics via the same interface.

Read all events in a bulk batch read:

Table 5.6. Batch Read of a JSON file

```
val eventsBatchDf = spark.read.schema(schema). json ("path / * . json")
```

Stream events as they arrive via streaming.

Table 5.7. Streaming Read of a JSON input stream

```
val eventStreamDf = spark.readStream.schema(schema). json ("path / * . json")
```

In the case of a batch read, all source events presented at the time of the read operation will be read in a bulk read operation and stored in an Apache Spark dataframe.

In the case of the streaming read, all source events present at the time of the read operation will be initially loaded into the target dataframe. The dataframe is unbounded, however. As new events arrive, new rows are added to the dataframe.

Data Cleaning and Transformation: Cleaning and transformation consists of Apache Spark and SparkSQL operations on the source dataframe. As discussed, dataframes in Spark are immutable. Every operation on the dataframe creates a new dataframe. Operations are distributed across the worker nodes in the cluster.

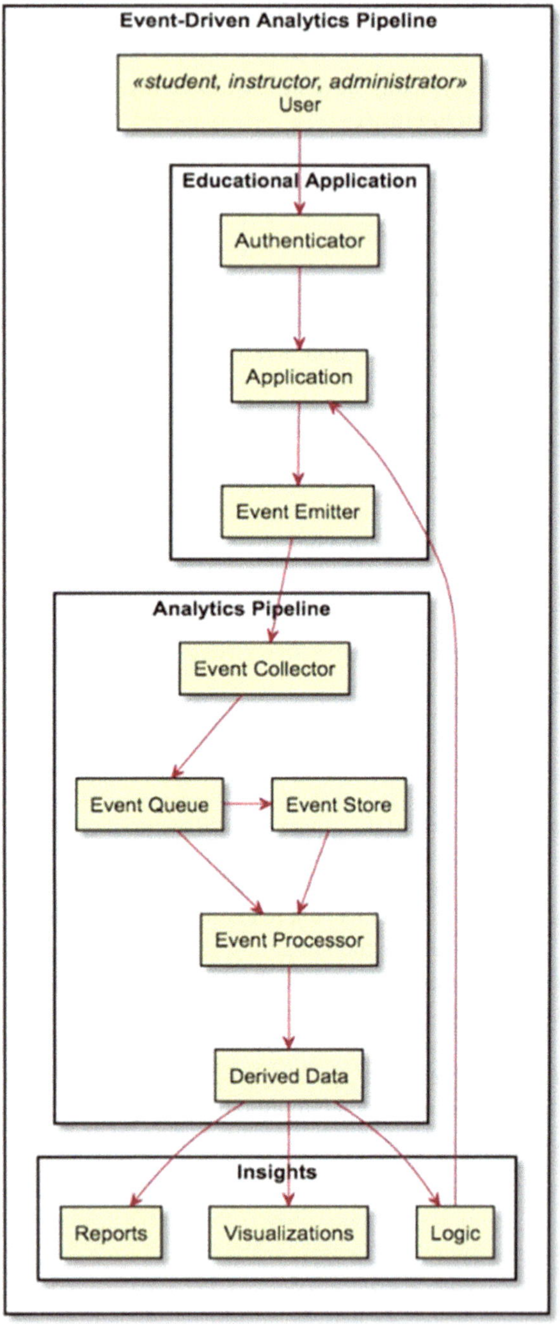

Fig. 7 The processing pipeline for analytics data for the mobile apps

Table 5.8. Filtering out unwanted data fields

```
// filter out events based on criteria,
// in this case columns not used in the processing

val 2Df = eventsStreamDf.drop("legacyData")

// use SQL−like syntax to group events based on some criteria
// in this case, by application and product title
// counted and sorted
// to produce a continuously updated dataframe containing
// the most common application/title combination

val activityByProductTitlesandApplicationStreamDf =
  v2Df
    . groupBy("session.studywiseApplication", "session.productTitle")
    . count
    . sort (desc ("count"))
```

Intermediate Storage: Whether transforming data for subsequent analysis, or producing a set of potentially valuable insights, it is useful to persist these results. The Apache Spark datasources API can write the data back into S3 cloud storage in a variety of formats including JSON or to a more optimized and compact format such as Parquet. These operations can also be performed in batch or streaming modes.

Table 5.9. Creating a Parquet File from raw JSON data

```
v2Df
  . writeStream
  . format ("parquet")
  . option ("path", "targetPath/v2DfStream . parquet")
  . start
```

5.3 *Filtering*

The data stream can also be filtered in order to produce more compact datasets for specific types of analysis and also to clean up the data. For example, during the test phase of the initial StudyWise deployment, the apps would sometimes produce duplicate records. By applying a filter to the stream, these duplicates can be eliminated. Other minor data issues have also been filtered out in a similar way.

It is also possible to filter the data based on any of the data fields in Table 1. A common filter used is to look at a particular title, type of question, correctness of answer, or level of confidence. Spark SQL makes the construction and application of such filters to dataframes straightforward.

Time Windowing: A very common way to want to filter data is by time. To facilitate this, a daily time stamp is added to the StudyWise data stream. With this, Spark SQL has a built-in Window function which allows the data to be grouped by user-specified time windows, such as hourly, daily, weekly, or monthly using SQL-like command. Operations of many types can be done within these windows, including calculating moving averages and ranking rows, operations difficult to do with standard SQL.

We have used SparkSQL Window functions, for example, to look at daily usage of each app and also to prepare data for calculating learning curves. While these types of calculations can be done by spreadsheets, such as Excel, Spark can do this on many millions or billions of records using parallel computation.

Versioning: Versioning components of the pipeline is a useful method for tracking features and compatibility as the pipeline evolves. Versioning applies to API endpoints and message/event schema. Increments to the major version number indicate "breaking" changes, while increments in the minor version indicate backward-compatible changes.

An example of a minor version change would be the addition of a new field that can be safely ignored. More drastic changes to an interface, such as a change in structure or names of existing fields, require a major version increment.

Schema Changes: By including versioning information in the event envelope, the processing pipeline can programmatically handle disparate versions of message formats through a process of transformation and normalization.

Table 5.10. Filtering events based on a specific software or message version.

```
val eventSampleDf.filter ($"session.softwareVersion" === "2.1.5")
```

Table 5.11. Defining a function to conditionally process events based on version.

```
// event normalization,  Scala  function
def normalizeEvent (version:String, event:String): String = {
  if ( version == "2.0"  ||  version == "2.1") {
        // transformation specific to v2
  }
  else if (version == "1.0" || version == "1.1" || version == " 1.0.1 ")  {
        // transformation specific to v1
  }
  else {
        // other or unrecognized versions
  }
}
```

Table 5.12. Registering a function as a UDF for event processing in SparkSQL

```
// event normalization, as registered UDF function
val normalizeEventUDF = spark.
                          udf.
                          register ("normalizeEvent", normalizeEvent)
```

Table 5.13. Applying the UDF to transform events in a dataframe

```
val dfTransformed =
   dfEvents
    . select (normalizeEventUDF($"session.softwareVersion", $"event", $"*"))
```

6 Managed Computing Environments and Cloud Computing

Managing the infrastructure associated with a processing pipeline can be complex and expensive.

A variety of resources must be managed in a processing environment. These include compute clusters, storage, processing code, recurring jobs, and users. In a secure environment, roles and permissions are enforced to limit access to resources.

In a self-hosted environment, administrators provision and manage these resources. In a managed environment, the service provider simplifies and automates the administration of these resources.

Each of the resources needed for a processing pipeline can be set up in one of several ways. An organization can do all of this in their own datacenter on their own hardware, with their dedicated staff to manage it. An alternative is to use cloud services to provide some or all of the storage, computing, and data management using such providers as AWS (https://aws.amazon.com/) and Azure (https://azure.microsoft.com).

Similarly, the software, such as Apache Spark, can also be installed, maintained, and managed by an organization's own personnel, either by directly obtaining it from the open-source repository or by using commercially packaged software distributions, such as Hortonworks (http://hortonworks.com/) or Cloudera (http://www.cloudera.com/).

There are also cloud-based providers, such as Databricks (http://databricks.com/) and Qubole (http://www.qubole.com/) which provide large-scale computing as a service, with data typically stored in Amazon S3 or on Azure.

Our organization chose to host its storage within its own Virtual Private Cloud (VPC) in AWS and to use Databricks for large-scale data processing and analysis.

6.1 Databricks

Databricks offers a managed, scalable, and enhanced cloud implementation of Apache Spark including tools to simplify and automate administration of the environment and also includes a notebook-oriented user interface to facilitate the organization, exploration, and analysis of large datasets. Among the features Databricks offers includes the following:

- graphical UI layer;
- cluster and job management;
- user, role, and permission management;
- improved scalability and elastic/autoscaling;
- compute cost optimization;
- vendor-specific enhancements to the processing pipeline;
- enhanced security; and
- RESTful APIs for user, job, and cluster management.

7 Data Storage and Formatting

When working with very large amounts of data, the specifics of how the data is stored and formatted can have a very large impact upon overall performance. Using the most efficient methods can greatly broaden the scope and types of analysis which are possible and expand the range of learning science questions which can be addressed.

7.1 Raw JSON in AWS S3 Cloud Storage

As the JSON data message packets arrive from each user's mobile device, they are validated and processed by an input server running in AWS and then stored in a flat file hierarchy in AWS S3. The files are stored within a Unix-like directory hierarchy with levels by/year/month/day with each file labeled with a timestamp which describes the data records within the packet.

This JSON directory hierarchy can be directly read into a Spark dataframe, with the system able to infer the data schema from the JSON records. However, reading the JSON directly from S3 files can be quite slow and for the large amounts of data that will be generated by StudyWise as usage grows, it was necessary to reformat the data into a more compact, easily read binary format, Parquet.

7.2 *Parquet Binary Files and Streaming to Improve Efficiency*

Parquet is a columnar, binary file format specifically developed to facilitate the processing of large amounts of data (http://parquet.apache.org/). This can be done both at the streaming and static file level. So, the JSON stream can be directed into a processing stream, the output of which is a Parquet formatted stream with the same content. For situations where the data does not need to be continuously updated, static Parquet files can be written.

Reading the data from a static Parquet file can considerably speed reading the data into Spark. For example, reading the raw JSON for the total data available at the moment of this writing takes about 45 min. To read the static, binary Parquet file of the same data takes 30 s. Thus, both in terms of time and in terms of cost, the use of Parquet has considerable benefits. As the dataset expands in size, these benefits will increase.

8 Learning Science and Analytics

A wide range of analysis can be done to advance learning science and to provide feedback to learners using the messaging data from StudyWise. At present, the StudyWise data is accessible only through Spark clusters specifically configured to do this within MHE's Databricks environment. Thus, all analysis, thus far, has been done within Databricks using Apache Spark.

Analysis which can be done includes constructing learning curves using well-known methods such as Bayesian Knowledge Tracing and Performance Factor Analysis. We have also looked at difference in performance as a function of question type. There are, for example, significant differences seen in performance between single-answer multiple-choice, fill-in-the-blank, and multiple-choice multi-answer modes of questions.

8.1 *Learning Curves for Learning Objectives*

One of the main methods for measuring learning in assessment systems, including StudyWise, is to look at how the performance of the users of a system improves with each attempt at answering the questions associated with a particular knowledge component or learning objective. For StudyWise, this is shown in Fig. 8, with shows that performance improves significantly between the first and second and the second and third appearances of an LO, at which point the LO can be said to be learned.

There are several methods of analysis to statistically estimate the probability of improved performance at each step in the learning process. One of the most widely

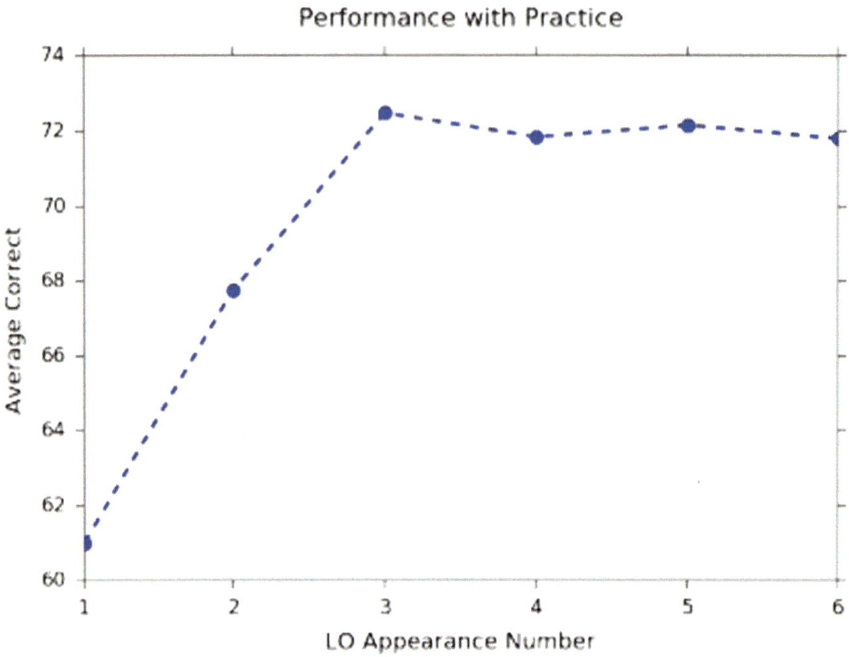

Fig. 8 Percent correct for all users as a function of appearance number for all LOs

used of these is Bayesian Knowledge Tracing, which was developed in the mid-1990s (Corbett & Anderson, 1994). Another commonly used method for measuring the growth of knowledge as study progresses is Performance Factor Analysis and its variations (Pavlik, Cen & Koedinger, 2009). Studies are currently in progress to apply both of these methods to the data being produced by StudyWise.

8.2 Confidence and Metacognition

One of the specifications for StudyWise which was agreed upon early in the development process was the desire to record not just the users' answers but to also ask the users to estimate their level of confidence in the answers they chose. This falls into the area of learning science called metacognition, the subject of which is a learner's self-awareness of their own level of knowledge. There is growing interest in studying the relationship between a learner's self-confidence and self-knowledge and their overall learning performance (Aghababyan, Lewkow, & Baker, 2017).

9 Data Visualization

A very important part of the exploration and analysis of large datasets in education is the use of visualization. In the environment we are using for the StudyWise data, there are a range of tools available for this. The Python and R computer languages have several powerful visualization packages available. All of these are available from within the Databricks environment.

9.1 Data Exploration and Visualization Using Built-in Tools

A very common method of organizing the analysis of large datasets is through the use of computing notebooks. In this model, computations in Python, R, Scala, or SQL can be interspersed with visualizations and graphs, which facilitates the exploration of the data. This can include basic plots of daily usage of the system and extend to very sophisticated learning science and statistical analysis.

Computing languages such as Python, R, and Scala have computing notebook systems available such as Jupyter http://jupyter.org (an outgrowth of the earlier iPython notebooks). Another open-source notebook, Apache Zeppelin (http://zepplin.apache.org), supports Apache Spark, Python, and SQL. In order to optimize the use of their computing environment, however, Databricks has developed their own proprietary notebook which can run Apache Spark code through the use of Scala, Python (Pyspark), R (SparkR), or SQL (SparkSQL).

The Databricks environment also includes a file system, called the Databricks File System (DBFS) which is a front end for Amazon S3 and which facilitates the organization of and access to very large datasets. Through DBFS, data can be read into a notebook for analysis. The notebooks also include built-in plotting routines which allows the quick construction of histograms, scatter plots, line plots, bar charts, pie charts, pivot tables, geographic maps, and others.

In addition to the quick, built-in plotting methods, the notebooks also have available the very powerful plotting routines built into Python, such as Matplotlib, Seaborne, and Bokeh and ggplot2 in R and Python. Thus, the exploration, analysis, and visualization of large dataset can be done within the context of a Databricks notebook. This facilitates the organization of the research as well as making it very easy to share results and to collaborate on research without having to duplicate code. There is also an interface to Github (https://github.com/) to allow detailed tracking and versioning of software.

10 Relationship Between Research and Production

Much of the research done on large educational datasets is done with the goal of making improvements to existing products. Such research can result in updates to the data API, adaptive algorithm, or educational design of a product. Product-targeted research projects may result in analyses which can directly provide feedback to users to help improve their educational outcomes.

In other cases, the outcome of the research could be a contribution to fundamental learning science which might not be immediately incorporated into the product from which the data was produced but will inform future development of other educational products.

The computing environment used for StudyWise allows for all of these possibilities. Cloud computing, such as AWS and Databricks, allows separate computing clusters to be set up for each project. Cloud storage, such as S3, can also be managed to direct data streams for a particular purpose and to also set up secure, isolated storage locations so that access can be carefully controlled. This allows projects that must use PII data, for example, to be clearly distinct from those that do not.

10.1 Development, Test, and Production Environment

StudyWise is a commercially available software product and has been developed in a way consistent with its commercial nature.

In particular, each of the components of the data transmission and processing pipeline has separate development, test, and production versions. This includes data intake, verification, and storage, with separate servers and S3 storage for each function. There are also unique data streams and processing computing clusters for each stage of development.

This allowed the developers to send trial data messages to a development area while the Analytics API was being developed and refined. These messages would vary in format, while the API was being finalized and refined.

During acceptance testing, a separate test area would have only data messages which, ideally, conform to the final format but which were not produced by actual users. This area can also be used to test the scalability of the application without interfering with end users.

The production area is reserved for actual user data from the end users. It is also the area which will need to be able to scale up as usage expands, although this functionality can be prototyped in the test environment.

This separation of environments allows modifications to be made to the software, the analytics data API, and the overall infrastructure without interfering with use by the real users. The fact that all of these components were built upon cloud-based serviced means that each could be implemented and tested without the need to acquire dedicated hardware for either storage or computing.

10.2 *Software Development Life Cycle for Educational Apps*

Up until recently, the research upon which an educational application was based would have been done on systems quite different from those upon which the production version would run. In particular, research groups often used computer languages, such as Matlab, which work well for doing research but are not designed to scale up for production systems.

A great advantage of using a framework like Apache Spark is that it can be used by data scientists and learning scientists to design and produce new algorithms and new processing streams which can then be moved into a production system with far less modification than was often the case previously.

Spark supports the use of Scale/Java, Python, R, and SQL on data from a common source and in a common format. So if researchers find that their research requires a particular data format, the production system can, if desired, adapt this. In the case of StudyWise, for example, the use of JSON was required by the data engineering group for company-wide compatibility, but the specifics of the API were developed jointly between learning scientists, business analysts, and data engineers.

Similarly, if the data engineers working on production systems find better ways of handling large amounts of data, their experience can be leveraged by researchers for their work because they are working within the same framework and using the same set of tools. The adoption of the Parquet file system to speed learning science analysis is an excellent example of this. Software engineers also have tools such as those for carefully tracking the version of software that can be very useful for keeping track of research.

With software engineers, data engineers, data scientists, and learning scientists all working in the same computing environment, the transfer of work from research to development to testing to production is greatly facilitated. Experience and expertise can also be shared in a way that has not been possible until the development of systems such as Apache Spark and Databricks. Each group can have their own separate areas and separate environments, but the transfer of algorithms and reporting tools between groups is much easier. And the development of shared expertise between groups benefits everyone.

11 Summary

Mobile devices such as smartphones and tablets can host educational applications which can be used anywhere, anytime, at the user's convenience. Such applications can be instrumented to emit data messages which can provide data on a user's learning progress. The data transmission, storage, security, and analysis used for such applications can be very similar to that which has been developed for the Internet of Things, where smart devices produce data messages on how the device is used.

Unlike most IOT devices, smartphones and tablets can also utilize on-device storage to allow the user interaction data messages to be stored for later transmission if a network connection is not available at the moment it is generated. This allows these educational apps to truly be used anywhere and anytime, including on airplanes or in very isolated areas where cellular data connections may not be available.

The infrastructure implemented for these mobile educational apps is now being used by about 5000 users who are answering several thousand questions per day. However, this infrastructure is designed to scale out to handle tens of millions of users answering millions of questions per day with no changes needed at any stage. Using cloud computing, this can all be done without the need to have a data center or to purchase any server or storage hardware. One only needs a checkbook backed by a large enough bank account to pay for the cloud storage and computing charges.

Given the great flexibility this allows students, teachers, developers, data engineers, and learning scientists, we expect that StudyWise is just the first of many applications like it to come. It puts learning directly into the hands of the users, directly alongside their social media apps, text messaging, games, email, and—for the old-fashioned—phone calls.

StudyWise uses recent results from learning science to help students master course material in an optimal way, all in the palm of their hand. At the same time, these apps are producing large amounts of educational data which will allow the continued improvement of the educational experience and also provide fundamental insight into the learning process.

Acknowledgements StudyWise was developed by a team of 15 developers, project managers, and data scientists lead by Technical Product Manager James Cooper, Business Product Manager Katie Ward, and Engineering Lead Tom Titchener. The infrastructure described was set up and is managed by the Data Engineering group lead my Matt Hogan and Matt Ashbourne and the Global Technology Services group lead by Boris Slavin.

References

Aghababyan, A., Lewkow, N., & Baker, R. (2017). Exploring the asymmetry of metacognition. In: *Proceedings of the Seventh International Learning Analytics; Knowledge Conference* LAK'17 (pp. 115–119). ACM, New York, NY, USA.

Bloom, B. E., Engelhart, M., Furst, E., Hill, W., & Krathwohl, D. (1956). *Taxonomy of educational objectives, handbook I: The cognitive domain*. New York: David McKay Co Inc.

Brown, P. C., Roedinger, H. L., & McDaniel, M. A. (2014). *Make it stick: The science of successful learning*. Cam-bridge, MA: Belknap Press: An Imprint of Harvard University Press.

Cepeda, N. J., Vul, E., Rohrer, D., Wixted, J. T., & Pashler, H. (2008). Spacing effects in learning, a temporal ridgeline of optimal retention. *Psychological Science, 19*(11), 1095–1102.

Corbett, A., & Anderson, J. (1994). Knowledge tracing: Modeling the acquisition of procedural knowledge. *User Model User-Adapted Interaction, 4,* 253–278.

Ebbinghaus, H. (1885). *Memory, a contribution to experimental psychology*. New York: Dover.

Kam, M., Kumar, A., Jain, S., Mathur, A., & Canny, J. (2009). Improving literacy in rural India: Cellphone games in an after-school program. In: Proceedings of IEEE/ACM Conference on Information and Communication Technology and Development. IEEE Press, Doha, Qatar (2009).

Karpicke, J., & Roediger, H. (2008). The critical importance of retrieval for learning. science. *Science, 319,* 966–968.
Leitner, S. (1972). So lernt man lernen. Der Weg zum Erfolg (How to learn to learn). Freiburg: Herder.
Mozer, M. C., & Lindsey, R. V. (2016). Predicting and improving memory retention: Psycho-logical theory matters in the big data era. In: M. Jones (Ed.), *Big data in cognitive science.* Taylor & Francis.
Pavlik, P. I., & Anderson, J. R. (2005). Practice and forgetting effects on vocabulary memory: An activation-based model of the spacing effect. *Cognitive Science, 29,* 559–586.
Pavlik, P. I., & Anderson, J. R. (2008). Using a model to compute the optimal schedule of practice. *Journal of Experimental Psychology: Applied, 14*(2), 101–117.
Pavlik, P. I., Jr., Cen, H., Koedinger, K. R. (2009). Performance factors analysis—A new alternative to knowledge tracing. In: *Proceedings of the 2009 conference on Artificial Intelligence in Education: Building Learning Systems that Care: From Knowledge Representation to Affective Modelling* (pp. 531–538). Amsterdam: IOS Press.
Pavlik, P. I., Jr., Kelly, C., & Maass, J. K. (2016). Using the mobile fact and concept training system (mofacts). In: A. Micarelli & J. Stamper (Eds.), *Proceedings of the 13th International Conference on Intelligent Tutoring Systems* (pp. 247–253). Switzerland: Springer.
Riedesel, M. A., Zimmerman, N., Baker, R., Titchener, T., & Cooper, J. (2017). Using a model for learning and memory to simulate learner response in spaced practice. In: E. André, R. Baker, X. Hu, M. Mercedes, T. Rodrigo, & B. du Boulay (Eds.), *Proceedings of 18th International Conference on th Artificial Intelligence in Education, AIED 2017*, Wuhan, China, June 28–July 1, 2017, (pp. 644–649). Springer International Publishing.
Roediger, H., & Karpicke, J. (2006). Test-enhanced learning: Taking memory tests improves long-term retention. *Psychological Science, 17,* 249–255.
Rohrer, D., & Taylor, K. (2007). The shuffling of mathematics problems improves learning. *Instructional Science, 35,* 481–498.
Settles, B. & Meeder, B. (2016). A trainable spaced repetition model for language learning. In: *Proceedings of the 54th Annual Meeting of the Association for Computational Linguistics* (pp. 1848–1858). Association for Computational Linguistics, Berlin, Germany.
Tsai, D. B. (2017). *Netflix's recommendation ML pipeline using Apache Spark* (2 2017) (Talk at Spark Summit East). http://databricks.com/session/netflixs-recommendation-ml-pipeline-using-apache-spark.

Framing Learning Analytics and Educational Data Mining for Teaching: Critical Inferencing, Domain Knowledge, and Pedagogy

Owen G. McGrath

This chapter reviews key challenges of learning analytics and educational data mining. It highlights early generation learning analytics pitfalls that could compromise the future of their use in technology-delivered instruction, especially if teachers are not well trained and adequately equipped with both technical and sociocritical literacy of this new field. Among the issues are potential for bias and inaccuracy in the algorithms involved, the propensity toward closed proprietary systems whose algorithms cannot be scrutinized, and the paucity of learning models typically considered. The new learning analytics and educational data mining systems bring with them a set of claims, aspirations, and mystique. These underlying technologies could be harbingers of future breakthroughs: a new generation of artificial intelligence systems adaptively responding to students' interactions with online teaching environments. However, current system implementations and research studies reveal an immaturity of methods and a tendency to focus narrowly on a small range of easily tracked user behaviors that are only indirectly associated with learning (Blikstein, 2013). The initial wave of studies and proof-of-concept systems seem at times like technologies in search of a problem, i.e., hammers in search of nails. There is a familiar risk here in allowing the technology developers to set the agenda—a risk that doomed previous generations of intelligent learning systems. Unless domain experts and stakeholders (i.e., teachers and teacher researchers) are trained up to critique and shape the design of these new technologies, the resulting systems will likely repeat the failures of the past: deployed as black box "expert systems" that confuse, constrain, or supplant teachers altogether while also jeopardizing the privacy and agency of students. Instead, this chapter argues, these technologies need to be conceived and designed within a broader context of supporting teaching, particularly teacher decision-making. The promise these systems hold can only be realized

O. G. McGrath (✉)
Educational Technology Services, UC Berkeley, Berkeley, CA, USA
e-mail: omcgrath@berkeley.edu

J. M. Spector et al. (eds.), *Frontiers of Cyberlearning*, Lecture Notes in Educational Technology, https://doi.org/10.1007/978-981-13-0650-1_2

if they are designed for the domain experts, i.e., teachers. Teacher training programs, in turn, need to add data science to the curriculum.

By many accounts, a measurement revolution is taking place in global secondary and tertiary education (Long & Siemens, 2011; Daniel, 2015). As with earlier technology movements in education, the actual outcome will depend on how well teachers are trained to understand, influence, and make use of the technology (Cuban, 2001; Jung, 2005; Kenny, 2006; Kozma, 2008). The risks around decision-making systems-based big data algorithms are only just starting to be understood, despite their widespread use in many industries (Jagadish, 2015; O'Neil, 2016). Given the black box approach to commercial learning analytics systems, the algorithms and models used for sorting and labeling students could also go by uninspected like a proprietary secret sauce. It would be all too easy for educators to stand aside as unquestioning and passive end users of these opaque systems deployed at the institutional level. Instead, this chapter argues, learning analytics and educational data mining systems should be designed for and by the domain experts, i.e., teachers and they should be implemented with transparency and openness so that their algorithms can be scrutinized and tested for fairness. If designed from the start to support the actual needs of teachers, these systems could be engineered to support teachers' inquiry and decision-making in pursuit of instructional effectiveness (Kumar et al., 2015). With data-driven information technologies as the key enablers, the learning analytics and educational data mining movement could offer new ways of asking questions about what gets taught and learned in school settings.

This technology-supported inquiry could yield a new understanding of learning outcomes, teacher effectiveness, personalization of learning, and perhaps even the core assumptions of requiring in-person education, which has been an organizing principle for most institutions of higher learning for centuries (Brown & Kurzweil, 2017). But how to engineer such systems reliably, what to measure, and how best to support teaching? These key questions are only just starting to be asked at this early stage. Early implementations and research studies of learning analytics and educational data mining reveal a narrowness of methods and a tendency to focus narrowly on a small range of easily tracked user behaviors such as the number of times they logged in, visited a web page, or lingered on a display of information. These limits have constrained the context and variables considered, and even so far, the new field has tended toward peripheral (albeit measurable) variables and narrow range of models of teaching and learning.

This chapter makes a case for teacher training and teacher research programs to engage with learning analytics and educational data mining not only to be critically aware of the key challenges revealed in early generation efforts but also to help shape the future of these new technologies. First is the need for teachers, as social scientists, to be critically literate in terms of the new technology: the role of algorithms, the means of inferencing, and the methods training with data. Learning analytics and educational data mining certainly bring with them a set of claims, aspirations, and mystique. Teachers in particular and teacher researchers as well need to consider critically key questions of fairness, reliability, and validity that lurk within these technologies. Critical literacy of these technologies, when used in supporting decision-making around instructional attainment and effectiveness, must be built upon familiar fundamental concerns with bias, model selection, validity, and reliability. In particular, teachers should feel empowered to consider critically the quality and provenance of the massive data used in these systems, the models of successful and failed learning used, the rate and accumulation of error, etc. Moreover, professional educators—as data scientists—also need to be empowered to call for the ongoing audit and scrutiny of the algorithms and data models employed. A second key area discussed in this chapter involves the theoretical models of teaching and learning upon which these new decision-making support systems are built. To date, most of the systems in this new era of learning analytics and educational data mining system are limited by their sources and methods to dealing only with a narrow range of directly observable online actions of learners, their outward digital behaviors, and some institutionally recorded categorical attributes. The data for these online behavioral traces are typically then analyzed in terms of correlates with assessment data, academic achievement measures, or normative digital behaviors of "successful" students.

Largely missing from the current focus on students' recordable interactions with online systems is much in the way of significant theorizing or even informed speculation about the relationship of teaching to student behavior in the broader contexts (e.g., classroom, institution), teacher attributes, or the material being taught. Teaching strategies, interactions, decision-making, attributes, etc., are absent as data or variables. Instead, the typical educational contexts considered are limited in scope to traces of online interactions, formative or summative assessment measures, and institutionally held categorical data (e.g., grade level, gender, SES, standardized achievement score history). The resulting approach toward teaching and learning that are implied in most early generation learning analytics and educational data mining systems is a simplistic, teacher-free view of learning as incremental behavioral pathways online that are either rewarded or remediated based on norms formed and update along the way through correlates of online success.

As advocated in this chapter, an alternative and more promising approach for the future envisions the scope and design of these learning analytics and educational data mining systems framed more broadly around questions and variables that more relevant to practitioners in the domain. These would include areas in which teachers bring together their content and pedagogical knowledge to design and carry out instructional activities: e.g., their structuring of material, selection of media and sequencing, the teacher/student discourse patterns, etc. The fields of teacher research and teacher training can bring to bear the domain knowledge to provide a crucial research and advocacy role that promotes and advances attention to such models, as opposed to the rather limited pedagogy (e.g., online lectures interspersed with computer-marked assignments) focused upon thus far (Daniel, 2010, 2012). What is needed are teaching and learning paradigms of content knowledge such that the design and use of the system will be based on a framework that considers both content knowledge and pedagogy (Shulman, 1986; Carlsen, 2001; Kleickmann et al., 2013). Priority should go to teachers' reflection and decision-making with helpful insights into the relationship between their understanding of subject matter and the instruction they provide to students.

As we will see in Section 1, to take up such an agenda would be a timely move for the fields of teacher training and research on teaching, given the rise of technology-augmented instruction in all levels of schooling. Indeed, as Section 2 will show, the convergence of networked information technology underlying learning analytics and educational data mining offers significant opportunities for expansive improvements to teaching and learning whether in traditional or virtual schools. Section 3 points particularly to the need for developing in teachers and teacher researchers the ability to consider critically both how these systems work and how educational data is mined. Section 4 looks at some guiding principles for the teacher training and teacher research fields' appropriate roles in the learning analytics and educational data mining era. These principles, framed in terms of teaching and learning, require paying attention to both when turning data into knowledge useful for decision-making.

1 Wired and Virtual Schools

Underlying and enabling the rise of learning analytics and educational data mining are the networked information technologies now reaching into formal education worldwide. In North America, secondary and tertiary education teaching and learning activities are increasingly carried out through and supported by Information and Communication Technology (ICT) both inside and outside the classroom. A convergence of enabling technologies (e.g., the Internet, mobile phones, tablet computing devices, cloud computing, satellite-based Internet access) has opened up transcendent possibilities for using networked computing and communications technologies to extend teaching and learning opportunities in unprecedented ways. In particular, the coming decades of ICT for education will likely be remembered as the dawn of technology-augmented teaching and fully online instruction. Accredited secondary and tertiary school systems delivering and managing instruction via technology within the classroom and blended or fully online instruction outside is becoming commonplace. With the rise of cyber-infrastructure in secondary and tertiary education, new opportunities surface when it comes to understanding learner's online activities. How, where, and when learner activity is captured and analyzed in academic online systems is particularly critical in these networked systems. On the flipside, the flexibility that Internet-based systems allows for in promoting easy integration of different technologies and platforms has repercussions for the engineering of these new systems: around the clock access to a multitude of distributed users can result in huge volumes of online learning data.

Whether it is online learning in traditional schools virtual schools or mega-schools, ICT-based online teaching and learning offer compelling opportunities to consider new approaches to teaching and learning, as a diverse and growing group of educational leaders and analysts agree (Moe & Chubb 2009; Daniel 2010). Whole books could be written in describing the many key enabling technologies that are allowing for online learning: the Internet, mobile phones, tablet computing devices, cloud computing, satellite-based Internet, etc. Whole books have been written about the wide range of possible teaching and learning modes, methods, and models that online teaching and learning might use. Vigorous debates and wide-ranging proposals already abound for possible organizational structures, methods of delivery, modes of institutional alignment, and assessment models for best implementing ICT-based online schools and ICT-based teacher training for secondary and tertiary education (Bramble & Panda, 2008). Across many of these varied proposals is also a shared sense that the sophistication and reach of ICT creates a historic opportunity to focus on designing personalized learning environments with revolutionary support for teacher decision-making.

2 Learning Analytics and Educational Data Mining

With the spread of networked information technology into secondary and tertiary education, the fields learning analytics and educational data mining emerged in the late 2000s as subfields of a wider movement toward web analytics and online usage data mining (Bach, 2010). It would be difficult to overstate the importance that web usage analytics and data mining already have as constitutive components of today's web-based e-commerce models and social computing paradigms. Tremendous amounts of money and research are being directed toward the art and practice of probing deeply into the mountains of activity data users leave behind in visiting online material. More controversial is the increasing deployment of browsing analytics and data mining for surveillance and profiling of users. Debates about the pros and cons of these kinds of tracking and monitoring technologies are only just beginning.

Although they are subfields of web usage analytics in general, learning analytics and educational data mining are not the same; it should be conceded. Nevertheless, they are paired throughout this chapter mainly because of the shared set of issues and challenges they present in their common implementations so far. The terms learning analytics and educational data mining have come to refer generally to a set of somewhat overlapping techniques for probing deeply into mountains of e-learner data. This informal use of the terms glosses over the extensive data structures and innovate techniques used to do the probing. The common use of the terms generally refers to computational techniques applied in order to uncover patterns in huge data sets about online teaching and learning. The underlying techniques draw on a variety of sophisticated and ever-improving machine learning algorithms. Encompassing a wide range of goals and approaches, learning analytics and data mining of user activity in e-learning systems have become research fields in their own right in recent years (Siemens & Baker, 2012). Typical approaches focus on how to find patterns in learner online behavior. Arranging various patterns into groupings (e.g., based on the activities, roles, and timing involved) can shed light on issues such as how to evaluate student progress or recommend learning pathway options. The variety of learning analytics and educational data mining investigations is also broad and ever increasing, but some of the better-known approaches include clustering, association analysis, and predictive analytics (Romero & Ventura, 2010).

As related fields, learning analytics and educational data mining also represent burgeoning research and policy areas where the teacher training and teacher research fields' traditional thought leadership and policy expertise will be much needed. A fair generalization can be made that much of the inquiry and practical wisdom developed so far center on applying computational techniques to large data sets about students. Applying tracking and data mining techniques in online teaching and learning contexts, learning analytics and educational data mining encompass a unique range of research questions and policy issues. Learning analytics and educational data mining efforts in secondary and tertiary education settings have served as the basis for discovering categories and characteristics in student enrollment patterns. In the context online learning environments, data mining projects have examined similarities across thousands of online sessions to reveal useful characteristic aspects of students' interaction with e-learning content as well (McGrath, 2009). The influence of learning analytics and educational data mining on secondary and tertiary education is potentially enormous. The easy response to this new technology, i.e., unwavering acceptance of it as a black box technology would be a tragic mistake in the face of required demand. With or without the teacher training program's involvement, many learning analytics and educational data mining-based attempts at creating metric-driven smart school will spring up in the coming decade. Within the context of online learning, an important set of strategy and policy considerations arises. With teaching and learning activities increasingly moving online, important research and policy questions surface as to how users are to be studied, how their usage patterns should be captured, how that user data will get analyzed, by whom and for what purposes.

3 Implications for Teacher Training Validity and Inferencing

With the early generation of learning analytics and educational data mining systems, important warnings have already been raised about both the myriad privacy concerns and the tremendous sociopolitical implications of the data mining revolution on a global scale. Comprehensive surveys of the privacy issues can be found in Ferguson (Ferguson et al., 2016). An overview of the critical data studies field is provided by Kitchin and Lauriault (2014) and Illiadis and Russo (2016). For education, some of the particularly salient concerns raised here include the ownership and commodification of learner data (Pardo & Siemens, 2014), governance and policy (Slade & Prinsloo, 2013), and the emerging data "divide" that mirrors the socioeconomic digital divide of previous decades (Dalton, Taylor, & Thatcher, 2016).

Meanwhile, even as we are rightly concerned about these critically important issues (e.g., confidentiality of learners' activities and the longer term data inequities), it is important in the near term to recognize as well a fundamental set of methodological problems within the emerging data sciences disciplines driving this movement. Namely, there is a significant methodological gap between the promise of the new technology and its ability to deliver reliable results. Learning analytics, educational data mining, and data science, in general, are beginning to experience growing pains as technology implementations move from the research environment to the real world. As recently acknowledged in a watershed report from the National Academies, the immaturity of data mining and data analytics as disciplines is a potential crisis if not quickly addressed. The data sciences, according to this report, are years away from being reliably principled reliability from an engineering perspective and conclusion validity from a statistical perspective (Jordan, 2013).

As a result, one immediate area in which learning analytics and educational research would benefit from more engagement from the fields of teacher training and teacher research would be in bringing statistical rigor to the information frameworks being deployed. Indeed, the common technical challenges that are bedeviling early generation learning analytics and educational data mining systems are age-old familiar issues for educational research and statistical inferencing: measurement error, sample size, over-fitting, etc. (Baker & Inventado, 2014). While e-commerce and social media system for search engines and recommender services may be able to tolerate high order error rates in their results, a system focusing on the fate and trajectory of individual student learners can scarcely tolerate fractional error rates. This typical challenge faced by designers of learning analytics and educational data mining systems stems in part from the relentless combining of disparate data sources—a technique that undergirds all web analytics technology. Digital systems cut across a wide range of teaching and learning activities in secondary and tertiary education today. The scope and reach of digital systems now increasingly extend to activities as they occur both inside and outside of physical classrooms, labs, and informal study areas. Electronic books, learning management systems, interactive student response systems, lecture capture systems, and digitally controlled smart classrooms are just a few examples of technology trends that potentially bring along with them an unprecedented amount of instrumentation quietly collecting lots of data about teacher and learner activities in and across these various spaces. In snapshots, these usage streams offer data that can be helpful for understanding and supporting teaching and learning. If combined across time and location, the varied data sources open windows onto even more interesting activity patterns and relations.

These mosaics, however, are very difficult to create and analyze in ways that meet traditional approaches to reliability and validity assumptions about data (Birgersson, Hansson, & Franke, 2016; Zhu et al., 2014; Doan, Domingos, & Halev, 2001). The reliability of traditional parametric statistical methods, for instance, requires as a starting point some assumptions about estimators and requirements about the probability distribution of the overall population from which data samples are drawn. In contrast, data mining approaches typically make no assumptions about models in the underlying data. Not making assumptions about models and distributions is partly seen as a way of allowing for serendipity. The exploratory knowledge discovery nature of data mining is valued for finding hidden patterns. More practically, the application of traditional parametric methods to big data can make exploration infeasible, resulting in either the discarding of much data or a computational complexity that makes timely results prohibitive. So data mining approaches relax the rigorous requirements of traditional parametric methods as a necessary cost in reliability and controlling uncertainty of achieving good enough results in a timely fashion (Larose, 2007). As a consequence divining rods, many implementers stray from inferential rigor and resort instead to heuristic techniques. These heuristic techniques such as nearest neighbor machine learning algorithms for classifying data by membership into groups. As the algorithm "learns" from training set data, it improves in its ability to assign class membership at some practical level of reliability that is often quite functional and suitable for some applications, such as profiling users of an e-commerce system or selecting customers as the audience for a marketing campaign.

Where the risks and consequences involved in misclassifying some of the data are acceptable, data mining's departure from traditional guidelines of reliability, error, and bias are deemed acceptable in some contexts (Glymour et al., 1997; Dasu & Johnson, 2003). Misclassifying a consumer for inclusion in a marketing campaign involves little impact. Someone getting a pop-up advertisement that turns out to be of no interest to them can dismiss it and move on. In contrast, misclassifying a learner regarding their progress in school may have a lasting impact. A student getting classified as needing remediation may find it very difficult to shake such a label (Prinsloo & Slade, 2016). While teaching itself involves plenty of informed guesses within the moment, the field of education has long embraced inferential methods for the many situations where informed guessing is not good enough. It is important, for example, to quantify certainty in deciding whether a learning outcome has been met, a new instructional method is effective, or a student should matriculate. The main and simplest point here is that basic notions of confidence intervals, sampling, and proportion estimates are already part of the traditional teacher training and teacher research toolboxes. The field of education can bring to the educational data mining and learning analytics conversations a balanced perspective on requirements for quantifying the degree of uncertainty and the use of statistical decision-making. As learning analytics and educational data mining are increasingly becoming available as mainstream research topics in educational research, there are plenty of opportunities to expand the focus to consider to engineer them better as reliable decision support systems (Pardo, 2014). Meanwhile, teachers, teacher training candidates, and teacher researchers alike must specifically develop critical and reflective perspective and stances toward these new technologies.

4 Implications for Teacher Research—More Theory, Thicker Description

As we've seen, teacher training programs and the field of teacher research need to become more critically engaged with learning analytics and educational data mining particularly regarding the reliability and validity of the answers being given. The second reason for critical engagement, we will see next, stems from the kinds of questions being asked. Many of the early generation systems developed and studied so far focused heavily on technology development and proof-of-concept prototypes, with the teaching and learning settings serving as mere background. Indeed, the educational questions, subjects, and issues in many studies, it seems, are chosen simply to provide algorithmic testbeds based on the convenient access to log data. As we will see, even in the case of production systems that have seen some success, the learning analytics and educational data mining approaches employed have demonstrated useful albeit very ***narrow*** insights: most commonly in detecting students who are in need of intervention or remediation.

This narrowness starts to make sense if we consider that typically is analyzed in early generation learning analytics and educational data mining systems: the so-called click streams left behind by students visiting, browsing, and interacting with e-learning content and tools. While the strength of the new technologies can be found in their ability to deal with huge and diverse data sets, a potential weakness stems from this same reliance on gathering pre-existing usage data. Behind the typical early generation learning analytics and educational data mining systems are evolving efforts to bring together more usage data regarding both source and volume. Most of these efforts, however, face practical hurdles: pulling together whatever usage data is available from disparate online tools and services and combining them by using loose-coupling and lightweight data standards. To accomplish these tasks, the functionality for combining and analyzing learning activity and learner information often gets boiled down to even simpler common denominators. Obviously, the scope of the patterns, arrangements, or groupings to be discovered depend heavily on the breadth and depth of the user activity streams in the original clickstream data.

Looking at some prominent research studies in the field, we can start to see the constraining effect of the data source availability. In the case of the Purdue University's Course Signals, for instance, the key data element used as a proxy for "effort" was simply the student's overall usage pattern in the course site within learning management system (Arnold and Pistilli, 2012). These traces of usage activity, combined with other educational analytics (e.g., test scores, GPA, standardized test scores, unit load, age, etc.) were mined to produce "actionable intelligence." Visualized in a rudimentary green, yellow, red dashboard rating for each student's potential risk of failure, the actionable information thereby gives instructors and support personnel high-level signals about student progress. The same constraining effect of the available data sources can also be seen in the units of analysis studied so far in the promising Open High School of Utah (OHSU) project, where learning analytics play a crucial role in mediating teacher and student interaction (Tonks, Weston, Wiley,

& Barbour, 2013). Given that students and teachers are not copresent in a physical school building, online analytics become essential in this virtual school situation for recording and monitoring individual student access to course materials, discussion forum activity, and their assessment results. In an online school, the volume from the various forms of user activity data captured grows by quickly by the day. In the context of the Moodle learning management system deployed for OHSU, instructors are provided with some monitoring capabilities as well as some predictive learning analytics about the students as derived from the thousands of hours of students accessing the virtual school's course sites and tools. Nevertheless, the breadth and quality of the data analytics here still depend on the what's available in the data source—in this case, Moodle activity logs.

A large cross-institutional open source project such as Moodle, for instance, involves scores of developers around the world over the years contributing to a shared code base. To facilitate distributed development, the design of the Moodle framework places minimal requirements on those who might want to create or integrate a new tool. By minimizing the overhead of tool creation and rewrites, however, the Moodle framework offers very little out-of-the-box functionality in the area of usage reporting, as Romero points out in his data mining study of Moodle use at the University of Cordoba (Romero, Ventura, & Garcia, 2008). The behind-the-scenes view of Moodle in operation reveals a piecemeal and heterogeneous affair. In particular, since responsibility for logging information about users' interaction within a running instance of Moodle is largely left up to individual tool developers, the usage data is inconsistent. In the case of OHSU, these limits have meant that learning analytics system is necessary but not sufficient for instructors in supporting teacher decision-making (Borup, Graham, & Drysdale, 2014). In the OHSU example, the deployment of these new technologies in a virtual school setting was shown to provide some benefits in narrow cases: monitoring, identifying students at risk, remediation, just-in-time alert systems, etc.

Of course, teaching and learning involve far more than just monitoring student presence and mitigating situations in which some students risk failing (Macfadyen & Dawson, 2010). First-generation learning analytics and educational data mining system have been shown to succeed in small online focused areas of early alert and remediation, but how to extend these new approaches to broader theoretical models and concerns of teaching and learning? Here, most observers do not yet have answers. For George Siemens, a major leader in the field, such issues are the main challenge for learning analytics and educational data mining if they are to survive. The next generation of learning analytics and educational data mining must focus aspects of pedagogy, he argues. To overcome the early generation limitation, argues Siemens, a new design approach for developing learning analytics and educational data mining for development must include learning from the start:

> Some analytics techniques, such as early warning systems [12, 13], attention metadata [14], recommender systems [15], tutoring and learner models [16], and network analysis [17], are already in use in education. A few papers in LAK11 presented analytics

> approaches that emphasized newer techniques, such as participatory learning and reputation mechanisms [18], recommender systems improvement [19], and cultural considerations in analytics [20]. Beyond these, however, there are limited first-generation LA techniques. The lack of defined identity of LA tools and techniques with an explicit learning focus is reflected in how analytics are described in papers and conference venues: "It's like Shazam", or "It's like Amazon or Netflix", or "It's like Facebook friend recommendations". This is not to criticize appropriating techniques from other fields for use in learning. Instead, it is a reflection that LA-specific approaches are still emerging and more research is required.
>
> (Siemens, 2012, p. 6)

Siemens does not say how to achieve a more theory-driven approach. However, he does correctly pinpoint a key relation where many of these factors would come into play at the earliest stage of learning analytics and educational data mining systems design: the tensions between bottom-up approaches based on available data and top-down approaches based on theoretical inquiry. Some new set of design processes is needed, Siemens asserts, for balancing local needs against the top-down constraints. What Siemens has put his finger on here, a process by which system functionality and data source descriptiveness would be better shaped by theory-driven questions, rather than the reverse.

Wider recognition of the need for more theory-driven approaches has begun to emerge as the single most important concern of the new these new fields (Dawson, Mirriahi, & Gasevic, 2015). Regarding learning analytics and educational data mining study results connecting to theoretical models of teaching and learning, the constraints of the data sources have limited the scope and power even in the few studies that have attempted modest theoretical claims (Tempelaar, Rienties, & Giesbers, 2015; Pardos, 2015). So another reason for teacher training programs and the field of teacher research to become more directly engaged in the future development of learning analytics and educational data mining include the need for more theory-driven approaches in these new fields (Dawson et al., 2015).

5 Conclusion

This chapter has considered the future of the learning analytics and educational data mining. The two fundamental shortcomings of these new fields are the limited instructional models considered and the relative immaturity of these new technologies when viewed from traditional perspectives of inferencing. In terms of models of instruction, the barriers preventing these systems from developing deeper insights into the teaching and learning activities seem mundane but vexing: the limited data sources upon which these systems can draw. In terms of the immaturity of these new technologies when viewed from traditional perspectives of inferencing and decision-making support, the potential for bias and inaccuracy in the algorithms involved is not merely an engineering problem. It points ahead to a perpetual need for transparency and openness so that algorithms are not concealed in proprietary black boxes where they might avoid scrutiny. Issues around the validity of inferential approaches employed and the narrowness of underlying data being mined point to political and policy questions that must be raised as learning analytics and data mining as decision-support systems are proposed for use in secondary and tertiary education. As we have seen, the challenges and issues seen in the early generation of learning analytics cannot simply be dismissed as growing pains.

This chapter has also pointed to the need for educational professionals to consider not only how such systems are designed and implemented, but also how they could be built better in the future. The influence of learning analytics and educational data mining on secondary and tertiary education is growing quickly. For the field of teaching, a passive response to this new technology, i.e., acceptance of it as a black box technology that cannot be questioned would be a mistake. Indeed, teacher training programs have before them a historic opportunity to influence fundamentally how learning analytics and educational data mining will be deployed and used. This is a role for which the teacher training and teacher research programs are uniquely suited: to influence research agendas, to form, fund, and nurture critical perspectives (Baepler & Murdoch, 2010). Bringing to bear wisdom from a century's worth of scholarship on teaching and learning would well befit educational research and teacher training programs, given their long-standing leadership in researching and assessing technology initiatives in teaching and learning. An important technology convergence is at hand again, one that holds out the promise of tracking, monitoring, measuring, and adapting teaching and learning activity in schools as a means of designing and assessing instructions with adaptive personalization. The field of education could bring to the educational data mining and learning analytics development not only domain expertise but also a balanced perspective on grounding the risks around of statistical decision-making. Finally this central role of the education domain experts, in turn, would necessarily require that educators become more literate in data science as well.

With or without the engagement from the fields of teacher research and teacher training, many learning analytics and educational data mining-based attempts at creating metric-driven smart schools will spring up in the coming decade try to address secondary and tertiary schooling from the perspective of measurement, accountability, and access (Daniel, 2012). The teacher training and teacher research fields' traditional roles as thought leaders in educational research have stemmed historically from their methodological expertise in collecting, managing, and analyzing data about teaching and learning. Teacher training and teacher research fields should extend that tradition by contributing to the evaluation and design of these new systems, bringing along core expertise in methods of educational research and inferencing. Teacher training and teacher research fields also possess unique capacity as a leading contributor to educational policy. By engaging more directly with learning analytics and educational data mining, the fields could develop teachers' critical literacy and expertise, while also shaping and advancing policies geared toward ensuring openness and transparency in how these new knowledge domains of learning analytics and educational data mining are implemented and managed. Professional educators in general also have a responsibility to serve policy advocates around best practices and watchdogs on the lookout for privacy and bias problems. These need already exist. Many more issues and opportunities will become known in the context of virtual school implementations. If professional educators take the leadership role in helping design and create model implementations of learning analytics and educational data mining, the fields of teacher training and teacher research would be in a strong position to ensure that the technology development and implementation are guided systematically by open debate, ethical policies, and grounded understanding of best practices.

References

Arnold, K. E., Pistilli, M. D. (2012). Course signals at Purdue: Using learning analytics to increase student success. In S. Buckingham Shum, D. Gašević, R. Ferguson (Eds.), *Proceedings of the 2nd International Conference on Learning Analytics and Knowledge (LAK '12)* (pp. 267–270). New York: ACM.

Bach, C. (2010). LA: Targeting instruction, curricula, and student support. In *Proceedings EISTA* 2010 June 29—July 2, 2010. Orlando, FL: International Institute of Informatics and Systemics.

Baepler, P., & Murdoch, C. J. (2010). Academic analytics and data mining in tertiary education. *International Journal for the Scholarship of Teaching and Learning, 4*(2), 1–9.

Baker, R. S., & Inventado, P. S. (2014). Educational data mining and learning analytics. In R. S. Baker & P. S. Inventado (Eds.), *Learning analytics* (pp. 61–75). New York, NY: Springer.

Birgersson, M., Hansson, G., & Franke, U. (2016). Data integration using machine learning. In *2016 IEEE 20th International Enterprise Distributed Object Computing Workshop (EDOCW)*, Vienna, Austria.

Blikstein, P. (2013). Multimodal learning analytics. In *Proceedings of the Third International Conference on Learning Analytics and Knowledge*. New York: ACM.

Borup, J., Graham, C. R., & Drysdale, J. S. (2014). The nature of teacher engagement at an online high school. *British Journal of Educational Technology, 45*(5), 793–806.

Bramble, W., & Panda, S. (2008). Organizational and cost structures for distance and online learning. In: W. Bramble, & S. Panda (Eds.), *Economics of distance and online learning*. London & New York: Routledge.

Brown, J., & Kurzweil, M. (2017). *The complex universe of alternative post-secondary credentials and pathways*. Cambridge, MA.: American Academy of Arts & Sciences.

Carlsen, W. S. (2001). Domains of teacher knowledge. In J. Gess-Newsome & N. G. Lederman (Eds.), *Examining pedagogical content knowledge* (pp. 133–144). Dordrecht, Netherlands: Kluwer Academic.

Cuban, L. (2001). *Oversold and underused: Computers in the classroom*. Cambridge, MA: Harvard University Press.

Dalton, C. M., Taylor, L., & Thatcher, J. (2016). Critical data studies: A dialog on data and space. *Big Data & Society, 3*(1).

Daniel, J. S. (2010). *Mega-schools, technology, and teachers: Achieving education for all*. London & New York: Routledge.

Daniel, J. (2012). Making sense of MOOCs: Musings in a maze of myth, paradox, and possibility. *Journal of Interactive Media in Education*.

Daniel, B. (2015). Big data and analytics in tertiary education: Opportunities and challenges. *British Journal of Educational Technology, 46*(5), 904–920.

Dasu, T., & Johnson, T. (2003). *Exploratory data mining and data cleaning*. New York: Wiley.

Dawson, S., Mirriahi, N., & Gasevic, D. (2015). Importance of theory in learning analytics in formal and workplace settings. *Journal of Learning Analytics, 2*(2), 1–4.

Doan, A., Domingos, P., & Halevy, A. Y. (2001). Reconciling schemas of disparate data sources: A machine-learning approach. *ACM Sigmod Record, 30*(2), 509–520.

Ferguson, R., Hoel, T., Scheffel, M., & Drachsler, H. (2016). Guest editorial: Ethics and privacy in learning analytics. *Journal of Learning Analytics, 3*(1), 5–15.

Glymour, C., Madigan, D., Pregibon, D., & Smyth, P. (1997). Statistical themes and lessons for data mining. *Data Mining and Knowledge Discovery, 1*(1), 11–28.

Iliadis, A., & Russo, F. (2016). Critical data studies: An introduction. *Big Data & Society, 3*(2).

Jagadish, H. V. (2015). Big data and science: Myths and reality. *Big Data Research, 2*(2), 49–52.

Jordan, M. I., et al. (2013). *Frontiers in massive data analysis*. Washington, D.C.: The National Academies Press.

Jung, I. (2005). ICT-Pedagogy integration in teacher training: Application cases worldwide. *Educational Technology & Society, 8*(2), 94–101.

Kenny, C. (2006). *Overselling the web: Development and the internet*. Boulder, CO: Lynne Rienner.

Kleickmann, T., Richter, D., Kunter, M., Elsner, J., Besser, M., Krauss, S., et al. (2013). Teachers' content knowledge and pedagogical content knowledge the role of structural differences in teacher education. *Journal of Teacher Education, 64*(1), 90–106.

Kozma, R. B. (2008). Comparative analysis of policies for ICT in education. In J. Voogt & G. Knezek (Eds.), *International handbook of information technology in primary and secondary education* (pp. 1083–1096). New York, NY: Springer.

Kitchin, R., & Lauriault, T. P. (2014). Towards critical data studies: Charting and unpacking data assemblages and their work. In J. Eckert, A. Shears, & J. Thatcher (Eds.), *Geoweb and big data* (The programmable city working paper 2; pre-print version of chapter to be published). University of Nebraska Press. Available at SSRN: https://ssrn.com/abstract=2474112 (Forthcoming).

Kumar, V. S., Somasundaram, T. S., Boulanger, D., Seanosky, J., & Vilela, M. F. (2015). Big data LA: A new perspective. In Kinshuk & Huang (Eds.), *Ubiquitous learning environments and technologies*. Berlin: Springer.

Larose, D. T. (2007). *Data mining methods and models*. New York: Wiley.

Long, P., & Siemens, G. (2011). Penetrating the fog: Analytics in learning and Education. *Educause Review, 48*(5), 31–40.

Macfadyen, L. P., & Dawson, S. (2010). Mining LMS data to develop an "early warning system" for educators: A proof of concept. *Computers & Education, 54*(2), 588–599.

McGrath, O. (2009). Mining user activity data in tertiary education open systems: Trends, challenges, and possibilities. In T. Kidd (Ed.), *Handbook of research on technology project management, planning, and operations*. Hershey, PA: Information Science Reference.

Moe, T., & Chubb, J. (2009). *Liberating learning: Technology, politics, and the future of American education*. San Francisco: Jossey-Bass.

O'Neil, C. (2016). *Weapons of math destruction. How big data increases inequality and threatens democracy*. New York: Crown.

Pardo, A. (2014). Designing learning analytics experiences. In *Learning analytics* (pp. 15–38). New York: Springer.

Pardo, A., & Siemens, G. (2014). Ethical and privacy principles for learning analytics. *British Journal of Educational Technology, 45*(3), 438–450.

Pardos, Z. A. (2015). Commentary on "Beyond time-on-task: the relationship between spaced study and certification in MOOCs". *Journal of Learning Analytics and Knowledge, 2*(2), 70–74.

Prinsloo, P., & Slade, S. (2016). Student vulnerability, agency, and learning analytics: An exploration. *Journal of Learning Analytics, 3*(1), 159–182.

Romero, C., Ventura, S., & García, E. (2008). Data mining in course management systems: Moodle case study and tutorial. *Computers & Education, 51*(1), 368–384.

Romero, C., & Ventura, S. (2010). EDM: A review of the state-of-the-art. *IEEE Transaction on Systems, Man, and Cybernetics, Part C: Applications and Reviews, 40*(6), 601–618.

Shulman, L. S. (1986). Those who understand: Knowledge growth in teaching. *Educational Researcher, 15*(2), 4–14.

Siemens, G. (2012, April). Learning analytics: Envisioning a research discipline and a domain of practice. In *Proceedings of the 2nd International Conference on Learning Analytics and Knowledge* (pp. 4–8). New York: ACM.

Siemens, G., & d Baker, R. S. (2012). Learning analytics and educational data mining: towards communication and collaboration. In *Proceedings of the 2nd International Conference on learning analytics and knowledge* (pp. 252–254). New York: ACM.

Slade, S., & Prinsloo, P. (2013). Learning analytics: Ethical issues and dilemmas. *American Behavioral Scientist, 57*(10), 1510–1529.

Tempelaar, D. T., Rienties, B., & Giesbers, B. (2015). In search for the most informative data for feedback generation: Learning Analytics in a data-rich context. *Computers in Human Behavior, 47,* 157–167.

Tonks, D., Weston, S., Wiley, D., & Barbour, M. K. (2013). "Opening" a new kind of school: The story of the Open High School of Utah. *The International Review of Research in Open and Distributed Learning, 14*(1), 255–271.

Zhu, H., Madnick, S. E., Lee, Y. W., & Wang, R. Y. (2014). *Data and information quality research: Its evolution and future.*

Learning Traces, Competence Assessment, and Causal Inference for English Composition

Clayton Clemens, Vivekanandan Kumar, David Boulanger, Jérémie Seanosky and Kinshuk

Abstract It is widely acknowledged that writing is a process and should be taught as a process. However, it is still assessed as though it is a product. Educational technology makes now possible for teachers to become observers of the writing process of their students to discover how their writing competences (e.g., grammatical accuracy, topic flow, transition, and vocabulary usage) develop over time. The present research proposes an innovative technique to identify the actual drivers of writing performance through a formal causality framework, unleashing a new source of potential insights to scaffold more effectively the writing process and guarantee more reliable success at the end.

Keywords Analytics of writing process · Causality · Competence · Big data Natural-language processing · Learning analytics

---

C. Clemens · V. Kumar (✉) · D. Boulanger · J. Seanosky
Athabasca University, 1200, 10011—109 St., Edmonton, AB T5J 3S8, Canada
e-mail: vive@athabascau.ca

C. Clemens
e-mail: clayton.clemens@gmail.com

D. Boulanger
e-mail: dboulanger1@athabasca.edu

J. Seanosky
e-mail: jeremie@rsdv.ca

Kinshuk
University of North Texas, Discovery Park, Suite E290D, Union Circle, Box 311068, Denton, TX 76203-5017, USA
e-mail: Kinshuk@unt.edu

J. M. Spector et al. (eds.), *Frontiers of Cyberlearning*, Lecture Notes in Educational Technology, https://doi.org/10.1007/978-981-13-0650-1_3

1 For Big Data in Education

Big data in business and industry come from a variety of sources: messages, tweets, likes, purchases, and other transactions. In education, the source of big data mostly comes from learning traces: low-level records of student activity within an online learning system. Educational big data are a comparatively new idea. The Internet has produced distributed online learning environments, which have in turn begotten a new paradigm, different from the centuries-old doctrines of instruction.

Learning traces themselves may be collected from a swath of different activities. The most basic kind of learning trace is a page-visit trail in an online learning environment. Page visits and link clicks, associated with timestamp information, comprise the most basic kind of trace: a student's path through a series of learning objects.

While navigational traces are helpful to assess how engaging the content is, learning traces may also be specific to individual subjects of instruction. Within each learning domain, there are particular actions that, when recorded, can be instrumental in determining a student's development in that subject. Similarly to navigational traces, virtual environments are ideally suited to gather these types of domain-specific actions within a system.

The ability to gather such granular information is new to education. In traditional settings, creating a log of every action a student took to construct an essay or complete a programming assignment would be an impossible task. As such, we have now entered an era where it is possible to view students' process, the exact series of steps they take to complete their assignments in their domain of study.

In English composition, the gap between process-based and product-based instruction was identified decades ago (Murray, 1972). As a result, writing has been taught as a process, but because of the limitations of traditional classrooms, it was never actually assessed as a process. Learning traces on a granular level allow instructors to begin to understand the nature in which learners and their work respond to the inputs of the curriculum and the environment, and lay the foundation for the generalized measurement of student competence in a subject.

With an arsenal of competence values based on the quantitative nature of student learning traces, it is possible to examine how, when, and why competences develop, and how they develop together as a collective ecosystem. It becomes possible to examine student cognition in regard to development of skills and knowledge. Moreover, understanding instruction as being a system of interventions to increase competences, and knowing the potential effects of increasing a particular skill, has enormous pedagogical value.

2 Competence

More broadly, competence is defined as having a required skill, knowledge, qualification, or capacity[1]. Sampson and Fytros (2008) condense definitions given by multiple authors in the literature to one specific definition: "A competence can be defined as a set of personal characteristics (e.g., skills, knowledge, attitudes) that an individual possesses or needs to acquire in order to perform an activity within a specific context." This definition captures the various aspects of competence, allowing for the definition of frameworks to evaluate competences in a structured and formal manner.

A large body of work surrounds the classification and quantification of competence. The aspects of competence (skills, knowledge, attitudes, and context) are often accounted for in these models, along with some rating or numerical assessment of the level of competence an individual may have. When models such as RDCEO[2] or HR-XML[3] are used consistently across a corporation or educational institution, they can standardize assessment and storage of individuals' competences, and optimize them in roles that best work with their existing skills and develop them further. Competence models also exist in conjunction with curriculum in the form of rubrics[4], or as universal tests for knowledge such as language (Verhelst, Van Avermaet, Takala, Figueras, & North, 2009).

The problem persists that students are usually tested for knowledge rather than for competence. Students are required to ingest a large amount of information, and then repeat or apply that information in the form of some assignment. While this format works for some subjects, many skills are reliant not only on the final outcome, but on the process of creation. Someone may be capable of creating the required deliverables for a test, but with a method that creates unseen systemic problems that may manifest in future work.

In the modern virtual environment, however, learning traces can inform the process of competence development at the assignment, topic, or course level. Where an instructor cannot sit on a student's shoulder, a software agent can sit in a text field or in a word processor and silently gather their keystroke input. This low-level data collection is a pure process. Useful in its own right, it is nonetheless maximized when combined with analysis and synthesis techniques into models of competence that track and quantify changes in competence.

---

[1]Dictionary.com (2017). Definition of "competence." Retrieved Aug. 10, 2017, from http://www.dictionary.com/browse/competence/.

[2]IMS Global Learning Consortium. IMS Reusable Definition of Competency or Educational Objective Specification. Retrieved Aug. 10, 2017, from https://www.imsglobal.org/competencies/index.html.

[3]IEEE Standard for Learning Technology-Data Model for Reusable Competency Definitions. (2008). IEEE Std 1484.20.1-2007, 1–32. http://doi.org/10.1109/IEEESTD.2008.4445693.

[4]Alberta Education, Canada (2000). English Language Arts K - Grade 9. Retrieved Aug. 10, 2017, from http://www.learnalberta.ca/ProgramOfStudy.aspx?lang=en&ProgramId=404703#.

3 Learning Traces

Learning traces represent the source of most educational big data. Learning traces are minute granular snapshots of student activity in a particular domain. As mentioned above, this is a description of each student's learning and creative process. Similar to how business intelligence has emerged for enterprises in response to large volumes of data (Cohen, Dolan, Dunlap, Hellerstein, & Welton, 2009), learning analytics has become the field for analyzing educational big data. The accepted definition of learning analytics is actually, "the measurement, collection, analysis and reporting of data about learners and their contexts, for purposes of understanding and optimizing learning and the environments in which it occurs."[5]

For some domains, even measurement and collection of data are a challenge. Some data are easy to measure, and some are difficult. At one extreme, navigational traces through a learning environment are very simple to log and track. Number of visits, time of visits, and path through the system tree all represent easily quantifiable aspects of that domain. On the other extreme lie physical activity and music, normally not considered to be programmatically traceable at all. However, even at these difficult extremes, research exists to quantify aspects of the activities. Wearable fitness technology is becoming ubiquitous in Western culture, and musical performance can be captured via MIDI controllers (Guillot, Guillot, Kumar, & Kinshuk, 2016). In the middle are activities that can be performed on the computer directly. Learning traces from activities like these only require that a listener be set up to capture the information as the student enters it. This could be a keylogger for writing-based assignments, or a method to capture the abstract syntax tree of the code from each compilation in a programming environment (Johnson et al., 2003; Kumar et al., 2015).

For writing particularly, it is simple to record each event that comprises a user's process. The layer of analysis and quantification is available in the form of natural-language processing (NLP) tools. Several aspects of English composition can be quantified, and NLP provides access to a swath of functionalities to aid in doing so. Part-of-speech taggers (Toutanova, Klein, Manning, & Singer, 2003) tag each word in a sentence or composition with a part of speech. Counts of different parts of speech provide a measure of how connected a document is (number of connecting words), how personal it is (number of personal pronouns), or how much imagery is present (number of adverbs and adjectives). Natural-language parsers (Klein & Manning, 2003) can break sentences down into their core components like noun phrases and verb phrases, giving a measure of average complexity. Sentiment analyzers can check the degree of positivity or negativity in individual words, phrases, or sentences (Nasukawa & Yi, 2003; Pang & Lee, 2008; Socher et al., 2013; Yi, Nasukawa, Bunescu, & Niblack, 2003). With knowledge of word lemmas and synonym sets (Miller, 1995) and other relations between words, it is possible to identify which related words and phrases are repeated between sentences and throughout the document. These semantic distances provide a measure of topic flow between sen-

[5]Siemens, G. (2011). 1st International Conference on Learning Analytics and Knowledge 2011. Retrieved Aug. 10, 2017, from https://tekri.athabascau.ca/analytics/.

tences and paragraphs (O'Rourke, Calvo, & McNamara, 2011). Matching systems can count the number of grammatical errors (using rule-based analysis of the text) and spelling errors (checking each word against a dictionary). Even simple word and syllable counts give a measurable impression of general complexity or readability using simple formulae (Flesch, 1948; Kincaid, Fishburne, Rogers, & Chissom, 1975).

NLP metrics, when associated with each learning trace event, provide a numeric evolution of student progression, not just a descriptive path. The metrics can be further combined to construct higher level measures of competence for different areas within the domain. As a simple example, taking the ratio of spelling errors in the document to the total number of words provides a measure of average spelling accuracy. The ratio of unique words in the document compared to the total number of words provides a measure of lexical diversity, and so on. With each event, these metrics and their competence derivatives will shift and flux, and hopefully grow as the student learns.

Certainly, tracking these competences over time is helpful for students and instructors. However, with this new wealth of statistical information, it is possible to go one step further and measure the effects of interventions upon different competences. Doing so requires the use of a set of tools to examine causal interactions from data.

4 The Next Step: Causal Models

The idea of causality is intrinsic to the human experience. It is part of humans' intuitive understanding about the way the world works (Russell, 1912). If a person takes a certain action, he or she can expect that it will have a certain effect. This intuition allows human beings to function through a variety of tasks in normal life despite the fact that notions of causation are often biased by perspectives, beliefs, and values. In order to make objective scientific statements about causality, its definition must be formalized.

The core concept of causation is that the occurrence of an event creates another event. If an action occurs, something reacts. If the first event did not occur, then the second will not, or would happen differently. Thus, the standard method for evaluating causal effects is by having an intervention (or treatment) and a counterfactual (what would have happened if the intervention did not take place).

It is not possible to see the effects of the intervention and the counterfactual simultaneously. The events are mutually exclusive. Therefore, the scientific way to test for causal effects is a randomized experiment. The treatment is randomly assigned within the sample, representing the intervention, and the remaining untreated portion of the sample represents the counterfactual. By comparing the two groups, the experimental and the control, it is possible to estimate the net causal effect of treatment: the difference in response from the two groups. Randomized experiments are ubiquitous throughout the sciences (Peirce & Jastrow, 1884).

In many situations, however, it is impossible to produce a randomized experiment to intervene. The real-world is often not as well controlled as a randomized experiment must be, and it is difficult to separate the real variables from confounders. Moreover, the variables experimented upon may not be the only ones present in the causal system. Finally, sometimes, it is simply impossible to intervene on certain populations. In these cases, the only tool at the researcher's disposal is data, a number of variables about the population that can be measured.

Statistics can be used on data to examine how two variables correlate. Correlation presents some of the same problems as randomized experiments, however, in that there may be more variables in the system confounding the results.

The solution is an even deeper formalism to causation, bringing it into mathematical notation and defining each of its properties in an axiomatic way (Spirtes, Glymour, & Scheines, 2000). One of the most important properties of causation is the notion of independence, that is, two variables have no effect on one another. Independence and conditional independence are also properties of probabilistic systems, which are extremely well defined and form the basis for many reasoning systems.

Causal systems can be represented by directed acyclic graphs (DAGs). $A \rightarrow B$ in a causal graph means that A causes B. $A \rightarrow B \leftarrow C$ means that A and C are common causes of B, and A and C are independent of one another. Causal DAGs are similar to the kinds of graphs used in Bayesian network systems.

There are three important axioms and one graphical relation that govern the connection between causality and probability. The Causal Markov condition assumes that each variable is independent of all of its non-descendants conditional upon its parents. The Causal Markov condition has a parallel in the realm of probability, which states a similar constraint for probabilistic systems.

Minimality is the second condition, and it assumes that there is no subgraph of a given causal system that also meets the Causal Markov condition. That is, that the causal system is the minimal representation of the Causal Markov condition.

Together, these two assumptions constrain the possible causal systems to the structures that are most common in science. Save for a few exceptions, all randomized experiments and all valid causal studies conform to these conditions.

A third axiom, faithfulness, enforces a stronger assumption. Faithfulness assumes that the conditional independence relationships in a probability distribution are the same as those present in the causal system that generated it. Faithfulness is more likely to be violated in the real-world systems than the Markov condition. Certain subsets of problems cause faithfulness to fail, and these generally fall under the banner of Simpson's paradox (Simpson, 1951).

Applying the Causal Markov and minimality conditions to a causal system produces a number of independence relations in the system, but it is not the entire set. A graphical relationship called dependence-separation or d-separation (Geiger, Paz, & Pearl, 1991) defines all and exactly the independence relations given by a causal graph. In formal terms, d-separation is defined as follows.

If X and Y are distinct vertices in a directed graph G, and $\mathbf{W}$ is a set of vertices in G not containing X or Y, then X and Y are d-separated given $\mathbf{W}$ in G if and only if there exists no undirected path U between X and Y, such that (1) every collider on U has a descendent in $\boldsymbol{W}$, and (2) no other vertex on U is in $\boldsymbol{W}$.

Causal inference uses these axioms and relations to produce a number of potential causal graphs from the conditional independence relations calculated from a dataset (Cramir, 1946; Fisher, 1915). These sets of graphs are called equivalence classes.

The condition of causal sufficiency separates algorithms into two broad types. Causal sufficiency is an assumption that the variables given in the data represent all of the common causes in the system. Namely that there are no confounders. Because this is so often the case, there is a class of algorithms that assumes causal sufficiency does not hold.

Causal algorithms (the PC algorithm in particular) begin with the complete undirected graph, and then remove adjacencies between variables if they are independent given any set. Two tests are conducted on triples of nodes, based on d-separation, to orient the nodes. The first is the collider test, which checks a triple of the form $X - Y - Z$ to see if the set that separated X and Z contains Y. If not, then the nodes can be oriented $X \rightarrow Y \leftarrow Z$. Following this, any remaining triples of the form $X \rightarrow Y - Z$ are oriented as $X \rightarrow Y \rightarrow Z$ because they cannot be colliders.

Undirected nodes are considered to be uncertain in the equivalence class. This means that the arrowhead could be at either end of the line, and the causal structure would be equivalent according to our principles and assumptions.

When the causal sufficiency condition is relaxed, algorithms can search for confounders. In order to properly represent latent variables, additional notation is needed. The equivalence classes or patterns for algorithms that do not assume causal sufficiency are represented as partial ancestral graphs (PAGs), which add a circle symbol ($\circ$) to the ends of arrows to indicate possible latent confounders. A circle means that there could be an arrowhead at that location, or that there could be a latent common cause between the two variables.

The FCI algorithm works similarly to the PC algorithm but begins with all adjacencies set to $\circ - \circ$. In the same way, arrowheads are oriented during the collider test, but the $\circ$ symbol still remains on one side. The away-from-collider test becomes powerful in FCI because it can determine when a legitimate one-way cause is occurring.

Equivalence class patterns, PAGs, and DAGs can show causal structure in terms of directions and which causes are responsible for which effects; however, they cannot in themselves show causal strengths and the nature of the effects. In order to discover this information, another statistical structure is needed.

For continuous variables, structural equation models (SEMs) can mathematically represent the causes and effects as a series of linear equations. For example, the structure $X \rightarrow Y \leftarrow Z$ has the following SEM model:

$$X = \varepsilon_X$$

$$Z = \varepsilon_Z$$

$$Y = \beta_1 X + \beta_2 Y + \varepsilon_Y$$

SEMs are produced from an equivalence class and instantiated from the original data. That is, the causal structure determines the equations in an SEM, based on which variables cause others. The data are used to apply values to the equation parameters. The error terms for each independent variable are the mean and standard deviation, accounting for the random variation.

Together, the causal DAG, the data, and the SEM produce a model of causality that is mathematically viable and can be tested for accuracy and goodness of fit (Bentler, 1990; MacCallum, Browne, & Sugawara, 1996; Schwarz, 1978). These methodologies can be applied to any statistical dataset. The next section will cover a case study in which these causal methods were applied to the learning analytics of writing competence.

5 The Case Study

The study in question (Clemens, 2017) made use of a custom-built simulator called WriteSim that takes completed papers from corpora (or any other source) and outputs a series of time-stamped records (also called writing events) for each document that represent a trace of the word-level transactions that might occur if a student had composed it. WriteSim used synonym sets to create deviations from the main text as the simulated "students" wrote. The simulator was programmed based on previous studies (Waes & Schellens, 2003) done in writing behavior and profiles. In these studies, students were asked to complete writing tasks. Their keystrokes were individually logged and placed into long streams, which were then painstakingly analyzed to determine a number of writing behaviors. The study examined how, when, and why students paused during writing, and when and why they revised errors in their writing. For each composition, and each student, the number and length of pauses were considered, the location of the pauses within the linguistic area, and whether the pauses were due to formulation (the writer considering what to write next) or revision (correcting existing errors in the document). Pauses and revisions were broken up by the point in the document at which they were completed: whether mid-sentence, mid-paragraph, or at the end of the main composition. The level or linguistic structure of each revision was determined: word, sentence, or paragraph. Additionally, revisions could be mechanical or structural (correcting mechanics like spelling and punctuation vs. reorganizing the document for better topic flow). All these parameters were taken into account by WriteSim and randomly generated in normal distributions during the creation and assignment of writing profiles to the essay writers. These writing profiles drove the writing process simulation for every student.

It is nevertheless important to acknowledge the scope of the simulator's limitations. The objective of the present research through this simulation is to highlight the potential of this new source of insights that would be unleashed by applying this formal approach to causality to the writing process. While this research claims that the causal analytical process is valid, the presented claims are only hypothetical given that the simulation process is not fully representative of the actual writing/revising process, that is, it does not do large-scale structural reconfigurations or does not change the order of phrases, sentences, or paragraphs. For example, this limitation will have the effect of making the topic flow information smoother than it would be if the real-world data were used. As students move and manipulate phrases, it is likely that metrics related to topic flow would tend to spike into local peaks and valleys more often throughout the process. Structure changes could be integrated into future iterations to make the simulator more comprehensive. Again, the hypotheses formulated in this study will only highlight directions for further research in the causal analysis of the writing process.

The result of the simulation was a batch of 744,848 writing events generated by simulating the writing process of 391 essays from the British Academic Written English corpus (Nesi, Sharpling, & Ganobcsik-Williams, 2004) written by 390 distinct students in higher education. As can be seen in Table 1, WriteSim generated in average for each of the 391 essays 1905 writing events, a little greater than the mean number of words per essay, that is, 1786 words. The average processing time per essay was calculated to be approximately 3 h and 20 min. To process all the 744,848 writing events generated from the 391 essays, it took, for a single server instance, 1304 h (54 days) of computing. The writing events were processed in a first-in-first-out (FIFO) queue since the competence assessment downstream attempted to reconstruct the timeline of competence growth. The data were simulated in this setting because of the large amount of time and computational power necessary to generate metrics for each of the events.

The SCALE (Smart Competence Analytics for Learning) (Boulanger, Seanosky, Clemens, Kumar, & Kinshuk, 2016; Boulanger et al., 2016) suite was the processor that assembled 65 metrics and competence information for each of the events in the dataset. Basic metrics included structure counts (number of words, sentences, paragraphs, etc.), word length counts (number of words longer than or equal to 5, 6, 7, or 8 characters), part-of-speech counts, specific word qualities, and error counts. These were combined into ratios and averages, indexes, rubric and essay scores, and finally six writing competences. The table of competences from the study is shown in Table 2.

Table 1 Descriptive statistics of the distributions in terms of the numbers of words, sentences, characters, writing events, and processing time per essay

	Min	Max	Q1	Q3	Median	Mean	SD
Writing events	1000	2229	1789.0	2019.5	1905	1904.98	143.70
Words	51	2162	1694.5	1926.0	1799	1785.55	219.24
Sentences	4	124	58.0	77.0	67	67.76	15.80
Characters	248	10120	7818.0	8964.0	8408	8270.22	1053.43
Processing time (h)	0.53	49.12	1.66	3.24	2.17	3.34	3.79

Table 2 Writing competences from SCALE

Competence	Description
Grammatical accuracy	Grammatical accuracy measures the student's competence in writing correct grammatical structures. It is based on the ratio of instances of incorrect grammar (based on grammar rule violations) to the total number of words in the document (length)
Spelling	Spelling measures the student's competence in spelling correctly. It is based on the ratio of misspelled words to the total number of words in the document
Topic flow	Topic flow is a measure of student competency in relating ideas to one another throughout the text. Topic flow is specifically based on the number of sentence-adjacent content words. Semantic distances are calculated for content words, and the competence is computed by comparing the content words to an ideal standard for topic flow
Transition	Transition is similar to topic flow but measures the overall connectedness of the student's composition. Transition competence is calculated by analyzing the number and distribution of connective words in the document
Vocabulary complexity	Vocabulary complexity is a formulaic manipulation of the Flesch–Kincaid readability index to measure the student's competence in creating a readable composition
Vocabulary usage	Vocabulary usage is a measure of the student's competence in using different kinds of words. It is based on the ratio of unique words to the total number of words in the document (using word lemmas)

The complete data were divided into 6 subsets, and upon each, 2 different causal inference algorithms were run, for a total of 12 causal models. The causal models were produced in TETRAD V, a program from Carnegie Mellon University that implements the algorithms from the literature on statistical causation (Spirtes et al., 2000). The six data segments consisted of both a vertical and horizontal split: each was a combination of a subset of metrics and variables, and a subset of events. The details from the study are shown in Table 3.

Out of these segments, the two most statistically significant results were the ones in which a minimal number of variables were used (Rows 2 and 5): namely, where only the competences were considered for causal analysis.

The results of the search over the final essay events using only the competence variables (Fig. 1) demonstrate several important relationships, both intuitive and surprising.

Intervening to increase vocabulary use increases essay score, but reduces transition. This phenomenon may indicate that increased vocabulary usage lowers the number of connective terms in the document. Intervening to increase grammatical accuracy increases essay score, and increases vocabulary complexity. If there are fewer grammatical errors in the document, its readability and overall grade will increase. Intervening to increase topic flow has a positive effect on essay score and transition. The more a composition flows well semantically, the more connective

Table 3 Data segments

Data included	Variables included	Description	Causal searches
Final record of each simulated student (390 events)	All available	All variables examined on a small sample size: the analysis expected from an automatic essay scoring system for traditional settings	Fast Greedy Equivalence Search (FGS) assuming causal sufficiency to obtain causal equivalence class. SEM constructed from a DAG within the FGS pattern. Estimation of SEM to determine fit to data. FCI search to examine potential latent common causes
Final record of each simulated student (390 events)	Competences and essay score only	Competence variables examined on a small sample size to use for comparison on the denser models	FGS search assuming causal sufficiency to obtain causal equivalence class. SEM constructed from a DAG within the FGS pattern. Estimation of SEM to determine fit to data. FCI search to examine potential latent common causes
Final record of each simulated student (390 events)	Competences, essay score, and first-order adjacencies as identified in Row 1	Expanded version of the competence set to include some clues about latent variables between competences	FGS search assuming causal sufficiency to obtain causal equivalence class. SEM constructed from a DAG within the FGS pattern. Estimation of SEM to determine fit to data. FCI search to examine potential latent common causes
All event records (744,848 events)	All available	The fully determined model, expected to be dense	PC pattern search with $\alpha = 0.001$ to obtain causal equivalence class assuming causal sufficiency. SEM constructed from a DAG within the PC pattern. Estimation of SEM to determine fit to data. FCI search to examine potential latent common causes. Regression tables for each competency and its direct adjacencies

(continued)

Table 3 (continued)

Data included	Variables included	Description	Causal searches
All event records (744,848 events)	Competences and essay score only	Competence variables examined in isolation to determine causal effects	PC pattern search with $\alpha = 0.001$ to obtain causal equivalence class assuming causal sufficiency. SEM constructed from a DAG within the PC pattern. Estimation of SEM to determine fit to data. FCI search to examine potential latent common causes
All event records (744,848 events)	Competences, essay score, and first-order adjacencies as identified in Row 1	Expanded version of the competence set to include some clues about latent variables between competences	PC pattern search with $\alpha = 0.001$ to obtain causal equivalence class assuming causal sufficiency. SEM constructed from a DAG within the PC pattern. Estimation of SEM to determine fit to data. FCI search to examine potential latent common causes

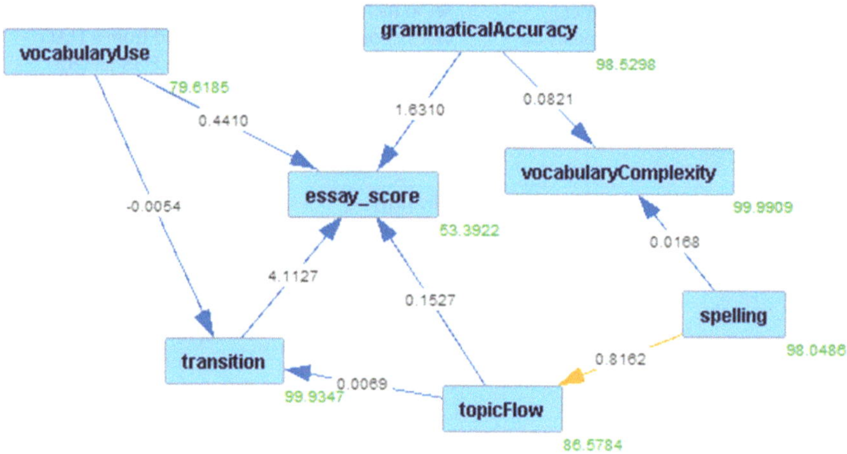

Fig. 1 Causal model of competence for completed essays

words are present to bring the ideas together. Intervening to increase spelling has a positive effect on vocabulary complexity. The better a document's mechanics, the more readable it is. Interesting to note is that essay score is always an effect of other competences, never a cause, lining up with intuition. Also interesting is that intervening on vocabulary complexity directly has no direct effect on essay score. It is better to focus on mechanics like spelling and grammar that will increase vocabulary

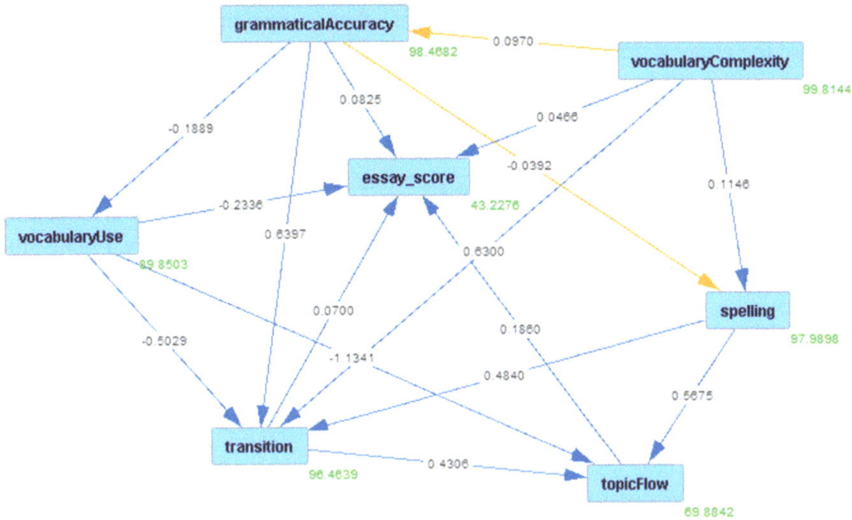

Fig. 2 Causal model of competence for all writing events

complexity, while simultaneously increasing essay score. Finally, spelling and topic flow have some sort of causal relationship, but its direction is uncertain. It is possible that when words are incorrectly spelled, it can confuse the calculation for semantic distances, and therefore reduce topic flow. It seems likely from intuition that spelling increases topic flow.

Adding in the developmental structure of the full set of events, the graph becomes much more complex, and some of the relationships change, illustrating the difference between final products, and the net effect of development (Fig. 2).

There are a number of relationships that remain consistent in this model. Essay score remains endogenous, fully qualified by other competences. This is expected, as the essay score will only grow as the document becomes more complete. Intervening on vocabulary use has a negative effect on transition, as in the previous model, but also is detrimental to essay score and topic flow. Vocabulary use is the only variable for which intervention produces negative effects. The result appears to be that students should focus on other competences during the development of the essays, rather than going for a diverse selection of words.

There are also a number of important differences with the complete data. The independent variables are uncertain because of the nature of the equivalence class. The effects between grammatical accuracy and spelling, and between grammatical accuracy and vocabulary complexity are ambiguous. In the complete data, it is evident that topic flow is a significant contributor to essay score, making it an important developmental competence. If a student maintains topic flow, his/her essay will steadily become better. The relationship between transition and topic flow is reversed in development. More connectivity results in better semantic flow. While this makes sense, it is conceivable that the causation could be in either direction. Both transition and topic flow are primarily effects of other competences, but both of them increase the essay score when intervened upon directly. Grammatical accuracy still increases essay score, but also has a positive effect on transition (possibly because correcting some types of grammatical errors leads to better use of connective words) and a negative effect on vocabulary use (perhaps because of the rule-based nature of the grammar checker, where correcting grammar can reduce the amount of creative words available). The causal direction between vocabulary complexity and spelling is reversed, and vocabulary complexity now affects essay score directly. Finally, the causal direction between spelling and topic flow is fixed in the direction that makes intuitive sense. Spelling also has a positive effect on transition.

6 Big Data Architecture

This research underscores the reality that capturing and analyzing the writing process of English essays is computing-intensive for a relatively small batch of 391 essays, and it demonstrates the need for more scalable solutions adapted to the writing process instead of only the final writing product. A related project (Lewkow et al., 2016) proposed a big data architecture that measured the writing competences of students, where the analytical solution focused only on assessing the students' competences over multiple writing activities and re-updated the assessment on any reattempt by the student of any of these activities. On the other side, the present case study reassessed the student's writing approximately every time a new word is added to the text. Consequently, many portions of the essay are unnecessarily and redundantly processed again and again. To adapt and scale natural-language processing to the writing process, it is proposed, as displayed in Fig. 3, to apply the Map-Reduce paradigm at the sentence level since sentences are the smallest units that NLP usually works with. This would provide the advantage of distributing the processing across a cluster of computing resources, while also avoiding reprocessing all the sentences that have not changed since the last edit. In general, the difference between two writing events is tiny and consists of the addition of a new word. In Fig. 3, it can be noted that the black arrows correspond to two map functions where (1) the text of an essay is split into its constituent sentences, and (2) each sentence is then analyzed by a part-of-speech tagger, named entity recognizer, lemmatizer, stemmer, spellchecker, etc., to derive and compute a set of writing metrics. The gray arrows correspond to reduce functions, where the various writing metrics are aggregated together to describe higher-level essay parts, such as pairs of consecutive sentences, paragraphs, the actual essay, and finally the set of all essays pertaining to a student. It means that every sentence or essay constituent, no matter the level, will ultimately be associated with a set of writing metrics as well as data describing (1) the essay to which it pertains, (2) the writing event from which it was calculated (e.g., the 300th writing event), and (3) its position within a higher-level essay part (e.g., second sentence within first paragraph). For example, an essay may consist of 10 sentences and 3 paragraphs. A student may want to add an adverb in Sentence 2 to enhance the meaning of an action verb. With

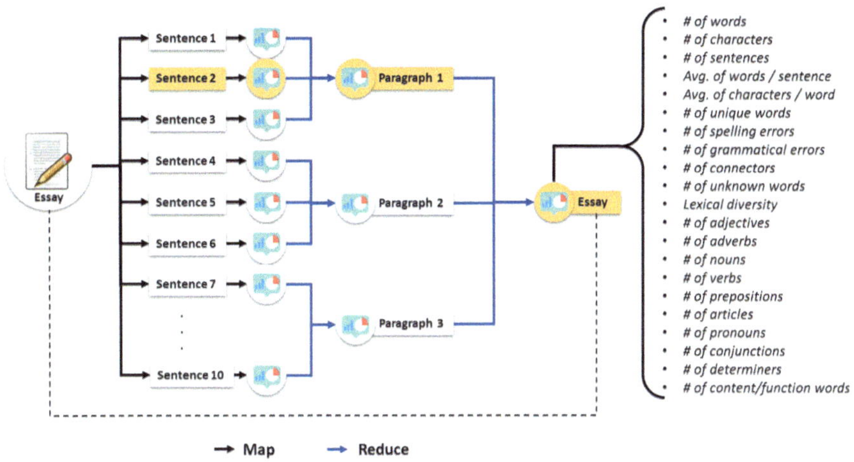

Fig. 3 Applying Map-Reduce framework to scale and adapt natural-language processing to the writing process

the proposed architecture, the updated essay text will again be sentence-split. Every sentence will then be compared against the sentences of the previous writing event to identify which sentences will have changed. In this case, only Sentence 2 will be required to be parsed again by the suite of NLP solutions (instead of re-parsing all 10 sentences), only the metrics of Paragraph 1 will have to be updated, and finally, the metrics of the encompassing essay will be recalculated. It is important to note that the map functions are significantly more computationally expensive than the reduce functions, which are merely aggregating functions.

Another measure of optimization that this research proposes is to unify the various disparate NLP solutions that often redo what other solutions have already performed. For instance, the SCALE suite consists of a conglomerate of NLP tools such as Stanford CoreNLP, Apache OpenNLP, and LanguageTool, which all need to perform part-of-speech tagging separately to feed their features that are unique to them. For instance, Stanford CoreNLP is the only tool that provides the lemma of every word, while OpenNLP, although less powerful than CoreNLP, gives the possibility to extract the n-grams of a text. Given that most of these software packages are open source, centralizing and reconciling certain NLP tasks become priority to improve the efficiency of writing analytics systems.

Figure 4 shows the implementation architecture and workflow of a big data writing analytics system, where data are ingested by the input API and placed into a distributed queueing system, which is implemented using Kafka. A collection service, implemented in Scala, pulls data from the queue and stores them in long-term storage, which is implemented using Hadoop Distributed File System (HDFS). The compute cluster runs models in parallel on the data in long-term storage and persists output views to the results store, implemented in MongoDB. Output views can then

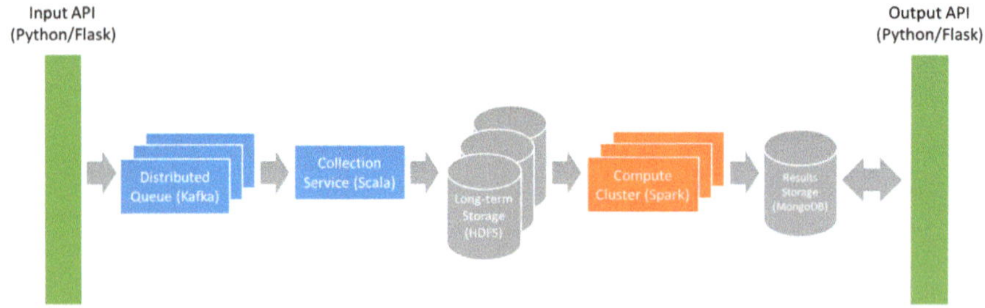

Fig. 4 Big data writing analytics architecture

be accessed through the output API. Both the input and output APIs are RESTful and coded in Python using Flask (Lewkow et al., 2016).

7 Conclusion

The case study presented in this chapter demonstrated the application of formal causal models to a set of 391 essays, whose writing processes were simulated by a tool called WriteSim. More than 744,000 writing events were generated to reconstruct the writing process of this batch of essays. Despite the fact that the conclusions drawn from the causal analysis performed on this dataset are only hypothetical given the limitations of WriteSim to fully represent the actual writing process, the use of formal causal inference and its resulting models represents another tool that educators can reliably use to determine how competences are built and developed. These types of systems, based on intervention, provide a powerful use case for educational big data. Learning traces represent powerful snapshots of student process and development, and leveraging them to gain pedagogical insights will pay dividends in the understanding of how learning works. This chapter concludes by proposing a big data architecture to scale and adapt NLP solutions for the analysis of the writing process in large-scale writing analytics systems.

Acknowledgements This research is supported by the Industrial Research Chair and Discovery programs of the Natural Sciences and Engineering Research Council of Canada, and the internal research funding programs of Athabasca University, Canada.

References

Bentler, P. M. (1990). Comparative fit indexes in structural models. *Psychological Bulletin, 107*(2), 238.

Boulanger, D., Seanosky, J., Clemens, C., Kumar, V., & Kinshuk. (2016). SCALE: A smart competence analytics solution for English writing. In *Proceedings of the 2016 IEEE 16th International Conference on Advanced Learning Technologies (ICALT)* (pp. 468–472). http://doi.org/10.1109/ICALT.2016.108.

Boulanger, D., Seanosky, J., Pinnell, C., Bell, J., Kumar, V., & Kinshuk. (2016). SCALE: A competence analytics framework. In Y. Li, M. Chang, M. Kravcik, E. Popescu, R. Huang, Kinshuk, & N.-S. Chen (Eds.), *State-of-the-art and future directions of smart learning* (pp. 19–30). Singapore: Springer. http://doi.org/10.1007/978-981-287-868-7_3.

Cohen, J., Dolan, B., Dunlap, M., Hellerstein, J. M., & Welton, C. (2009). MAD skills: New analysis practices for big data. *Proceedings of the VLDB Endowment, 2*(2), 1481–1492. http://doi.org/10.14778/1687553.1687576.

Clemens, C. (2017). *A causal model of writing competence* (Master's thesis). Retrieved from https://dt.athabascau.ca/jspui/handle/10791/233.

Cramir, H. (1946). *Mathematical methods of statistics*. Princeton: Princeton University Press.

Fisher, R. A. (1915). Frequency distribution of the values of the correlation coefficient in samples from an indefinitely large population. *Biometrika, 10*(4), 507–521. Retrieved from http://www.jstor.org/stable/2331838.

Flesch, R. (1948). A new readability yardstick. *Journal of Applied Psychology, 32*(3), 221.

Geiger, D., Paz, A., & Pearl, J. (1991). Axioms and algorithms for inferences involving probabilistic independence. *Information and Computation, 91*(1), 128–141. http://doi.org/10.1016/0890-5401(91)90077-F.

Guillot, C., Guillot, R., Kumar, V., & Kinshuk. (2016). MUSIX: Learning analytics in music teaching. In Y. Li, M. Chang, M. Kravcik, E. Popescu, R. Huang, Kinshuk, & N.-S. Chen (Eds.), State-of-the-Art and Future Directions of Smart Learning (pp. 269–273). Singapore: Springer. http://doi.org/10.1007/978-981-287-868-7_31.

Johnson, P. M., Kou, H., Agustin, J., Chan, C., Moore, C., Miglani, J., ... Doane, W. E. J. (2003). Beyond the personal software process: Metrics collection and analysis for the differently disciplined. In *Proceedings of the 25th International Conference on Software Engineering, 2003* (pp. 641–646). http://doi.org/10.1109/ICSE.2003.1201249.

Kincaid, J. P., Fishburne, R. P., Jr., Rogers, R. L., & Chissom, B. S. (1975). Derivation of new readability formulas (Automated Readability Index, Fog Count and Flesch Reading Ease Formula) for Navy enlisted personnel.

Klein, D., & Manning, C. D. (2003). Accurate unlexicalized parsing. In *Proceedings of the 41st Annual Meeting on Association for Computational Linguistics* (Vol. 1, pp. 423–430). Stroudsburg, PA, USA: Association for Computational Linguistics. http://doi.org/10.3115/1075096.1075150.

Kumar, V., Kinshuk, Somasundaram, T., Harris, S., Boulanger, D., Seanosky, J., ... Panneerselvam, K. (2015). An approach to measure coding competency evolution. In M. Chang & Y. Li (Eds.), *Smart learning environments* (pp. 27–43). Berlin, Heidelberg: Springer. http://doi.org/10.1007/978-3-662-44447-4_2.

Lewkow, N., Feild, J., Zimmerman, N., Riedesel, M., Essa, A., Boulanger, D., ... Kode, S. (2016). A scalable learning analytics platform for automated writing feedback. In *Proceedings of the 3rd (2016) ACM Conference on Learning @ Scale* (pp. 109–112). New York, NY, USA: ACM. http://doi.org/10.1145/2876034.2893380.

MacCallum, R. C., Browne, M. W., & Sugawara, H. M. (1996). Power analysis and determination of sample size for covariance structure modeling. *Psychological Methods, 1*(2), 130.

Miller, G. A. (1995). WordNet: A lexical database for English. *Communications of the ACM, 38*(11), 39–41. https://doi.org/10.1145/219717.219748.

Murray, D. M. (1972). Teach writing as a process not product. *The Leaflet, 71,* 11–14.

Nasukawa, T., & Yi, J. (2003). Sentiment analysis: Capturing favorability using natural language processing. In *Proceedings of the 2nd International Conference on Knowledge Capture* (pp. 70–77).

Nesi, H., Sharpling, G., & Ganobcsik-Williams, L. (2004). Student papers across the curriculum: Designing and developing a corpus of British student writing. *Computers and Composition, 21*(4), 439–450. http://doi.org/10.1016/j.compcom.2004.08.003.

O'Rourke, S. T., Calvo, R. A., & McNamara, D. S. (2011). Visualizing topic flow in students' essays. *Educational Technology & Society, 14*(3), 4–15.

Pang, B., & Lee, L. (2008). Opinion mining and sentiment analysis. *Foundations and Trends in Information Retrieval, 2*(1–2), 1–135. https://doi.org/10.1561/1500000011.
Peirce, C. S., & Jastrow, J. (1884). On small differences in sensation.
Russell, B. (1912). On the notion of cause. *Proceedings of the Aristotelian Society, 13,* 1–26. Retrieved from http://www.jstor.org/stable/4543833.
Sampson, D., & Fytros, D. (2008). Competence models in technology-enhanced competence-based learning. In H. H. Adelsberger, Kinshuk, J. M. Pawlowski, & D. G. Sampson (Eds.), *Handbook on information technologies for education and training* (pp. 155–177). Berlin, Heidelberg: Springer. http://doi.org/10.1007/978-3-540-74155-8_9.
Schwarz, G. (1978). Estimating the dimension of a model. *The Annals of Statistics, 6*(2), 461–464. Retrieved from http://www.jstor.org/stable/2958889.
Simpson, E. H. (1951). The interpretation of interaction in contingency tables. *Journal of the Royal Statistical Society. Series B (Methodological), 13*(2), 238–241. Retrieved from http://www.jstor.org/stable/2984065.
Socher, R., Perelygin, A., Wu, J., Chuang, J., Manning, C., Ng, A., & Potts, C. (2013). Recursive deep models for semantic compositionality over a sentiment treebank. In *Proceedings of the Conference on Empirical Methods in Natural Language Processing (EMNLP).*
Spirtes, P., Glymour, C. N., & Scheines, R. (2000). *Causation, prediction, and search.* MIT press.
Toutanova, K., Klein, D., Manning, C. D., & Singer, Y. (2003). Feature-rich part-of-speech tagging with a cyclic dependency network. In *Proceedings of the 2003 Conference of the North American Chapter of the Association for Computational Linguistics on Human Language Technology* (Vol. 1, pp. 173–180). Stroudsburg, PA, USA: Association for Computational Linguistics. http://doi.org/10.3115/1073445.1073478.
Verhelst, N., Van Avermaet, P., Takala, S., Figueras, N., & North, B. (2009). *Common European framework of reference for languages: Learning, teaching, assessment.* Cambridge University Press.
Waes, L. V., & Schellens, P. J. (2003). Writing profiles: The effect of the writing mode on pausing and revision patterns of experienced writers. *Journal of Pragmatics, 35*(6), 829–853. http://doi.org/10.1016/S0378-2166(02)00121-2.
Yi, J., Nasukawa, T., Bunescu, R., & Niblack, W. (2003). Sentiment analyzer: Extracting sentiments about a given topic using natural language processing techniques. In *3rd IEEE International Conference on Data Mining* (pp. 427–434). http://doi.org/10.1109/ICDM.2003.1250949.

Clayton Clemens holds a Master of Science in Information Systems, with a specialization in natural-language processing, learning analytics, and causal inference. Clayton works full-time as a business analyst for the City of Edmonton, Alberta, where he leverages his knowledge of computational techniques to support continuously improving recreation opportunities for citizens.

Dr. Vivekanandan Kumar is a Professor in the School of Computing and Information Systems at Athabasca University, Canada. He holds the Natural Sciences and Engineering Research Council of Canada's (NSERC) Discovery Grant on Anthropomorphic Pedagogical Agents, funded by the Government of Canada. His research focuses on developing anthropomorphic agents, which mimic and perfect human-like traits to better assist learners in their regulatory tasks. His research includes investigating technology-enhanced erudition methods that employ big data learning analytics, self-regulated learning, co-regulated learning, causal modeling, and machine learning to facilitate deep learning and open research. For more information, visit http://vivek.athabascau.ca.

David Boulanger is a student and data scientist involved in the learning analytics research group at Athabasca University. His primary research focus is on observational study designs and the application of computational tools and machine learning algorithms in learning analytics including writing analytics.

Jérémie Seanosky is an undergraduate student and research assistant at Athabasca University. His areas of research interests include big data learning analytics, learning analytics software sensors, hardware sensors for both learning and sports analytics, fail-safe data collection, analysis, visualization, automated assessment, solutions for securing the privacy and anonymity of students in the learning analytics world, virtual and augmented reality-based training, and video-based analytics.

Dr. Kinshuk is the Dean of the College of Information at the University of North Texas, USA. Prior to that, he held the NSERC/CNRL/Xerox/McGraw Hill Research Chair for Adaptivity and Personalization in Informatics, funded by the Federal Government of Canada, Provincial Government of Alberta, and by national and international industries. His work has been dedicated to advancing research on the innovative paradigms, architectures, and implementations of online and distance learning systems for individualized and adaptive learning in increasingly global environments. Areas of his research interests include learning analytics; learning technologies; mobile, ubiquitous, and location-aware learning systems; cognitive profiling; and interactive technologies. For more information, visit http://www.kinshuk.info/.

QUESGEN: A Framework for Automatic Question Generation Using Semantic Web and Lexical Databases

Nguyen-Thinh Le, Alexej Shabas and Patrick McLaren

Abstract Semantic web and lexical databases offer multifaceted purposes. In this chapter, we present an automatic question generation framework for teachers that deploys semantic web and lexical databases for generating questions for a specific lesson topic. This framework is intended to assist teachers in preparing questions for their lessons. We investigated two research questions: (1) "which semantic/lexical database is more appropriate for which learning domain?" and (2) "can a vector space model-based ranking algorithm enhance the relevance of generated questions?"

Keywords Semantic database · Term frequency · Term relevance
Vector space model · Question ranking

1 Introduction

Asking questions is one of the most important techniques in teaching and learning (Mason, 2011; Schank & Cleary, 1995; Dewey, 1966). In 1912, Leven and Long found that teachers spent approximately 80% of the school day by asking questions. This fact was replicated by their study of classroom teachers and their use of questioning in the 1980s (Leven & Long, 1981). Several studies confirmed the high usage of questions in the classroom. Tofade, Elsner and Haines (2013) found that 80% of a teacher's school day was taken up asking questions to students, and Fischer (2005) reported that instructors asked more than 300 questions per day.

However, many studies have reported that most of the teachers, tutors, and students do not use deep questions, which are supposed to evoke high-order cognitive requirements (Chafi & Elkhouzai, 2014; Graesser, Ozuru, & Sullins, 2009). Thus, students have a limited exposure to more beneficial inquiry. Approximately, 60% of teacher's questions evoke lower-order cognitive requirements, whereas 20% invoke higher-order cognitive requirements, leaving 20% that represent procedural day-to-

N.-T. Le (✉) · A. Shabas · P. McLaren
Department of Computer Science, Humboldt-Universität zu Berlin, Berlin, Germany
e-mail: nguyen-thinh.le@hu-berlin.de

J. M. Spector et al. (eds.), *Frontiers of Cyberlearning*, Lecture Notes in Educational Technology, https://doi.org/10.1007/978-981-13-0650-1_4

day questions (Dickman, 2009). Despite the prioritization of higher-order questions in theory, teachers actually ask a disproportionate number of lower-order questions (Dickman, 2009; Harvey & Goudvis, 2007; Myhill & Dunkin, 2005). A recent study conducted in Germany with 143 school teachers (Le & Pinkwart, 2016) shared a similar picture of question usage. The study found that teachers used questions to enhance understanding (22.83%), to stimulate interaction (19.8%) between teachers and students, and to motivate students (19.29%). The remaining questions used by teachers were categorized as recalling knowledge (12.69%) and stimulating reflection (6.6%). A small proportion of questions were used to enhance the analytical ability of students (6.6%) and to assess their learning progress (8.13%).

Training teachers to ask effective questions at the right moment is desirable in the learning process. While teachers can attend training seminars for improving questioning skills (e.g., Chicago Center for Teaching, 2016; Ontario Ministry of Education, 2011; Department for education and skills, Cambridge University Press, 2004; Intel Teach Program, 2007), such training programs will cost them time and money. Can a computational technology-enhanced framework be deployed to help teachers better prepare questions and use more higher-order questions?

In the next section, we briefly review question generation systems for education. Section 3 is devoted to describe the adaptive question generation framework and its application. In Sects. 4 and 5, we investigate the research question "which semantic database is more apt to which learning topic?" and "Can a vector space model-based ranking algorithm enhance the relevance of generated questions?" Section 6 summarizes the conclusions.

2 Technology-Enhanced Question Generation Systems

Numerous question generation systems have been developed over the past two decades. Le et al. (2014) reviewed and classified question generation systems into three classes according to their educational purposes: (1) knowledge/skills acquisition, (2) knowledge assessment, and (3) educational systems that use questions to provide tutorial dialogs. Since this chapter focuses on question generation systems aimed at enhancing questioning skills and supporting teachers in preparing questions, knowledge/skills acquisition question generation systems are briefly reviewed. Several automatic question generation systems aim at improving reading and writing skills. The LISTEN tutor generates questions automatically to enhance student's reading comprehension of English texts (Mostow, Nelson, & Beck, 2013). Questions are used for various reasons in this reading tutor such as assessing comprehension and engagement, aiding comprehension, teaching self-questioning, modeling and assessing self-questioning, and helping learn vocabulary (Mostow, 2011; Mostow et al., 2010). For Japanese, a reading tutor was developed to provide comprehension questions (Kawamura, 2012). This system has been online since 1999 and was accessed 1500 times per day as reported by Kawamura (2012). While these two review question generation systems aimed at enhancing the reading skills of students, Liu, Calvo and Rus (2012) introduced a system (G-Asks) for improving students' academic writing skills (e.g., citing sources to support arguments, presenting the evidence in a persuasive manner). Evaluation studies have shown that the system could generate questions as useful as human supervisors and significantly outperformed human peers and generic questions in most quality measures after filtering out questions with grammatical and semantic errors (Liu et al., 2012). Other systems are intended to develop student's knowledge of in specific learning domains. For example, Chaudhri et al. (2013) deployed a structured database, constructed by biologists consisting of 5500 biology concepts. Based on this concept database, the authors used 30 question templates to generate questions. Along this line, Jouault, Seta and Hayashi (2016) recently proposed generating semantics-based questions by querying information from the large linked open data sources DBpedia (http://dbpedia.org/) and Freebase (https://www.freebase.com/) to facilitate learners' self-directed learning. Using this system, students in self-directed learning were asked to build a timeline of events of a period in history with causal relationships between these events given an initial document. The system's concept map is updated with every student modification and enriched with related concepts that can be queried from both linked open data sources. Using these related concepts and their relationships, the system generates questions for the student to lead them to a deeper understanding without forcing them to follow a fixed path of learning. Jouault et al. (2016) reported that the generated questions could cover more than 80% of the questions generated by humans to support knowledge acquisition. Similarly, Le and Pinkwart (2015) proposed to use WordNet (Miller, 1995) in order to generate questions that aim at stimulating brainstorming for argumentation. We have selected WordNet as a semantic source for our question generation, because it is a rich lexical database that is able to provide hyponyms (related concepts) to a queried concept.

Most existing question generation systems have demonstrated their usefulness for enhancing students' reading, writing skills or knowledge. They lack the capability to support teachers in preparing effective questions that can be used in a classroom setting, particularly for classroom discussions. In the following, we propose a framework for question generation for teachers.

3 A Framework for Generating Adaptive Questions

3.1 The Conceptual Design

During the design phase of a framework for generating questions, Le and Pinkwart (2016) studied the practice of classroom questioning of 143 teachers in German schools. The study reported that the Bloom's question taxonomy (Anderson & Krathwohl, 2001) is known and used by 31.25% of teachers. The only other known taxonomy, Wilen's taxonomy (Wilen, 1991), is used by only 3.25%. The rest (65% of teachers) do not know any other question taxonomies. This is despite there being more than 21 question taxonomies available (Wilen, 1991). The aim of this adaptive question generation framework is to provide teachers (especially pre-service teachers) with a tool to apply one of these systematic question taxonomies (e.g., Bloom's taxonomy, Wilen's taxonomy, Socratic taxonomy, etc.). Being familiar with and using these question taxonomies gives teachers awareness of the cognitive level of their students and lets them ask appropriate questions (i.e., low-order or high-order). Based on one study's result (Le & Pinkwart, 2016), the framework for generating adaptive questions is designed to support teachers in three steps.

First, teachers are able to modify initial question templates, which have been pre-specified in the framework. Since in a study by Le (2015) found that people from different groups perceive questions differently, teachers should adapt the question templates to their individual group of school students. These question templates are used to generate questions (in the next section, we explain how question templates are used). Figure 1 illustrates how to adapting question templates for an individual student group. It shows a teacher selecting Bloom's taxonomy among other available supported question taxonomies. For each question taxonomy, the framework provides a list of initial question templates according to each type of question. For example, for Bloom's taxonomy, initial question templates for the classes "knowledge", "comprehension", "application", "analysis", "synthesis", and "evaluation" have been specified in advance. The teacher can choose the most appropriate question taxonomy for the specific purpose the teacher has in mind.

Next, a teacher inputs a lesson topic as a term into the question generation framework. When generating questions, the teacher has two options: selecting a semantic/lexical database [e.g., WordNet (Miller, 1995), ConceptNet (http://conceptnet.io), DBPedia (Bizer et al., 2009)] or choosing to generate questions without using a semantic/lexical database. If the teacher chooses a semantic database, the question generation framework connects to the semantic/lexical database, forwards the lesson topic as input, and retrieves semantically related terms. The retrieved terms are used to fill the question templates in order to generate questions. If the teacher chooses the option without using a semantic/lexical database, the question templates will be filled with the lesson topic they entered. Figure 2 shows an example of a user generating questions for the topic "graph" of a lesson in computer science. The teacher inputs the lesson topic "graph" into the system, chooses Bloom's question taxonomy, and selects the option without using any semantic/lexical database and the questions for the lesson topic "graph" are generated accordingly, as illustrated in Fig. 2.

After generating questions, the third step for the teacher is to choose questions that may be relevant and useful for his/her specific lesson topic and add them to a memory list. Then, he/she can print out the list of selected questions that can be used in the class (cf. Fig. 3).

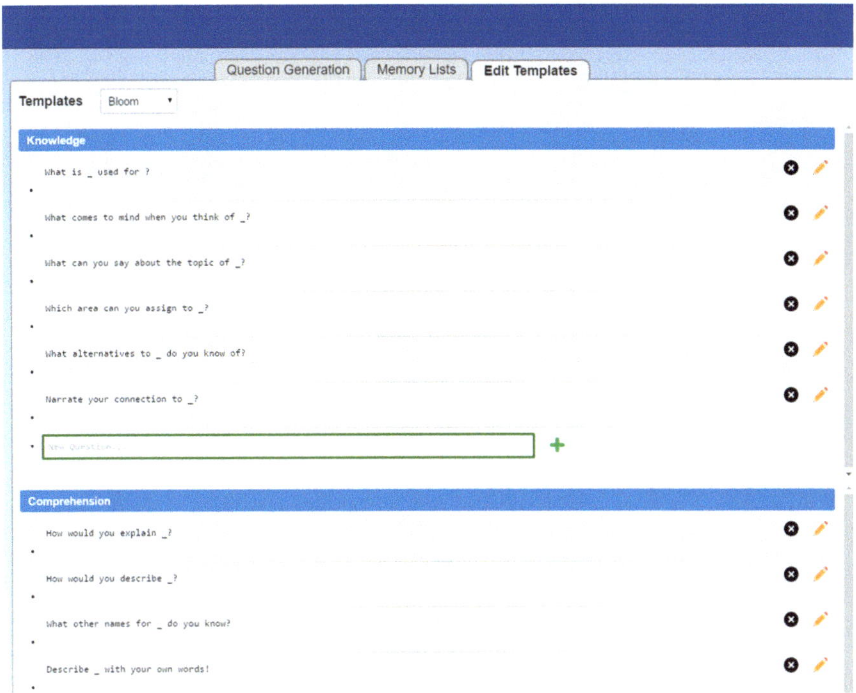

Fig. 1 Step 1: Adapting questions according to an individual student group

3.2 The Template-Based Question Generation Approach and Implementation

In order to support teachers in generating questions of different cognitive levels, we propose using the template-based question generation approach, which is widely employed in question generation systems (Le et al., 2014). For each question taxonomy, the system is initialized with a set of question templates. For example, Fig. 1 illustrates some question templates for Bloom's taxonomy, which has six question levels. Each template has a placeholder, which is to be filled with the lesson's topic or with a semantically related term.

The architecture of the question generation framework consists of front-end and back-end, which are divided by the dashed horizontal line (Fig. 4). The front-end is implemented as a single page user interface. The back-end represents a RESTful web service, which performs business logic and provides the data for the front-end.

Figure 4 shows three main functionalities of the framework: question template view, question generator view, and question watchlist view. The question template view enables the teacher to prepare the phrasing of questions according to the individual student group (e.g., age of the students). He/she can choose appropriate question taxonomy and modify the initial question templates. The question generator view

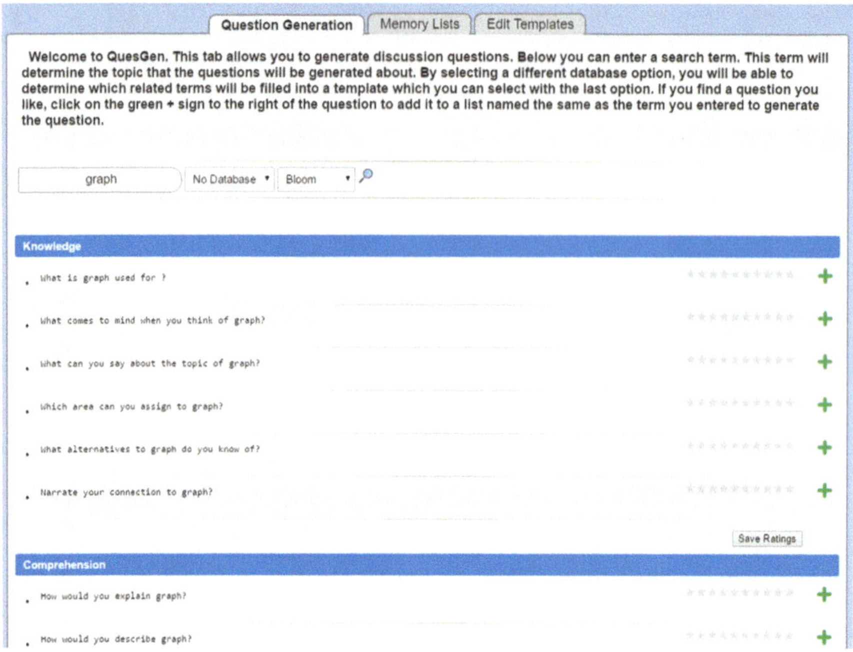

Fig. 2 Step 2: Generating questions for the lesson topic "graph"

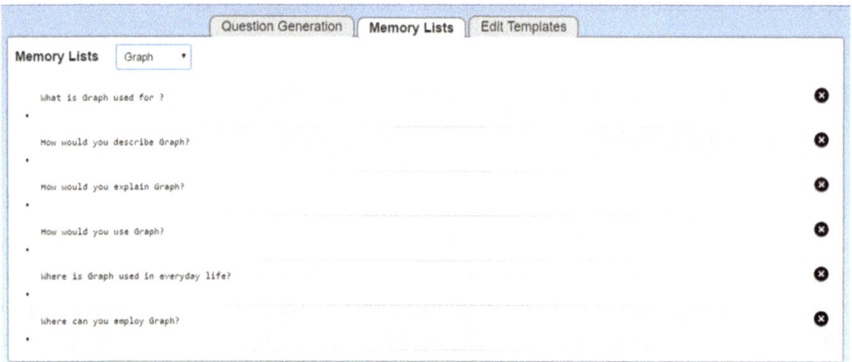

Fig. 3 Step 3: A list of selected relevant questions for the lesson topic "graph"

represents the central functionality of the application (Fig. 2). Here, the teacher has two options: (1) generate questions using a semantic web or a lexical database; (2) generate questions without using a semantic web database. Using a semantic web [e.g., ConceptNet, DBPedia (http://de.dbpedia.org)] or a lexical database [WordNet for English (Miller, 1995) and GermaNet for German (http://www.sfs.uni-tuebingen.de/GermaNet)], the lesson topics can be filled with other meaningful semantically related concepts. When using a semantic web or lexical database, the lesson topic

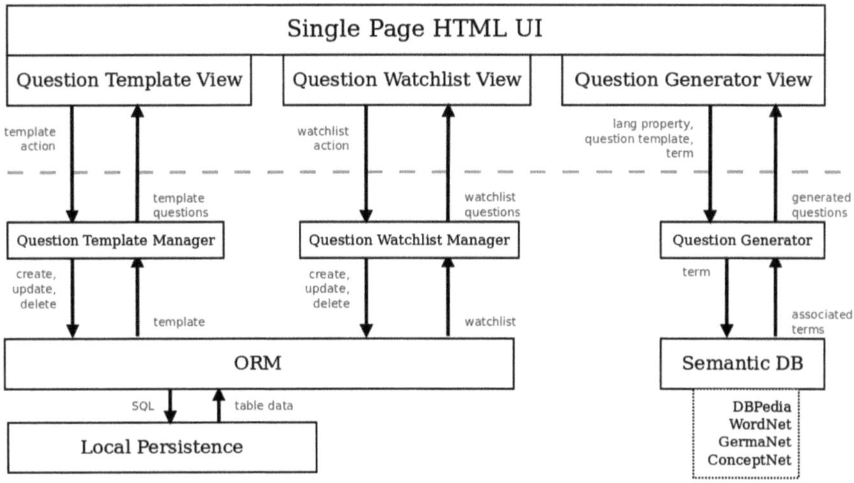

Fig. 4 The architecture of a question generation framework

is sent to the selected database through the corresponding external API. The current implementation supports integration with WordNet and ConceptNet for the English language as well as DBPedia and GermaNet for the German language. Next, the framework retrieves a list of related semantic terms from the chosen semantic/lexical database (e.g., "graph" yields "echocardiogram", "echoencephalogram", "ballistocardiogram", etc. from the WordNet API). Each question template for the selected question taxonomy is then filled with one of the retrieved semantically related terms. The filled question templates result in questions that may be relevant and useful for a given lesson topic.

When generating questions with no database selected, the term representing the lesson topic (e.g., "graph") is used to fill the question templates (these may have been adapted by the teacher to suit their particular student group).

The question watchlist view allows the teacher to choose appropriate questions, to view, and to print out a list of chosen questions.

4 Term Relevance Analysis

Semantically related terms retrieved from the semantic/lexical databases may have little relation to an intended lesson topic and may create semantically meaningless sentences. In this section, we investigate the research question "which semantic/lexical database yields the most relevant semantically related terms for each learning domain?"

4.1 Methodology

In order to investigate the research question specified above, we take three learning domains: Computer Science, History, and Politics. We choose these learning domains as case studies because Computer Science is a common subject of STEM (Science, Technology, Engineering, and Mathematics), and History and Politics are two typical candidates in social science. In this study, we compare two databases: WordNet and ConceptNet for lesson topics to be held in English (we are aware that there also exist other semantic/lexical databases in English, but at this moment, only two databases in English have been integrated in the question generation framework).

To analyze the relevance of retrieved semantically related terms from a semantic/lexical database with respect to the specific learning domain, the statistical measure TF-IDF (term frequency—inverse document frequency) is applied. TF-IDF is a technique that measures the relevance of a word in a particular document in relation to the inverse proportion of that word over the whole document corpus. This technique is usually used to measure the relevance of a word in document queries in the area of information retrieval, e.g. in Koujalagi (2015) and Ramos (2003). Term frequency refers to the proportion of occurrences of a word to the total number of words in a document. Since some words, e.g., stopping words, articles or prepositions would occur more frequently and inflate this measure, inverse document frequency is used to punish generally common words' high frequency (Manning, Raghavan, & Schütze, 2009). The TF-IDF relevance score for a term $\boldsymbol{t}$ in a document $\boldsymbol{d}$ of a corpus of $\boldsymbol{N}$ documents is calculated by the formula:

$$\text{TF - IDF}(t, d) = \text{tf}(t, d) \times \text{idf}(t)$$

where $\mathbf{tf}(\boldsymbol{t},\boldsymbol{d})$ is the term frequency of the term $\boldsymbol{t}$ in the document $\boldsymbol{d}$ and $\mathbf{idf}(\boldsymbol{t})$ is the inverse document frequency of a term in the corpus of $\boldsymbol{N}$. The inverse document frequency is calculated by the formula:

$$\text{idf}(t) = \log(N/\text{df}(t))$$

where $\mathbf{df}(\boldsymbol{t})$ is the document frequency is defined to be the number of documents in the corpus that contain the term $\boldsymbol{t}$.

TF-IDF scores increase the frequency of a term occurring in that document scaled down by the frequency the word occurs in a document corpus. Therefore, the higher the term frequency value in a document and lower the frequency the word occurs in a document corpus, the higher the TF-IDF value is.

In order to calculate the TF-IDF measure, a corpus of documents is required. We assemble three corpuses from textbooks for three learning domains. These textbooks are downloaded as text files from the Internet Archive (https://archive.org/) including 21 computer science textbooks, 20 politics textbooks, and 8 history textbooks. Each textbook was 100 KB or larger.

In each learning domain, a sample of 10–20 lesson topics is collected for the analysis. These lesson topics are randomly selected words from the alphabetical index of each textbook. These selected words are then input into the question generation framework to generate questions using only the English semantic/lexical databases (WordNet and ConceptNet). The terms retrieved from the semantic/lexical databases are used to measure their TF-IDF relevance in a specific learning domain, each is represented by a corpus of collected textbooks. The TF-IDF relevance of each term is averaged over the documents in the corpus of each learning domain.

4.2 Results

For the learning domain "politics", the following words were collected as lesson topics: "government", "law", "authoritarian", "aristocracy", "libertarian", "property", "power", "sovereign", "left", "right", "justice system", "state", "negotiation", "monarchy", "corruption", "executive system", "constitution", "warfare", and "democracy". These lesson topics were input into the question generation framework QUESGEN.

Figure 5 shows the TF-IDF relevance scores (that are averaged over many documents) of terms that were retrieved after inputting the lesson topics into the question generation framework. WordNet produced a high number of terms with non-zero TF-IDF relevance score for the learning domain "politics", but ended up with lower TF-IDF relevance scores for the non-zero results. That means, WordNet returned a longer list of semantically related terms including more false positives (i.e., terms whose TF-IDF scores are 0). In another word, from WordNet the system retrieved many non-relevant related terms. On the contrary (Fig. 6), ConceptNet did not return as many semantically related terms as WordNet, but the retrieved ones from ConceptNet had higher TF-IDF scores on average over documents. This indicates that for the learning domain "politics", ConceptNet provides more relevant concepts (66%) than WordNet (34%), when it does, in fact, and then delivers any.

For the learning domain "history", the following words were used as input for lesson topics: "Latin", "archaeology", "region", "past", "humanities", "historian", "Greek", "document", "primary source", and "period". ConceptNet only found one semantic-related term for each of the lesson topics "Greek", "document", and "period", and every retrieved term had the TF-IDF score of 0. This shows that ConceptNet did not have many relevant terms in the learning domain "history", and that the terms it could find had low TF-IDF relevance score. This means, the terms retrieved from ConceptNet were not relevant to the input lesson topics. WordNet produced about 30 semantically related terms for the 10 input lesson topics. For six lesson topics, the retrieved terms had non-zero relevance TF-IDF score (Fig. 7). This indicates that WordNet returns more relevant terms than ConceptNet in the "history" learning domain.

For the learning domain "computer science", the following words were used as lesson topics: "artificial intelligence", "binary", "heuristic", "computer vision",

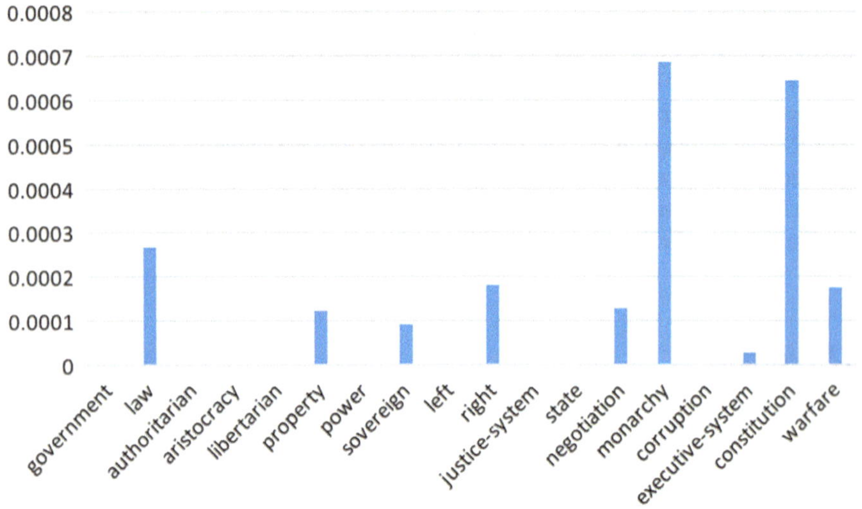

Fig. 5 Average TF-IDF for retrieved semantically related terms from WordNet for the learning domain "politics"

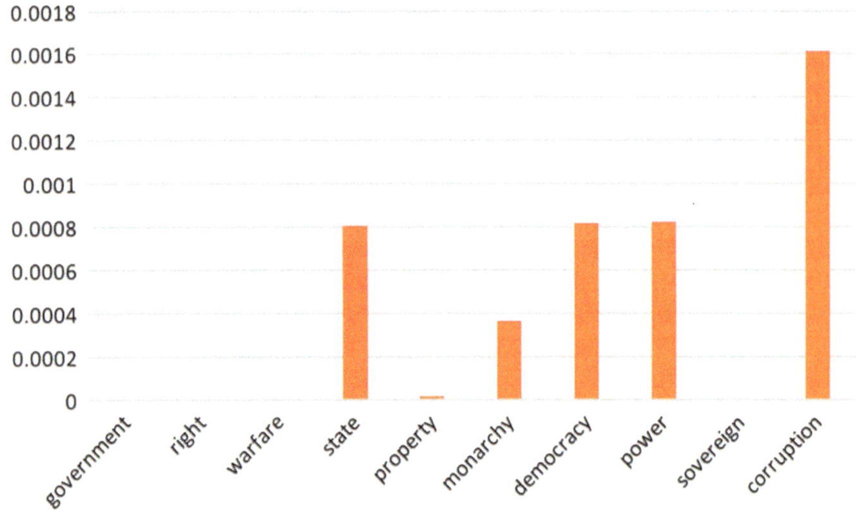

Fig. 6 Average TF-IDF for retrieved semantically related terms from ConceptNet for the learning domain "politics"

"data structure", "machine learning", "formal methods", "database", "performance", "complexity", "operating system", and "computer architecture". In this learning domain, ConceptNet outperformed in terms of the TF-IDF relevance (ConceptNet 78%, WordNet: 22%). ConceptNet returned more relevant terms than WordNet.

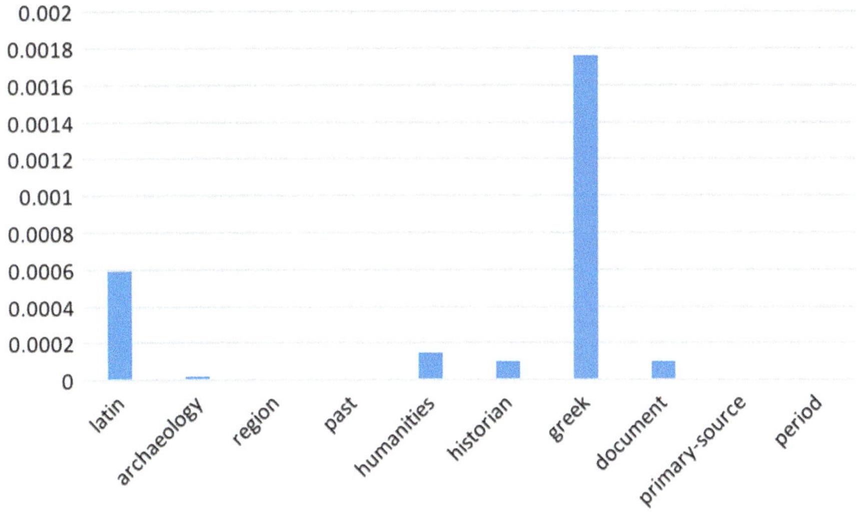

Fig. 7 Average TF-IDF for retrieved semantically related terms from WordNet for the learning domain "history"

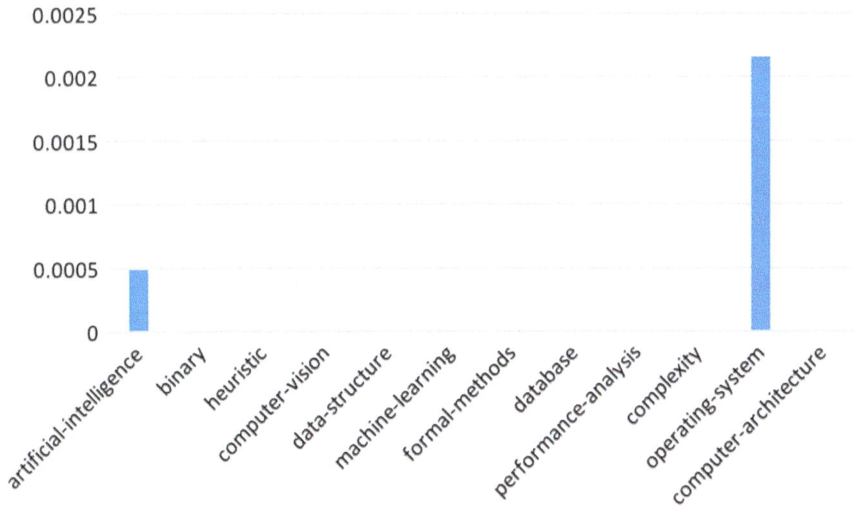

Fig. 8 Average TF-IDF for retrieved semantically related terms from WordNet for the learning domain "computer science"

Figure 8 shows that WordNet returned a larger amount of semantically related terms with non-zero TF-IDF score than ConceptNet (Fig. 9). However, the TF-IDF score of most of retrieved terms from WordNet is not high. On the contrary, ConceptNet returned less semantically related terms, however, these terms had high scores of relevance (Fig. 9).

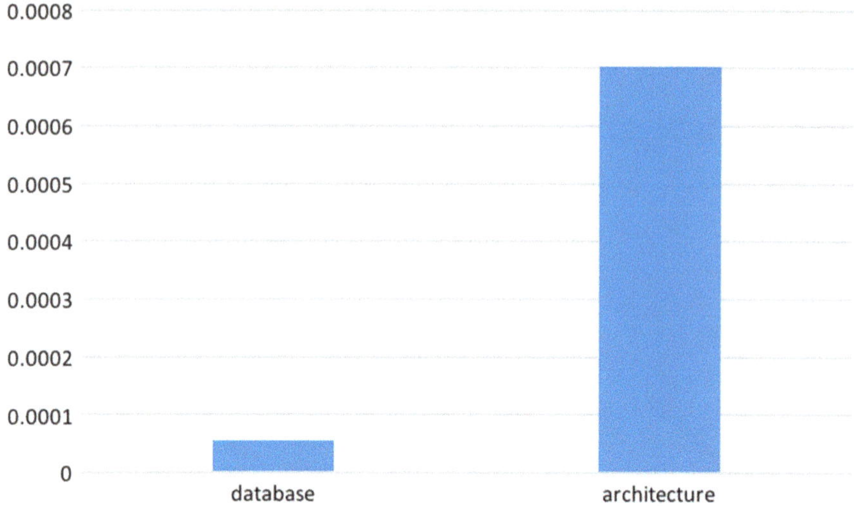

Fig. 9 Average TF-IDF for retrieved semantically related terms from ConceptNet for the learning domain "computer science"

4.3 Discussion

We have applied TF-IDF in order to find appropriate sematic/lexical databases for three learning domains: "history", "computer science", and "politics". WordNet is more appropriate than ConceptNet to find relevant semantically related terms for generating questions in the "history" domain. On the contrary, in the domains of "politics" and "computer science", ConceptNet provides more relevant semantically related terms than WordNet.

Going forward, the TF-IDF analysis may require a larger corpus size and document size. This would create a more representative distribution of the words in the English language and therefore make the statistic less sensitive to outlier documents. In addition, the tradeoff between corpus size and corpus quality is certainly something continued research.

5 Question Ranking Evaluation

One remarkable problem of question generation is that generated questions are not always relevant to a given topic. This occurs when using semantic/lexical databases as investigated in Sect. 4. Thus, a possible solution for selecting relevant questions is ranking their relevance with respect to a specific topic. For ranking questions, several approaches might be applied. The approach taken by Heilman and Smith (2010) generated a large amount of questions from an input text and deployed a statistical ranker to rank the relevance of questions. Another approach filters out appropriate sentences from a text using concepts, which have a specific semantic similarity (Adamson et al., 2013) and questions are generated from these sentences. The approach of Chali and Hasan (2015) assigns a topic to each text that contains information about that topic. Then, questions about a specific topic are generated using the assigned texts. Ranks are assigned using latent semantic analysis (Blei, Ng, & Jordan, 2003). That is, the ranking algorithm searches for sub-topics in the assigned texts and measures the semantic similarity between the identified sub-topics in the generated questions. These three approaches all require an original text to rank generated questions, and thus might not be suited to ranking questions generated using the framework QUESGEN.

Which approach is most effective at ranking questions that are generated using semantic/lexical databases? This is the research question we take a closer look at in the following. For example, the lesson topic "computer" might generate "what is mainframe for?" or "what is associated with voltage?" We investigate ranking approaches to find most relevant questions for the lesson with the topic "computer".

5.1 Methodology

There are several approaches we considered for ranking generated questions: Latent Dirichlet Allocation (LDA, Blei et al., 2003), latent semantic analysis (LSA, Bhagwant, 2017), vector space model (VSM, Turney & Pantel, 2010)

In order to discern how applicable each of these approaches is, we consider two approaches to filling a question template with a concept word: one that represents lesson topic or one that represents a term semantically related to a lesson topic. For instance, the question "What is a compiler for?" is made up of "What is a _ for?" and the concept word "compiler". As the question template remains the same across different concept words the LDA, LSA, or VSM rank of the question can be reduced down to the concept word.

LDA is a technique that can be used to model topics in a document. LDA represents a document as a statistical distribution of different topics and each topic is represented as a statistical distribution of words. LDA is used to rank automatically generated questions (Chali & Hasan, 2015), text summaries (Arora & Ravindran, 2008), automatic completions for search engine queries (Li et al., 2017), and search recommendations e.g., websites (Xu, Zhang, & Yi, 2008). Since LDA requires large corpuses to derive statistical distributions of different topics, our generated questions might not be well suited to be ranked with this method.

VSM is usually used to measure the semantic similarity in information retrieval and is deployed in search engines, e.g., in Apache Lucence (http://lucence.apache.org). In addition, this technique is also used in information filtering (Musto, 2010), image retrieval (Magalhaes & Rueger, 2007), or searching for example code for a specific API (Nguyen, Nguyen, Phan, Nguyen, & Nguyen, 2017). Since the vectors of VSM in our scenario are easy to interpret, they can be manipulated.

Another approach is building a new matrix structure. LSA is an extension of VSM. Where VSM represents documents as vectors and semantic similarity is calculated in document vector space, LSA documents are transformed into smaller concepts using the "singular-value decomposition" technique and semantic similarity is calculated in concept vector space. Since singular-value decomposition does co-occurrence analysis, the semantics of a document are reduced to a concept word. This makes the co-occurrence analysis unnecessary. In the next section, we present a vector space model-based algorithm for ranking questions that are generated based on a lesson topic using semantic web/lexical databases.

5.2 Ranking Algorithm and Integration in the Question Generation Framework

The ranking algorithm has the following input parameters:

- A lesson topic: e.g., "object"
- A subject: e.g., computer science
- A generated list of concept words that are related to the lesson topic: e.g., "class", "object-oriented programming" (OOP), "accusative object"
- A semantic/lexical database: e.g., ConceptNet.

The subject parameter is relevant, because the same lesson topic could be in the context of both subjects, computer science and English. The following describes how the ranking algorithm works:

- Input: a lesson topic, a subject, a list of concept words, a semantic/lexical database
- Output: concept words associated with relevance value.

- Step 1: filter concept words that belong to the context of the subject
- Step 2: create a matrix RK_M *relation x concept word*
- Step 3: calculate the relevance value for each concept word in the context of the lesson's subject using RK_M and cosine similarity
- Step 4: return a map of concept words and relevance values for each lesson topic.

The first step of the ranking algorithm is removing all concept words that are not related to the subject. There could be some concept words that are not relevant to the lesson topic. For example, given as input the lesson topic "object", subject "computer science", a list of concept words ("class", "object-oriented programming", and "accusative object"), we use the semantic relations of the chosen semantic/lexical database (e.g., ConceptNet has been chosen to generate questions and has the relations: "IsA", "RelatedTo", "DerivedFrom", "PartOf", "HasA") to check whether a concept word is related to a subject. Since "accusative object" is not related to the subject "computer science", it can be removed. As a result, the output includes "class" and "object-oriented programming".

The second step of the ranking algorithm is creating a matrix *relation x concept word*. The columns represent the lesson topic and filtered concept words. The rows of the matrix are created according to the following procedure:

- Look for words in the semantic/lexical database that are related to the lesson topic.
- For each word, a row in the matrix is created.

For example, given a lesson topic "object-oriented programming" and a list of filtered concept words ("constructor" and "polymorphy"), the lesson topic "object-oriented programming" is related to the following words in ConceptNet: "computer science", "constructor", "polymorphy", and "object". The matrix is created as illustrated in Table 1.

Each cell in the matrix is initiated with value 0. In each row, if the column name is related to the parameterized word **x** in a relation, then the value in the corresponding cell of the matrix is incremented by one. For example, following relations exist in ConceptNet: IsA("polymorphy", "computer science"), RelatedTo("polymorphy", "modification"), RelatedTo("computer science", "constructor"), RelatedTo("constructor", "object"), RelatedTo("object-oriented programming", "computer science"), RelatedTo("object-oriented programming", "constructor"), RelatedTo("object-oriented programming", "polymorphy"), RelatedTo("object-oriented programming", "object"). The matrix would be filled as follows.

The fourth step is to calculate the relevance value. Therefore, we apply the cosine similarity measure, which is usually deployed in VSM, between the lesson topic and the concept word. Continuing with the example above (Table 2), the concept word "constructor" has the relevance value 0.71, "polymorphy" has 0.5. Based on these values of cosine similarity, we can imply that "constructor" is more relevant than "polymorphy" with respect to the lesson topic "object-oriented programming".

In Sect. 3, we introduced the developed question generation framework QUESGEN. We extended this framework with the VSM-based ranking algorithm, which returns the relevance value for each generated question in case a semantic web/lexical database is employed. One could define a limit value and each concept word with a relevance value less than the limit value should be removed from the list of concept words. This way, we could use only the most relevant concept words to fill in the question templates. The problem is that the relevance values could be very different

Table 1 A matrix is created based on Relation and Concept word

	Object-oriented programming	Constructor	Polymorphy
Rel(**x**, Computer Science)	0	0	0
Rel(**x**, constructor)	0	0	0
Rel(**x**, polymorphy)	0	0	0
Rel(**x**, object)	0	0	0

Table 2 Matrix is filled with a number of relations

	Object-oriented programming	Constructor	Polymorphy
Rel(**x**, Computer Science)	1	1	1
Rel(**x**, constructor)	1	0	0
Rel(**x**, polymorphy)	1	0	0
Rel(**x**, object)	1	1	0

for different lesson topics, and thus it would be problematic to define a perfect static limit value. Another approach is to select only a number ***k*** of best concept words. This approach is also problematic, because potential good concept words that are not among the ***k*** best concepts would also be eliminated. We propose combining these two approaches to select relevant concept words. That is, the relevance values are interpreted as a probability. Every time, when the concept words are filled in the question templates, a concept word will be randomly selected, but a concept word with a higher relevance value will be more probable. Based on the relevance values, more relevant questions will be generated than less relevant ones.

5.3 Evaluation

The goal of the evaluation is to investigate the hypothesis that the question generation framework using the VSM-based ranking algorithm (QuesGen V2) yields more relevant generated questions than the version without ranking algorithm (QuesGen V1). To test this hypothesis, the experiment was designed and consisted of three steps: (1) working with one version of the question generation framework, (2) working with the second version of the framework, (3) filling a questionnaire. Fifty percent of the study participants were assigned the version QuesGen V1 for the first step, then the version QuesGen V2 for the second step. Vice versa, another fifty percent of the study participants were assigned with version QuesGen V2 first, then QuesGen V1. For both steps, the participants were asked to choose some lesson topics in computer science and to generate questions with the two versions using the same set of lesson topics. The participants were asked to select the questions (using the tool of question generation framework, see Sect. 3), which are useful for the chosen lesson topics.

The two versions of the question generation were web-based and available on the Internet during the experiment period. The questionnaire was also hosted online, so that the study participants could answer the questionnaire after finishing their experiment with both versions of the question generation framework.

Participants were sourced by contacting 25 schools in Berlin and via the "Bildungsserver"[1] platforms of each federal state in Germany. Each participant was required to be a computer science teacher. We were able to acquire ten participants, nine of which were computer science school teachers and one of which was a university professor. Since the professor teaches computer science, this subject was also included in the analysis. The participants had an average of 11.7 years of teaching experience. One participant could not access version 2, hence, there were ten subjects for version 1 and nine for version 2.

5.4 *Results and Discussion*

The answers for the questionnaire indicate the subjective impact of the ranking algorithm for questions' relevance. Table 3 shows that for both versions, the number of useful questions was 18. The total number of useful questions generated by version V2 was less than version V1, because version V2 had one user less than version V1.

With respect to the relevance of the generated questions to the lesson topics, Table 4 shows the distribution of participants' ratings on the scale between 1 and 10, where 1 means "*all generated questions are related to completely another lesson topic*" and 10 means "*all generated are related to the chosen lesson topic*". It is remarkable that for both versions, the rating value 2 dominated with 30% for QuesGen V1 and 55.56% for QuesGen V2 (cf. Table 4). The mean rating values for QuesGen V1 and QuesGen V2 were 3.8 and 3.4, respectively. These mean ratings showed a low relevance of generated questions for both versions and no significant difference between the ratings for the two versions could be found. Thus, the hypothesis that the VSM-based ranking algorithm improves the relevance of generated questions can be rejected.

Table 3 Number of useful questions selected by participants

	QuesGen V1	QuesGen V2
# Participants	10	9
# Total of useful questions	176	164
# Average of useful questions	17.6	18.22

Table 4 Subjective ratings of study participants for the two versions of QUESGEN

	1	2	3	4	5	6	7	8	9	10
V1 (%)	10	30	10	10	20	10	0	10	0	0
V2 (%)	0	55.56	11.11	0	22.22	0	0	11.11	0	0

[1]On the Bildungsserver platforms in Germany, information about education in each federal state is published.

With respect to the monotony/diversity of generated questions, study participants were asked to rate on a scale between 1 and 10, where 1 means "*the generated questions were the same or similar and the set of generated questions was very monotonous*" and 10 means "*the set of generated questions was very divers and contains many different interesting questions*". The mean values of the ratings for QuesGen V1 and QuesGen V2 were 3.6 and 3.1, respectively. These values were below the average value (5), and therefore seem to indicate that the generated questions from both versions of the framework were monotonous. In addition to the option of answering specific questions, the study participants could also give their comments in free-form. The following is a summarization of the pros and cons of QuesGen V1:

- Pros: higher quality of generated questions; using more diverse concepts related to the lesson topics; higher number of relevant questions;
- Cons: for many lesson topics, questions could not be generated, i.e., related concept words could not be found in the semantic database (e.g., computer architecture, HTML); the generated questions are semantically not related to the input lesson topics.

The following is a list of pros and cons the participants gave for QuesGen V2:

- Pros: at least useful questions for a lesson topic; more generated questions;
- Cons: many lesson topics could not be found, however, better than QuesGen V1; for the lesson topic "loop", generated questions are totally not semantically related to the lesson topic; many unknown/irrelevant concepts with generated questions.

From the participant's comments, we can derive that QuesGen V1 generated more relevant questions, while V2 covered more lesson topics. These comments also reject our hypothesis that the developed question ranking algorithm would result in more relevant questions. This result could be explained by the fact that ConceptNet contains little relations for the input lesson topics, and thus, the information the ranking algorithm uses is incomplete. Note, that the conclusion that the ranking algorithm did not enhance the relevance of generated questions is based on subjective answers of study participants. More quantitative research is required to confirm this claim.

6 Conclusions

In this chapter, we introduced an automatic question generation framework, which aims at helping teachers prepare lower- and high-cognitive level questions for their lessons. The framework addresses the concern reported in many studies that most teachers use lower-cognitive questions in their classes. Since semantic/lexical databases are intended to be deployed to extend the number of generated questions related to a lesson topic, we investigated the appropriateness of several semantic/lexical databases (WordNet, ConceptNet) for different learning domains: "history", "computer science", and "politics". Using TF-IDF technique, we found that

WordNet is more appropriate than ConceptNet in the "history" domain. However, in the domains of "politics" and "computer science", ConceptNet provides more relevant terms than WordNet.

In order to enhance the relevance of generated questions, we developed a vector space model-based ranking algorithm and hypothesized that it could result in more relevant questions. However, an evaluation study with nine teachers and one computer science professor rejected this hypothesis. This result suggests to us that we must improve our ranking algorithm, for example, by building a context model, which specifies the context of a lesson topic.

References

Adamson, D., Bhartiya, D., Gujral, B., Kedia, R., Singh, A., & Rose, C. P. (2013). Automatically generating discussion questions. In *Artificial Intelligence in Education* (pp. 81–90).

Anderson, L. W., Krathwohl, D. R., et al (Eds.) (2001). A taxonomy for learning, teaching, and assessing: A revision of Bloom's taxonomy of educational objectives. Allyn & Bacon. Boston, MA (Pearson Education Group).

Arora, R., & Ravindran, B. (2008). Latent dirichlet allocation based multi-document summarization. In *Proceedings of the 2nd Workshop on Analytics for Noisy Unstructured Text Data* (pp. 91–97).

Bhagwant. (2017). Latent semantic analysis tutorial. Available: https://technowiki.wordpress.com/2011/08/27/latent-semantic-analysis-lsa-tutorial/.

Bizer, C., Lehmann, J., Kobilarov, G., Auer, S., Becker, C., Cyganiak, R., & Hellmann, S. (2009): DBpedia – A crystallization point for the Web of Data. *Web Semantics: science, services and agents on the world wide web,7*(3), 154–165.

Blei, D. M., Ng, A. Y., & Jordan, M. I. (2003). Latent dirichlet allocation. *Journal of Machine Learning Research, 3,* 993–1022.

Cambridge University Press. (2004). Teaching repertoire: Pedagogy and practice-teaching and learning in secondary schools Unit 7: Questioning. Department for Education and Skills. DfES Publications.

Chafi, M. E., & Elkhouzai, E. (2014). Classroom interaction: Investigating the forms and functions of teacher questions in Moroccan primary school. *Journal of Innovation and Applied Studies, 6*(3), 352–361.

Chali, Y., & Hasan, S. A. (2015). Towards topic-to-question generation. *Journal Computational Linguistics, 41*(1), 1–20.

Chaudhri, V. K., Cheng, B., Overholtzer, A., Roschelle, J., Spaulding, A., Clark, P., Greaves, M., & Gunning, D. (2013). Inquire Biology: A textbook that answers questions. *AI Magazine, 34*(3).

Chicago Center for Teaching. (2016). The power of questions. http://teaching.uchicago.edu/teaching-guides/asking-effective-questions/. Last Access: July 13, 2016.

Dewey, J. (1966). *Democracy and education: An introduction to the philosophy of education.* New York: The Free Press. http://www.archive.org/stream/democracyandedu01dewegoog. Last Access: April 3, 2017.

Dickman, N. E. (2009). The challenge of asking engaging questions. In J. Rege (Ed.), *Currents in Teaching and Learning, 2*(1).

Fischer, R. (2005). Questions for thinking. In English! Winter, 6–9.

Graesser, A. C., Ozuru, Y., & Sullins, J. (2009). What is a good question? In M. G. McKeown & L. Kucan (Eds.), *Threads of coherence in research on the development of reading ability* (pp. 112–141).

Harvey, S., & Goudvis, A. (2007). *Strategies that work: Teaching comprehension for understanding and engagement* (2nd ed.). Stenhous Publishers.

Heilman, M., & Smith, N. A. (2010). Good question! Statistical ranking for question generation. In *Proceedings of the annual conference of the North American Chapter of the Association for Computational Linguistics* (pp. 609–617).

Intel Teach Program. (2007). Designing effective projects: Questioning, the Socratic questioning technique.

Jouault, C., Seta, K., & Hayashi, Y. (2016). Content-dependent question generation using LOD for history learning in open learning space. *Japan Society of Artificial Intelligence, 34*(4).

Kawamura, Y. (2012). Reading Tutor, A Reading Support System for Japanese Language Learners. *Acta Linguistica Asiatica, 2*(3).

Koujalagi, A. (2015). Determine word relevance in document queries using TF-IDF. *International Journal of Scientific Research, 4*(8). https://doi.org/10.15373/22778179.

Le, N. T. (2015). Using Semantic Web for Generating Questions: Do Different Populations Perceive Questions Differently?. *Transaction on Computational Collective Intelligence,* 17.

Le, N. T., Kojiri, T., & Pinkwart, N. (2014). Automatic Question Generation for Educational Applications - the state of Art. In T. V. Do, H. A. L. Thi, N. T. Ngugen, (Eds.), *Advances in Intelligent Systems and Computing (282) - Advanced Computational Methods for Knowledge Engineering - Proceedings of the 2nd International Conference on Computer Science, Applied Mathematics and Applications (ICCSAMA)* (pp. 325–338). Berlin, Germany, Springer Verlag.

Le, N.-T., & Pinkwart, N. (2015). Evaluation of a question generation approach using open linked data for supporting argumentation. Special Issue on Modeling, Management and Generation of Problems/Questions in Technology-Enhanced Learning—*Journal Research and Practice in Technology Enhanced Learning.*

Le, N.-T., & Pinkwart, N. (2016). Ein adaptierbares Fragengenerierungs-Framework zur Unterrichtsvorbereitung. In *Proceedings of the DELFI Workshop on "Blended Learning konkret: Didaktische Szenarien für den täglichen Unterricht".*

Leven, T., & Long, R. (1981). *Effective instruction.* Washington, D.C.: Association for supervision and Curriculum Development.

Li, L., Deng, H., Dong, A., Chang, Y., Baeza-Yates, R., & Zha, H. (2017). Exploring query auto-completion and click logs for contextual-aware web search and query suggestion. In *Proceedings of the 26th International Conference on World Wide Web* (pp. 539–548).

Liu, M., Calvo, R. A., & Rus, V. (2012). G-Asks: An intelligent automatic question generation system for academic writing support. *Dialogue and Discourse, 3*(2), 101–124.

Magalhaes, J., & Rueger, S. (2007). High-dimensional visual vocabularies for image retrieval. In *Proceedings of the 30th Annual International ACM SIGIR Conference on Research and Development in Information Retrieval* (pp. 815–816).

Manning, C. D., Raghavan, P., & Schütze, H. (2009). An introduction to information retrieval.

Mason, J. (2011). Cognitive engagement and questioning online. In A. Mendez-Vilas (Ed.), *Education in a technological world: Communicating current and emerging research and technological efforts.*

Miller, G. A. (1995). WordNet: A lexical database for English. *Communications of the ACM, 38*(11), 39–41.

Mostow, J. (2011). Questions and answers about questions and answers: Lessons from generating, scoring, and analyzing questions in a reading tutor for children, Invited talk at AAAI Symposium on Question Generation. Arlington, VA, USA.

Mostow, J., Beck, J., Cuneo, A., Gouvea, E., Heiner, C., & Juarez, O. (2010). Lessons from project LISTEN's session browser. In C. Romero, S. Ventura, S. R. Viola, M. Pechenizkiy, & R. S. J. d. Baker (Eds.), *Handbook of educational data mining* (pp. 389–416). Taylor & Francis Group.

Mostow, J., Nelson, J., & Beck, J. E. (2013). Computer-guided oral reading versus independent practice: Comparison of sustained silent reading to an automated reading tutor that listens. *Journal of Educational Computing Research, 49*(2), 249–276.

Musto, C. (2010). Enhanced vector space models for content-based recommender systems. In *Proceedings of the 4th ACM Conference on Recommender Systems* (pp. 361–364).

Myhill, D., & Dunkin, F. (2005). Questioning learning. *Language and Education, 19*(5), 415–427.

Nguyen, T. V., Nguyen, A. T., Phan, H. D., Nguyen, T. D., & Nguyen, T. N. (2017). Combining Word2Vec with revised vector space model for better code retrieval. In *Proceedings of the 39th International Conference on Software Engineering Companion* (pp. 183–185).
Ontario Ministry of Education. (2011). Asking effective questions. Capacity Building Series, #21.
Ramos, J. (2003). Using Tf-Idf to determine word relevance in document queries.
Schank, R., & Cleary, C. (1995). *Engines for education*. New Jersey: Lawrence Erlbaum Associates.
Tofade, T., Elsner, J., & Haines, S. T. (2013). Best practice strategies for effective use of questions as a teaching tool. *American Journal of Pharmaceutical Education, 77*(7), Article 155.
Turney, P. D., & Pantel, P. (2010). From frequency to meaning: Vector space models of semantics. *Journal of Artificial Intelligence Research, 37,* 141–188.
Wilen, W. W. (1991). *Questioning skills for teachers.* What Research Says to The Teacher Series. Washington, D.C.: National Education Association.
Xu, G., Zhang, Y., & Yi, X. (2008). Modelling user behaviour for web recommendation using LDA model. In *Proceedings of the 2008 IEEE/WIC/ACM International Conference on Web Intelligence and Intelligent Agent Technology* (Vol. 3, pp. 529–532).

A Big Data Reference Architecture for Teaching Social Media Mining

Jochen Wulf

Abstract The analysis of big data represents an important capability for companies and in research and teaching. Data scientists, confronted with complex system configuration and implementation tasks, require affordable and state-of-the-art solutions, which are flexibly configurable to enable diverse analytical research scenarios. In this research, we describe an architecture for the collection, preprocessing, and analysis of social media data based on Hadoop, which we used in a master-level course. We demonstrate how to configure and integrate different components of the Hadoop/Spark ecosystem in order to manage the collection of large data volumes as social media data streams over Web APIs, distributed data storage, the definition of schemas, data preprocessing, and feature extraction, as well as the calculation of descriptive statistics and predictive models. Three exemplary student projects, shortly described in this paper, demonstrate the versatility of the presented solution. Our results can serve as a blueprint for similar endeavors at other educational institutions.

Keywords Analytics · Big data in education · Hadoop · Secondary data research

1 Introduction

Big data, i.e., the emergence of high volume, velocity, and variety data and technology to generate insights from this data, is predicted to have a strong impact on industry and society. There is rich evidence, where data-driven decisions indeed represent a significant driver for competitive advantage and growth (Davenport, 2014). Social media analytics, in particular, provides valuable customer insights, and competitive intelligence (Weiguo & Gordon, 2014). In science and research, the extensive use of secondary data sources, such as social media or sensor data, represents a foundation for novel research questions and methods (Dhar, 2013) and allows the study of

J. Wulf (✉)
University of St. Gallen, Mueller-Friedberg-Strasse 8, 9000 St. Gallen, Switzerland
e-mail: jochen.wulf@unisg.ch

J. M. Spector et al. (eds.), *Frontiers of Cyberlearning*, Lecture Notes in Educational Technology, https://doi.org/10.1007/978-981-13-0650-1_5

novel social phenomena that remain difficult to observe (Lazer & Radford, 2017). Researchers are equipped with affordable means to collect and leverage data, which is claimed to shift the scientific paradigm toward computational methods (Chang, Kauffman, & Kwon, 2014).

The above-described shift requires novel capabilities for scientists and teaching staff, which are often described under the term "data science" and include considerable programming and system configuration skills (Davenport & Patil, 2012). Information technology-related aspects represent a particular challenge, due to the multitude, heterogeneity, and complexity of available technology options (Chen & Zhang, 2014; Pääkkönen & Pakkala, 2015).

Scientist requires affordable state-of-the-art tools, which are flexibly adaptable and extendable to the research contexts. Most data analytic instruments are designed for clearly defined business contexts and lack such capabilities (Herschel, Linden, & Kart, 2014). The analysis of social media data, in particular, involves high data volumes and varieties that require scalability and cannot be handled by classic tools for data management and analytics (Bello-Orgaz, Jung, & Camacho, 2016; Gandomi & Haider, 2015).

Among the various technologies that address challenges related to data volume and variety, the Hadoop and Spark ecosystem has proven particular relevancy (Tambe, 2014). Hadoop is an open-source ecosystem for scalable distributed computing (White, 2015), which supports the complete data management lifecycle (including data acquisition, storage, transformation, and analysis). Spark is an important processing component in this ecosystem and implements multistage in-memory primitives (Zaharia et al., 2012).

Hadoop and Spark are fast-evolving and dynamic technologies, the implementation and configuration of which requires considerable knowledge and expertise. Apart from sandboxes provided by commercial Hadoop distributors[1] for testing and learning purposes, there are no out-of-the-box solutions. Due to the constant further development of the Hadoop and Spark platforms, application knowledge is sparse and not well documented. Hence, there is a considerable demand for developing and publishing big data analytics implementations (in terms of system configurations and the programming of data analytics tasks). The prototype in this paper presents a solution for collecting large-scale stream data from social media over the Web, data preparation, and implementing different analytical scenarios. It is designed to process volumes of over a terabyte of social media data.[2] Our presented big data architecture for social media analytics can guide infrastructure implementations in other educational institutions. Further, the described research projects provide inspirations for designing and showcasing big data applications in the educational context.

---

[1] An example is the virtual machine provided by Cloudera (http://www.cloudera.com/content/www/en-us/documentation/enterprise/latest/topics/cloudera_quickstart_vm.html, accessed on January 15, 2016).

[2] When connecting the Twitter Streaming API, for example, one terabyte is roughly 5 months of tweet data.

2 Foundation

Hadoop is a general-purpose storage and analysis platform for big data, which is managed as an open-source project by the Apache Software Foundation. It is conceptually rooted in research on distributed file systems conducted at Google (Ghemawat, Gobioff, & Leung, 2003), the first large-scale operational implementation of Hadoop took place at Yahoo! in 2008 (Shvachko, Kuang, Radia, & Chansler, 2010). Hadoop is a software framework written in Java, which supports the distributed storage and processing of very large datasets on computer clusters, which are built from commodity hardware. Whereas the Hadoop platform originally covered a distributed filesystem, a resource management platform and an implementation of the MapReduce programming model, a variety of additional and alternative functional components emerged, which is referred to as the Hadoop ecosystem. We will below discuss those components, which are relevant for our prototype implementation.

The *Hadoop Distributed Filesystem (HDFS)* is designed for a reliable storage of very large datasets and for the support of highly scalable processing tasks (Shvachko et al., 2010). It consists of a namenode and multiple datanodes. The namenode maintains the HDFS namespace, i.e., the hierarchy of files and directories, and the mapping of data blocks to datanodes. The content of each file is split into large blocks (default is 128 MB), which are independently replicated across multiple datanodes (default is three). HDFS does not require a specific filetype or data format, which leads to a high versatility. If an application wants to read a file, it contacts the namenode, receives the locations of the data blocks, and reads the blocks from the datanodes, which are closest to the client. During operation, datanodes send heartbeats to the namenode. In case of datanode outages, a namenode coordinates the creation of new data block replicates, enabling a high overall resilience against datanode outages. HDFS is primarily applicable for the storage of immutable files, not for the management of concurrent write operations.

Spark is an open-source cluster-computing framework which supports in-memory processing (White, 2015). Unlike Hadoop's traditional execution engine, which bases on MapReduce, Spark keeps large working datasets in memory between processing jobs and thus is particularly suitable for iterative algorithms (particularly used in machine learning applications) and interactive analyses. A core concept of Spark is Resilient Distributed Datasets (RDDs), which partition data across machines and are created by referencing data in stable storage or other RDDs [so-called transformations, (Zaharia et al., 2012)]. Apart from RDDs, Spark provides modules for machine learning (MLib), graph processing (GraphX), stream processing (Spark Streaming), and SQL (Spark SQL). Spark SQL supports a limited set of SQL syntax queries as well as HiveQL (see below).

Flume supports the ingestion of high-volume event-based data into Hadoop data storage (White, 2015, p. 381). In order to use Flume, an agent is required, which is a long-lived Java process. The agent specifies the configurations for the three flume components: source, channel, and sink. A source produces events and delivers them to the channel, which is responsible for buffering the events and forwarding them to a sink. The source component describes where the data originates from. Flume supports popular network streams (such as Avro, Thrift, Syslog, and Netcat), spooling directory sources, http sources, and outputs from executed commands (among others). Channels are repositories, on which events are staged by the source. Events may either by stored in-memory (memory channel) for a high throughput but with the risk to lose staged data in case of agent failures. Alternatively, events are staged in a persistent storage (file channel, JDBC channel, or Kafka channel). Although the primary sink is HDFS, flume supports other destinations (such as HBase, Hive, Avro, and Solr). A configuration for na HDFS sink includes the file type (either text or sequence files), the approach for rolling the files (either time-, size-, or event-oriented), and optionally data bucketing and directory and file naming policies.

Hive is an open-source warehousing solution, which supports queries expressed in a declarative language (HiveQL) (Thusoo et al., 2010). HiveQL statements are subsequently converted to Spark jobs. Hive supports schema-on-read, i.e., schemas are not defined at the time of data extraction but after loading. HiveQL allows tables containing primitive types, arrays and maps, and nested compositions. Apart from simple data manipulation statements (such as load, select, group by, and join), HiveQL allows for user-defined functions, which enable complex text processing and maths tasks.

H2O is an open-source framework with an engine for parallel processing, libraries for analytics, maths, and machine learning, as well as data preprocessing and evaluation support (Landset, Khoshgoftaar, Richter, & Hasanin, 2015). H2O comes with an own engine for parallel processing, which processes large data volumes completely in-memory. However, it may alternatively run on the Spark execution engine. H2O offers a web-based user interface and alternatively supports Java, R, Python, and Scala.

3 Solution Architecture

For our big data analytics prototype, we used different components from the Hadoop/Spark ecosystem. The solution architecture is depicted in Fig. 1. It contains the key components of a big data reference architecture (see for example Pääkkönen & Pakkala, 2015) and describes data sources, data extraction, data storage, data loading, data processing, and data analysis.

At the data ingression layer, this architecture is generally flexible to connect to multiple *REST APIs*. For demonstration, we connected two social media streams. Twitter offers a stream of sample tweets, consisting of a random selection of around 1% of the complete firehose.[3] Data is provided in JSON format and, apart from the tweet text, contains contextual information about the tweet and the issuer.[4] Meetup is a social networking portal which supports the organization of offline group meetings

[3]https://dev.twitter.com/streaming/reference/get/statuses/sample (accessed on January 16, 2016).
[4]https://dev.twitter.com/overview/api/tweets (accessed on January 18, 2016).

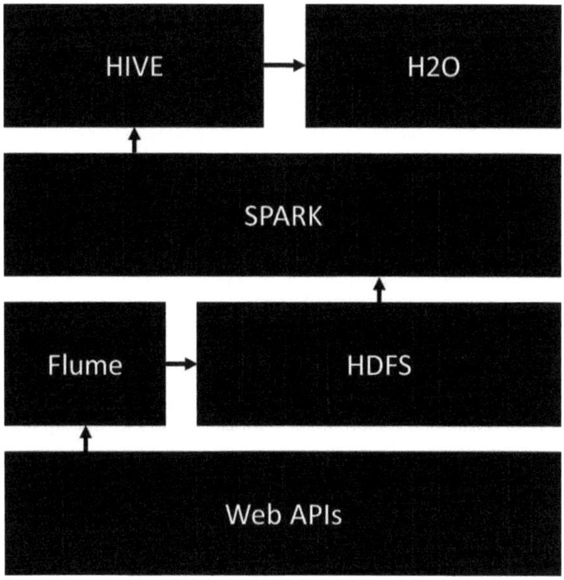

Fig. 1 Solution architecture for big data analytics

around the world. It offers various APIs,[5] of which we connect to the RSVP stream (providing real-time RSVP notifications in JSON), the open events stream (providing event information of public meetup groups in JSON), and the open comments stream (providing real-time event comment notifications in JSON).

For data collection, we used *Flume*. In order to connect to the Twitter API, we apply a prebuilt mechanism, which specifically supports accessing the Twitter sample stream.[6] For connecting the Meetup streams, we created an exec source, which launches a cURL command to connect to the API endpoint and consumes the output (see Fig. 2). We use a memory channel, which stores events in the memory leading to a high throughput while risking the loss of events in case of agent restarts. The maximum number of events the channel will take from a source or give to a sink per transaction (transactionCapacity) is 10,000 and equals the maximum number of events stored in a channel (capacity). The maximum number of events processed in a single batch (batchSize) is 10,000. The maximum interval at which a file is rolled (rollIntervall) is 1800 s, and the maximum file size (rollSize) is 67,108,864 bytes.

In *HDFS*, data is stored as plain text (fileType: DataStream) with text values (writeFormat). For naming, local timestamps are used and the files are stored under a specific path each day (and hour respectively). We partition the data on HDFS by day and hour, respectively, in order to enable the querying of meaningful data subsets. The overall daily data volume from Meetup is about 500 MB, and Twitter accounts for about 7 GB.

[5]http://www.meetup.com/meetup_api/ (accessed on January 18, 2016).

[6]https://github.com/cloudera/cdh-twitter-example (accessed on January 18, 2016).

```
MeetupAgent.sources = r1
MeetupAgent.channels = c1
MeetupAgent.sinks = s1

MeetupAgent.sources.r1.type = exec
MeetupAgent.sources.r1.command = curl -i http://stream.meetup.com/2/rsvps
MeetupAgent.sources.r1.channels = c1
MeetupAgent.sources.r1.restart = true

################## SINK ##################################
MeetupAgent.sinks.s1.channel = c1
MeetupAgent.sinks.s1.type = hdfs
MeetupAgent.sinks.s1.hdfs.path = hdfs://hdp.serveraddress:8020/user/root/flume/meetupRSVP/%Y/%m/%d/
MeetupAgent.sinks.s1.hdfs.useLocalTimeStamp = true
MeetupAgent.sinks.s1.hdfs.fileType = DataStream
MeetupAgent.sinks.s1.hdfs.writeFormat = Text

MeetupAgent.sinks.s1.hdfs.batchSize = 10000
MeetupAgent.sinks.s1.hdfs.rollSize = 67108864
MeetupAgent.sinks.s1.hdfs.rollInterval = 1800
MeetupAgent.sinks.s1.hdfs.rollCount = 0

#################### CHANNEL #########################
MeetupAgent.channels.c1.type = memory
MeetupAgent.channels.c1.capacity = 10000
MeetupAgent.channels.c1.transactionCapacity = 10000
```

Fig. 2 Exemplary configuration for accessing the Meetup RSVP stream

```
CREATE TABLE raw_rsvps (json string)
LOCATION '/user/root/flume/meetupRSVP';

CREATE TABLE rsvps as
SELECT
 get_json_object(json, "$.event.event_id") as eid,
 get_json_object(json, "$.event.event_name") as ename,
 get_json_object(json, "$.event.time") as etime,
 get_json_object(json, "$.group.group_city") as gcity,
 get_json_object(json, "$.group.group_country") as gcountry,
 get_json_object(json, "$.group.group_topics.topics_name") as gtopics,
 get_json_object(json, "$.group.group_topics.urlkey") as gurlkey,
 get_json_object(json, "$.member.member_id") as mid,
 get_json_object(json, "$.rsvp_id") as rid
FROM raw_rsvps;
```

Fig. 3 Exemplary Hive statements

```
val sqlContext = new org.apache.spark.sql.hive.HiveContext(sc)
sqlContext.sql("HiveQL statement")
```

Fig. 4 Execution of HiveQL statements in the Spark shell

We use *Hive* to subsequently process the data. As shown in Fig. 3, we create a table with one event (as a raw string) per row before using the get_json_object function, built in by Hive, to select the JSON objects, which are of interest to us. Subsequently, we use different statements provided by the Hive Query Language for retrieval (e.g., select, join, and group by), descriptive analyses (e.g., analyze table), and text processing (e.g., explode and ngrams).

In order to execute HiveQL statements in *Spark*, we create a HiveContext, which inherits from the SQLContext and adds HiveQL functionalities (Apache, 2015). Figure 4 shows the code snippet required to execute HiveQL statements in the Spark shell.

After data preparation in Hive/Spark, we can access and further analyze the data in H2O. H2O can be executed as a regular Spark application. After launching H2O services in the Spark cluster, we can access H2O via a Web UI. As a first step, the data (in this case HIVE tables) needs to be imported. Thereafter, we parse the data (specifying among others data type, separator, and header). Further, we define column types, which were not set automatically, prior to finalizing the parsing job. In a next step, we can look at various descriptive statistics for data exploration. Finally, we can select and define an analytical model, calculate it, and export the results.

4 Results

The above-described system architecture for big data analytics serves as a basis for various research and student projects, of which we describe three in the following.

4.1 Analysis of Twitter Sentiment Data of a U.S. Presidential Candidate

There is considerable research addressing whether and to which degree sentiment analyses of social media data complements or even substitutes traditional polls. Mueller (2015) implements a sentiment analysis of tweets related to the 2016 Republican candidate Donald Trump, in order to demonstrate basic concepts of sentiment analysis. He starts by selecting tweets containing either the words *Donald* and *Trump* or the hashtag *@realdonaldtrump* with Hive queries. He subsequently uses a dictionary to calculate the sentiment scores for the individual tweets (again with a series of Hive queries). The sentiment scores for each day were summed up with the built-in aggregate function sum() and a group by statement. Figure 5 shows the results for 4 days. The results were compared with poll data, providing weak evidence for correlations.

4.2 Differences in the Usage of Twitter Between IOS and Android Device Users

Besenbruch (2015) uses Twitter data to analyze whether there are differences in the usage of Twitter between IOS and Android device users. To prepare for model calculation, he extracted features about the tweet (e.g., # favorites and language), the user (e.g., # followers and user verification), and the context (e.g., geolocation and timezone) from the JSON objects. Further, he used hive text processing (e.g., rlike, sentences, and explode), built-in aggregate functions and hive joins to calculate the tweet length, the number of hashtags per tweet, and to distinguish IOS from Android users. Thereafter, he used the percentile function and arithmetic operations to create

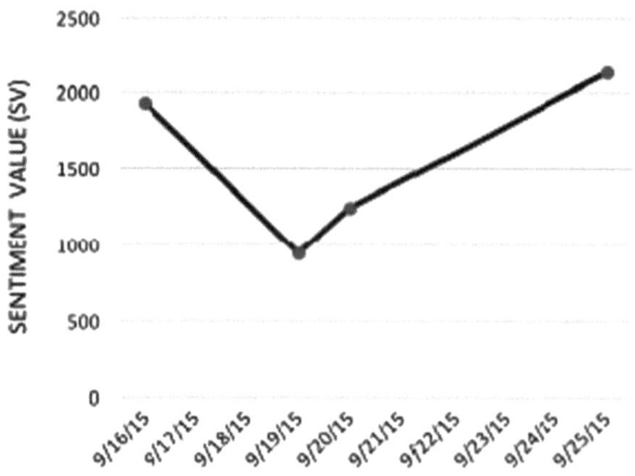

Fig. 5 Overall sentiment value over time (Mueller, 2015)

descriptive statistics. The prepared features were then used to calculate a regression model, which predicts whether an IOS or an Android system is used.

Hive tables stored in HDFS can be imported and parsed by H2O. As part of the generalized linear models module, H2O supports logistic regression models. A binomial logistic regression for predicting system usage shows that language (particularly English-C8, Japenese-C9, and Spanish-C10, see Fig. 6) and time zone are the strongest predictors, as IOS vs Android market shares vary considerably between different regions.

4.3 Analysis of Meetup RSVPs: How About Fake RSVPs

Jung-Loddenkemper (2015) uses Meetup data and Hive to analyze whether individuals manipulate the declared number of accompanying guests in order to increase the attractiveness of events directed at singles. After extracting the relevant JSON objects, he uses Hive table-generating and string functions as well as relational operators to select the events specifically addressing singles. He then uses aggregate functions and arithmetic operations to calculate the distribution of accompanying guests per RSVP. A comparison of single-specific events with all events shows conspicuous differences for the maximum declarable number of accompanying guests of 99 (see Fig. 7). The results provide evidence that hosts of single event indeed manipulate the number of accompanying guests for an RSVP to make their events look more popular, to attract more guests, and ultimately to generate higher revenues.

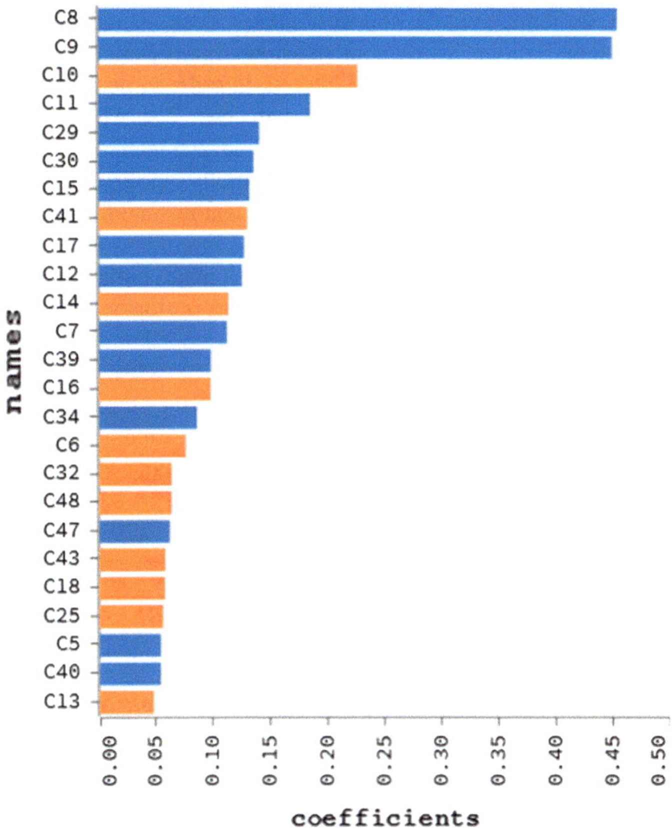

Fig. 6 Standard coefficient magnitudes of logistic regression

#guests	total	single	Δ	Δ/total
1	0.680047119	0.548278757	-0.131768361	-.240330962
2	0.177147517	0.154911839	-0.022235678	-.143537629
		…		
99	0.006705328	0.022670025	0.015964697	.704220529

Fig. 7 Distribution of accompanying guests per RSVP (totally compared to single-specific events) (Jung-Loddenkemper, 2015)

5 Conclusion

The analysis of big data represents an important capability, not just for companies but also in research and teaching. Data scientists, confronted with complex system configuration and implementation tasks, require affordable and state-of-the-art solutions, which are flexibly configurable to enable diverse analytical research scenarios.

In this research, we implement the collection, preprocessing, and analysis of social media data based on Hadoop. We demonstrate how to configure and integrate different components of the Hadoop/Spark ecosystem in order to manage the collection of large data volumes as social media data streams over Web APIs, distributed data storage, the definition of schemas, data preprocessing, and feature extraction, as well as the calculation of descriptive statistics and predictive models. Three exemplary research projects, shortly described in this paper, demonstrate the versatility of the presented solution.

Due to size limitations, we refrained from discussing the configuration and administration of the server cluster including the possible utilization of platform as service offerings (such as Amazon's Elastic MapReduce service[7]). For an initial discussion of associated issues, we point to (White, 2015, pp. 283–344). The prototype can serve as a blueprint for similar endeavors at other institutions supporting the analysis of large and poly-structured secondary data sources. In the future, we plan to include further data sources and to support a wider variety of analytical scenarios.

References

Apache. (2015). Spark SQL, dataframes and datasets guide. Retrieved from http://spark.apache.org/docs/latest/sql-programming-guide.html.

Bello-Orgaz, G., Jung, J. J., & Camacho, D. (2016). Social big data: Recent achievements and new challenges. *Information Fusion, 28,* 45–59.

Besenbruch, C. (2015). Analyzing differences between IOS and Android device users. In *Data science seminar 2016*. University of St. Gallen.

Chang, R. M., Kauffman, R. J., & Kwon, Y. (2014). Understanding the paradigm shift to computational social science in the presence of big data. *Decision Support Systems, 63,* 67–80.

Chen, C. P., & Zhang, C.-Y. (2014). Data-intensive applications, challenges, techniques and technologies: A survey on big data. *Information Sciences, 275,* 314–347.

Davenport, T. H. (2014). *Big data at work: Dispelling the myths, uncovering the opportunities*. Harvard Business Review Press.

Davenport, T. H., & Patil, D. (2012). Data scientist. *Harvard Business Review, 90,* 70–76.

Dhar, V. (2013). Data science and prediction. *Communications of the ACM, 56*(12), 64–73.

Gandomi, A., & Haider, M. (2015). Beyond the hype: Big data concepts, methods, and analytics. *International Journal of Information Management, 35*(2), 137–144. https://doi.org/10.1016/j.ijinfomgt.2014.10.007.

Ghemawat, S., Gobioff, H., & Leung, S.-T. (2003). *The Google file system*. Paper presented at the ACM SIGOPS operating systems review.

Herschel, G., Linden, A., & Kart, L. (2014). Magic quadrant for advanced analytics platforms, Gartner, Inc. Retrieved from.

Jung-Loddenkemper, A. (2015). Analysis of meetup RSVPs: How about fake RSVPs. In *Data science seminar*. University of St. Gallen.

Landset, S., Khoshgoftaar, T. M., Richter, A. N., & Hasanin, T. (2015). A survey of open source tools for machine learning with big data in the Hadoop ecosystem. *Journal of Big Data, 2*(1), 1–36.

Lazer, D., & Radford, J. (2017). Data ex Machina: Introduction to big data. *Annual Review of Sociology, 43,* 19–39. https://doi.org/10.1146/annurev-soc-060116-053457.

[7]https://aws.amazon.com/de/elasticmapreduce/ (accessed on January 19, 2016).

Mueller, M. (2015). Analysis of twitter sentiment data of a U.S. presidential candidate. In *Data science seminar*. University of St. Gallen.

Pääkkönen, P., & Pakkala, D. (2015). Reference architecture and classification of technologies, products and services for big data systems. *Big Data Research*.

Shvachko, K., Kuang, H., Radia, S., & Chansler, R. (2010). *The hadoop distributed file system*. Paper presented at the 2010 IEEE 26th Symposium on Mass Storage Systems and Technologies (MSST).

Tambe, P. (2014). Big data investment, skills, and firm value. *Management Science, 60*(6), 1452–1469.

Thusoo, A., Sarma, J. S., Jain, N., Shao, Z., Chakka, P., Zhang, N., … Murthy, R. (2010). *Hive-a petabyte scale data warehouse using hadoop*. Paper presented at the 2010 IEEE 26th International Conference on Data Engineering (ICDE).

Weiguo, F. A. N., & Gordon, M. D. (2014). The power of social media analytics. *Communications of the ACM, 57*(6), 74–81. https://doi.org/10.1145/2602574.

White, T. (2015). *Hadoop: The definitive guide* (Vol. 4). O'Reilly Media, Inc.

Zaharia, M., Chowdhury, M., Das, T., Dave, A., Ma, J., McCauley, M. … Stoica, I. (2012). *Resilient distributed datasets: A fault-tolerant abstraction for in-memory cluster computing*. Paper presented at the Proceedings of the 9th USENIX Conference on Networked Systems Design and Implementation.

Jochen Wulf is postdoctoral research fellow at the Institute of Information Management at University of St. Gallen (IWI-HSG) Switzerland. His research focuses on socio-technical systems and large-scale data processing systems, consumer-centricity, and IT service management. He authored more than 50 scientific publications. His research has been published in journals such as *Business & Information Systems Engineering (BISE)* and *Electronic Markets (EM)*, and presented at conferences such as International Conference on Information Systems (ICIS), European Conference on Information Systems (ECIS), and the International Conference on Wirtschaftsinformatik.

Big Data in Education: Supporting Learners in Their Role as Reflective Practitioners

Sabine Seufert and Christoph Meier

Abstract Recent discussions on the topic of big data in education currently revolve heavily around the potential of learning analytics to increase the efficiency and effectiveness of educational processes and the ability to reduce dropout rates (with focus on prediction and prescription). This chapter refers to the pedagogical perspective to provide learners with appropriate digital tools for self-organization, and enable them to further develop their competences and skills. The normative orientation towards the reflective practitioner in the digital age highlights the necessity to foster reflection on big data approaches in education. For this, a conceptual framework for digital learning support is introduced and illustrated via four case studies. This conceptual framework can be applied in two ways: first, it serves as a heuristic model for identifying and structuring the design questions that must be answered by developers of learning environments. Second, the conceptual framework provides guidance when it comes to generating and detailing relevant research questions that can then be transferred and processed in specific research designs.

Keywords Reflective practitioner · Big data · Learning analytics · Big nudging Gamification

1 The Second Machine Age: Augmentation as a Key Challenge

Digitalization in an advanced form is about the expansion of the Internet from web initially connecting information (e.g. webpages), then people (social software) and now objects (Internet of Things) (Seufert & Vey, 2016). It is, also, about processes and control systems that work mostly digitally, Big Data, elaborate predictive and

S. Seufert (✉) · C. Meier
University of St.Gallen, St.Gallen, Switzerland
e-mail: sabine.seufert@unisg.ch

C. Meier
e-mail: christoph.meier@unisg.ch

J. M. Spector et al. (eds.), *Frontiers of Cyberlearning*, Lecture Notes in Educational Technology, https://doi.org/10.1007/978-981-13-0650-1_6

prescriptive analytics and growing use of artificial intelligence and digital assistants in decision-making. And, lastly, it is about the discovery of hidden connections in the enormous volume of data in the digital universe. Computing has moved from mechanical machines that undertook simple arithmetic to those that could be programmed digitally to intelligent machines that can learn and reason from completely unstructured data (machine learning).

With high hopes for a miraculous digital welfare economy on the one hand and fears of the end of jobs and prosperity on the other, we must not overlook the implications of human augmentation based on digital technologies. Currently, little attention is paid to this aspect in the educational debate—even though there are already important books out there on this aspect (e.g. Frank Pasquale's "The Black Box Society" (Pasquale, 2015) and Eli Pariser's "The Filter Bubble" (Pariser, 2011)). There is a risk that even digitally skilled teachers are overwhelmed by the intensive and fast moving technological, social, and economic developments and not well prepared for the upcoming technological advances such as transformative Artificial Intelligence.

Discussions on big data in education currently focus mostly on the potential of learning analytics to increase the efficiency and effectiveness of educational processes (for example, how to reduce dropout rates). Helbing et al. recently emphasized that our society is "at a digital crossroad" (Helbing et al., 2017): "If ever more powerful algorithms would be controlled by a few decision-makers and reduce our self-determination, we would fall back in a Feudalism 2.0, as important historical achievements would be lost." Helbing et al. argue for a shift from remote control based on data-driven top-down decision making to self-control. Educational policy makers have to develop a vision for the successful partnership of human and machine (in particular due to transformative Artificial Intelligence and emotional robotics), with the aim to win synergies through complementary competences.

Against this background, this contribution develops a general discussion about being competent in a digital world and about human augmentation as a key challenge in the fourth industrial revolution. The overarching research question is how to provide learners with appropriate digital tools to enable self-organization and further development of individual competences and skills: how to exploit the potential of big data in education to support learners as so called "reflective practitioners"?

As a starting point, we will elaborate what competent use of Big Data and Artificial Intelligence means. Based on this discussion, we propose the normative orientation of being a reflective practitioner in a digital society ("digital citizen"). This normative orientation provides the required foundational base for dealing with issues related to the competent use of big data for learning system developers. We propose a conceptual framework for digital learning support based on Big Data, Learning Analytics and Gamification and illustrate this on the basis of 4 cases. The conceptual framework allows for progress in two ways: First, it serves as a heuristic model for identifying and structuring the design questions that must be answered by training course providers. Second, it provides support for generating and detailing relevant research questions that can then be transferred and processed in specific research designs.

2 Competent Use of Big Data and Artificial Intelligence

Big Data and analytics currently are a burgeoning field of research and development (Abdous, He, & Yen, 2012; Ali et al., 2012; Dyckhoff et al., 2012). With regard to Big Data in education, what does "being *digital competent*" mean in light of these developments? The European commission (EU, 2006) provides the following definition: "Digital competence involves the confident and critical use of Information Society Technology (IST) for work, leisure and communication. It is underpinned by basic skills in ICT: the use of computers to retrieve, assess, store, produce, present and exchange information, and to communicate and participate in collaborative networks via the Internet." The EU framework of digital competences identifies the key components of digital competence in 5 areas: information, communication, content creation, safety and problem solving. To be competent requires knowledge and instrumental skills, advanced skills and appropriate attitudes. However, with advanced cognitive computing systems these key competence areas require higher order skills in terms of complementary competences driven by augmentation. The following situation provides an example of what it means to be digitally competent—here understood as competent use of augmentation:

Imagine the following situation

You feel really bad physically and decide to visit the emergency service at a local hospital. When it is your turn, two physicians enter, an elderly physician on duty together with his youngish assistant. The elderly physician says he commands 30 years of experience, he will find out what is wrong with you. The youngish assistant says he works with a computer database which comprises the knowledge of 600 years of western medical practice.
Who would you rather turn to?

This (admittedly hypothetical) scenario demonstrates the developments in medical diagnoses and why we need to come to terms with the changes in human–machine interaction (Holzinger, 2016). In the healthcare system, one person will soon generate 1 million GB of health-related data during her or his lifetime—equivalent to about 300 million books (Karin Vey, IBM Research, personal communication). One example of augmentation is interactive machine learning in health informatics. The following quote demonstrates how in this field humans and machines interact with complementary competences (Holzinger, 2016, p. 119):

> The goal of Machine Learning (ML) is to develop algorithms which can learn and improve over time and can be used for predictions. Most ML researchers concentrate on automatic machine learning (aML), where great advances have been made, for example, in speech recognition, recommender systems, or autonomous vehicles. Automatic approaches greatly benefit from big data with many training sets. However, in the health domain, sometimes we are confronted with a small number of datasets or rare events, where aML-approaches suffer of insufficient training samples. Here interactive machine learning (iML) may be of

> help, having its roots in reinforcement learning, preference learning, and active learning. The term iML is not yet well used, so we define it as '*algorithms that can interact with agents and can optimize their learning behavior through these interactions, where the agents can also be human.*' This '*human-in-the-loop*' can be beneficial in solving computationally hard problems, e.g., subspace clustering, protein folding, or k-anonymization of health data, where human expertise can help to reduce an exponential search space through heuristic selection of samples. Therefore, what would otherwise be an NP-hard problem, reduces greatly in complexity through the input and the assistance of a human agent involved in the learning phase (Fig. 1).

Decisions on all management levels increasingly have to be made in consideration of computer-based data analyses as well as one's own gut feeling. Decision makers have to learn in what cases algorithms can help them to detect distortions in their thinking and when intuition in form of condensed knowledge needs to come into play. It is about being able to design flexible decision processes, understanding the role of digital tools and using them well versed. A cognitive assistant that is equipped with artificial intelligence can make statistically sound proposals based on enormous data volumes. Nonetheless, these results are limited. The proposals are valid only for a specific area that we specify for the machine and a question that we trained with the system. The human on the other hand is able to make a holistic evaluation of the situation. A decision maker has to know about the different competences and limitations of machines on the one hand and humans on the other hand and be able to design adequate decision processes.

We argue that—as digitalization of knowledge work advances—not so much workforce substitution through automation but rather augmentation of knowledge work becomes the real new challenge. It is important to see work not as a zero-sum game where machines gain an ever-increasing part. Many things that today cost a knowledge worker a lot of time. For example, time-consuming search for sources of information can be performed by computer systems in the future. However, significant improvement in research requires cooperation of machines and humans—so that the sources and knowledge collected will be usable not only in new and better

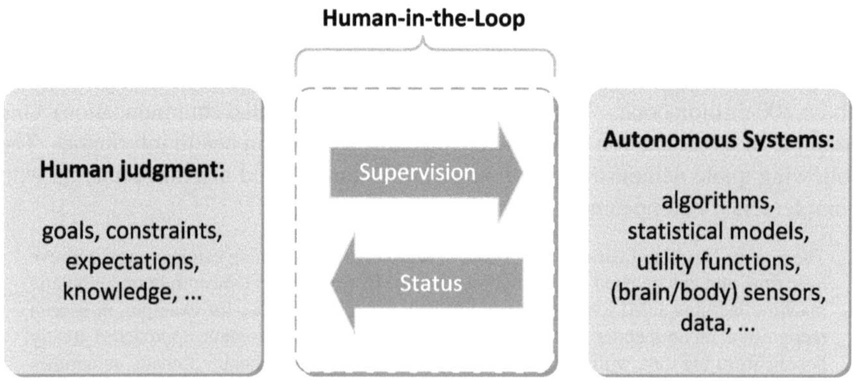

Fig. 1 The phenomenon "Human-in-the loop" (HITL) (Rahwan, 2016)

ways but also in a considerably more economically manner. This allows better support of decisions. However, without humans providing direction, machines provide only fragmented or irrelevant results. Therefore, having humans in the loop (HITL) in augmentation is important (Rahwan, 2016).

Today, many apps already learn from human behavior in order to improve their ability to offload routine work (e.g. sms systems, cognitive automation). The same is true for AI as for example in medical diagnosis. One of the main challenges in developing such systems is that the AI engineers training the systems using huge amounts of data (Big data) usually are not domain experts. Therefore, any biases or errors in the data will create models that reflect those biases and errors. That is the reason why Holzinger (Holzinger, 2016, p. 3) demands a human lens for AI: "Human-in-the-loop machine learning (or interactive machine learning) is work that is trying to create systems to either allow domain experts to do the training or at least be involved in the training by creating machines that learn through interactions with experts. (…) At the heart of human-in-the-loop computation is the idea of building models not just from data, but also from the human perspective of data."

Recently, Rahwan (2016) emphasized the need for a scaled-up version of HITL in his blog: a "Society-in-the-Loop" approach for developing AI-systems with wide societal implications. Similarly, Helbing et al. (2017) describe a future scenario: from programmed computer to programmed society and programmed citizens: "Everything started quite harmlessly. Search engines and recommendation platforms began to offer us personalized suggestions for products and services. This information is based on personal and meta-data that has been gathered from previous searches, purchases and mobility behavior, as well as social interactions. (…) The more is known about us, the less likely our choices are to be free and not predetermined by others. But it won't stop there. Some software platforms are moving towards "persuasive computing." In the future, using sophisticated manipulation technologies, these platforms will be able to steer us through entire courses of action, be it for the execution of complex work processes or to generate free content for Internet platforms, from which corporations earn billions. The trend goes from programming computers to programming people."

Leaders, educational policy makers, and responsible educational developers (including teachers who develop competences for digital citizenship), must understand this connection and develop a vision for the successful partnership of human and machine—human values and big data/artificial intelligence—with the aim to win synergy through complementary competences. In the next section, we will further elaborate on these complementary competences in order to clarify the implications for being digitally competent in the new domain of man–machine interactions.

3 Digital Competences as Core Competences: What Is Really New?

> Imagine a situation where the amount of data about our world determines how well we can see and understand it. It, then, becomes clear that we are moving from a time of darkness, where we did not see enough to make good decisions, into a digital age where we tend to be blinded by information, i.e. suffering from extreme information overload. To master this situation, we will need suitable filters, something like 'digital sun glasses'. Whoever builds these filters will determine what we see [1]. This creates possibilities to influence people's decisions in such subtle a way that they would consider these decisions their own, while they have been actually remote controlled. (Helbing, 2017)

In the last few decades, computers have posed a daunting challenge for us. In particular, in order to achieve better results, we had to learn how to adapt to the functioning of the machine. Now we are experiencing a radical change. The interaction with the system becomes increasingly natural. We can easily communicate with the systems—through our language and our gestures. Nevertheless, there are important differences in the communication with machines compared to the communication with humans (Seufert & Vey, 2016). The former is purely objective and specific in depth. A person, in contrast, would initiate a richer, more extensive exchange—for example, introduce more context, associations, and metaphors. Moreover, dialog between people includes three further levels: self-disclosure, relationship level, and appeal character (Schulz von Thun, n.d.).

Big data and artificial intelligence challenge us to identify and develop our core competences. This is about raising our cognitive-emotional skills to a higher level. For us humans, it will be important in the future to be able to distinguish between accessibility through language expression and the restrictions mentioned above with respect to communication levels. We will be able to interoperate with data in a new way, compensate for local data space, and navigate in hybrid worlds. For example, we will make decisions in groups in immersive data spaces. This in many ways new interaction with digital content requires new skills. AI challenges us to identify and develop our core competences. It is about raising our *cognitive-emotional skills* to a higher level (augmentation skills). Highly developed skills, such as abstraction ability, generalization, creativity, and empathy are increasingly in demand.

Highly developed skills such as the ability for abstraction, generalization, creativity, and empathy are increasingly called for (OECD, 2016) as shown in Fig. 2.

The core competences represented above are interlinked with each other as all three areas relate to changing interactions with machines, cognitive systems and wearables of all kinds. However, for each of these three core competences several important sub-competences can be pointed out:

Expertise Competence: "Critical Thinking"

- Rethinking Research: Finding the right information in huge amounts of data in an efficient manner (e.g. by asking adequate questions based on a sound epistemological foundation).

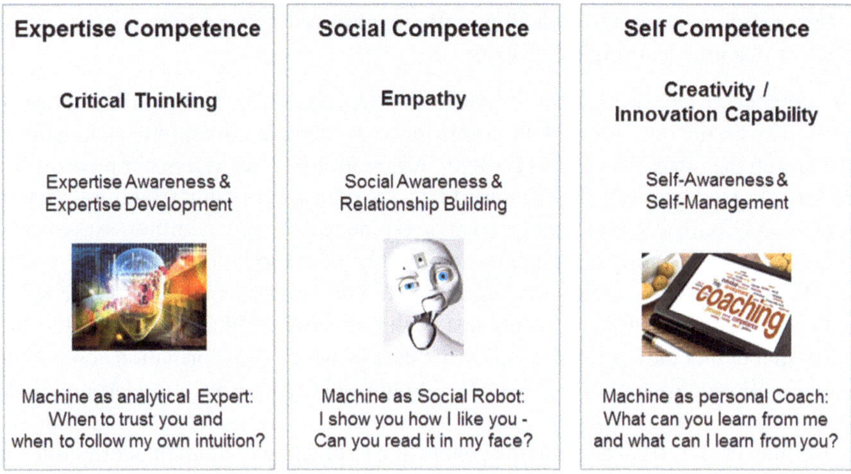

Fig. 2 Complementary Core Competences of digital competences (as transversal competences) *Source* Seufert 2017

- Decision Planning: Comprehensive presentation of alternatives and recommendations, with confidence levels and transparent sources (evidence-based).
- Discovery: Finding and identifying hidden connections, or recombining data from huge data spaces to create something new.

Social Competence: "Empathy"

- The capacity to place oneself in another's position. Empathy is seeing with the eyes of another, listening with the ears of another and feelings with the heart of another.
- Identification/evaluation of moral competence in social robots as an emerging category of collaborative machines (see e.g. http://www.hansonrobotics.com/robot/sophia/)
- Willingness and ability to enhance empathy through the interaction with social robots.

Self-Competence: "Creativity, Innovation Capability"

- Higher order learning competences, experimentation, and reflection as metacompetences.
- Lateral thinking, creative thinking, divergent thinking, and playful thinking.
- Dealing with uncertainty, risk taking, and rule breaking.
- Deliberate practice in the active maintenance of superior domain-specific performance (in spite of general age-related decline).

– New learning strategies in dealing with cognitive computing systems (e.g. interactive machine learning [HITL])

The competent use of big data in education depends on both, the competence of developers on the one side and the competence of users (learners) in the educational systems on the other side. In this context, information literacy is a major prerequisite for self-directed learning. The Stanford History Education Group (Stanford History Education Group, 2016) has analyzed civic online reasoning via online assessments, focusing on "the ability to judge the credibility of information that floods young people's smartphones, tablets, and computers" The researchers described the information competence of the students just with one word—"bleak". They state: "we worry that democracy is threatened by the ease at which disinformation about civic issues is allowed to spread and flourish" (Stanford History Education Group, 2016, p. 5).

Helbing et al. (2017) come to the conclusion to practice fundamental principles in order to take the right decision at the digital crossroad. For that reason, the researchers propose several fundamental principles, for example to support informational self-determination and participation and to promote responsible behavior of citizens in the digital world through digital literacy and enlightenment (Helbing et al., 2017).

For us, the challenge is how to transfer these fundamental principles to the educational system. For a start, we propose to clarify the normative orientation of learning. In doing so, we will employ an "old model", the concept of 'reflective practitioners'. Subsequently, we will clarify generic approaches to big data and learning analytics in order to promote the role model of a reflective practitioner as a role model in the digital world.

4 Normative Orientation: The Reflective Practitioner in the Digital Age

The concept of 'reflective practitioner' was proposed by Schön (1983) and has since become well established. It highlights reflective abilities of individuals. Such reflective abilities are relevant, for example, in the process of preparing, realizing/delivering, and controlling work activities. Beyond that, reflection may also pertain to oneself and also to the environment of work activities. Being reflective, therefore refers to conscious, critical and responsible evaluations of (1) one's own activities and competences (e.g., personal knowledge and results of task performance), (2) the personal process of competence development (e.g., formal and informal learning and the outcomes) and (3) the conditions for performing work (e.g., organizational structures or tools and resources available for task performance) (Dehnbostel, 2003, S. 42).

In the context of digital transformation, being a reflective practitioner refers to someone who reflects on her or his own competences (e.g., digital literacy), on relevant work environments (e.g., conditions and tools for remote collaboration) and work results (Dehnbostel, 2003).

In many corporate sectors, specific knowledge and specific skills have become a determining factor for the success of companies and organizations. Due to the dynamic nature of these changes, it is virtually impossible to predict which requirements and demands companies will face in the future, and which skills will be crucial for success. In consequence, traditional normative guidelines for the design, structure, and promotion of learning and competence development need to be reformulated (Seufert & Diesner, 2010). It is important that critical reflection necessarily be ethical in the context of a radically technologized twenty-first century. While digital technology and the online world provide significant opportunities to education, these same opportunities can be leading to new risks and less self-control (Helbing et al., 2017).

The new points of departure for educational management can be developed on the basis of contrasts between "old work/old learning" in a remote-controlled society following the role model of a technocratic problem solver versus "new work/new learning" in a self-controlled society based on critical reflection and balanced ethics (see Table 1).

5 Analytics in Education: A Framework and Four Cases

In the context of a more general shift from "old work/old learning" to "new work/new learning", learners—as reflective practitioners—need to take over more responsibility in managing the process of learning (Seufert et al., 2017a). Accordingly, greater emphasis is placed on the importance of self-organization, self-control, and self-determination. And there is a wealth of digital media available that support learners in planning, organizing, and controlling their own learning—ranging from task management via mind mapping and note taking to gathering community support for personal learning achievements (e.g. stikk.com).

While much of the interest in Big Data and Learning Analytics is currently focused on prediction, reflection (i.e., monitoring and understanding) may in fact become more widely relevant (Siemens & Gasevic, 2012; Gaviria et al., 2011). All the more so, as learners take on more responsibility in managing their own learning processes. However, those employing Learning Analytics (LA) applications need to be aware that "competing methods, technologies and algorithms applied to the same set of data, will result in different outcomes, and thus may lead to different consequences in terms of decision making based on these outcomes" (Greller & Drachsler 2012, 50; Kelly et al., 2015).

Employing LA in order to support learning, therefore, requires specific competences—on the part of institutions, teachers/facilitators, and learners. Table 2 provides an overview of relevant LA competences modeled on the taxonomy of cognitive process dimensions (Anderson & Krathwohl, 2001).

Table 1 Points of Departure for new working and learning environments (Seufert, 2013)

Remote-controlled society Technocratic problem solvers	Self-controlled society Reflective practitioners in the digital age
"Old Work/Old Learning"	"New Work/New Learning"
Work & work environment	
Stable and predictable environment with clearly defined organizational units	Unstable, dynamic and unpredictable environment and permeable organizational boundaries
Physical presence in the defined work environment	Real and virtual work environments as well as work in distributed/virtual teams
Paternalistic and transactional leadership	Transactional and transformational, meaningful leadership
Employees = learners who are passive ("consume" learning); "learning delivery"	Employees = learners who shape and co-produce; co-creation in work and learning
Modalities of learning	
Learning by individuals	Learning by individuals, teams and organizations
Formally organized, "off-the-job" learning processes	Formal and informal learning "off/near/on-the-job"
Externally controlled learning	Autonomous and self-directed learning
leveling of heterogeneity in the learning process	responding to and use of heterogeneity in the learning process
Point of Departure and Objectives for Learning	
Learning targeted exclusively to current needs	Learning targeted to current as well as future demands and needs
Learning and knowledge sharing according to organizational guidelines (conveying answers)	Learning and knowledge exchange as part of the culture of a learning organization (enabling problem-solving)
Available content (e.g. courses/expertise) as starting point for training	Complex and real problems as starting point
Knowledge transfer and development of knowledge pool (behaviorist view of learning)	Developing skills and competence (cognitive-constructivist perception of learning)
Learning at specified times	Learning as and whenever needed
Learning effected by 'teachers';'Teachers' as "intermediaries"; instruction	Learning supported by 'teachers', managers, colleagues and media (instruction and construction)
Measurement of learning success	Measurement of the success of knowledge transfer and the impact of learning
Focus on utilization of existing knowledge/existing skills	Balance of utilizing existing knowledge/existing skills with the exploration of new knowledge/new skills

Table 2 A taxonomy for learning analytics activities

The cognitive process dimension	Main Goal Reflection by learner	Main Goal Prediction (and prescription) by system
Remember Retrieve relevant information	Identify strategies to retain access to information and datasets	Information retrieval and integration of data from different sources
Understand Construct meaning from instructional messages	Interpret (visualized) datasets	Visualization of datasets
Apply Carry out/employ a procedure in a given situation	Use of techniques that match one's own strengths	Instructional messages, including feedback; Resource suggestions; Answers to frequently asked questions; Suggestions for novices
Analyze Break material into constituent parts and determine how parts relate to another and to an overall structure or purpose	Deconstruct own biases	Learner stratification Deviations from suggested paths
Evaluate Make judgments based on criteria and standards	Engage in self-assessment (e.g., reflect on personal progress)	Computer-based Assessment; Judgements based on learner profiles
Create Put elements together to create a new whole, reorganize into a new pattern or structure	Generate an innovative learning portfolio using personal datasets	Generation of personalized learning paths; Algorithms for learner profiles

With regard to employing Big Data and Learning Analytics as a means to support (digital) learning, we propose a set of generic approaches based on a 2×2 matrix (Fig. 3). One dimension is set up via the distinction of reflecting on past learning activities on the one hand versus predicting next/future learner activities on the other hand. Reflection here refers to critical self-evaluation on the basis of different datasets (Greller & Drachsler, 2012, p. 41):

- OWN datasets created in the process of learning or supporting learning (in the case of teachers respectively facilitators);
- Datasets created by OTHERS (e.g., a teacher reflecting on his or her own teaching style based on datasets generated by the students).

Prediction refers to anticipating learner activities (e.g., further reducing investment in classwork or discontinuing with classwork altogether). Prediction is a precursor of prescription and interventions that aim at dealing with a predicted event (e.g. a student discontinuing classwork) (Siemens, 2011).

The other dimension is set up via a distinction between learning activities by individual learners on the one hand and social learning activities on the other. Much work

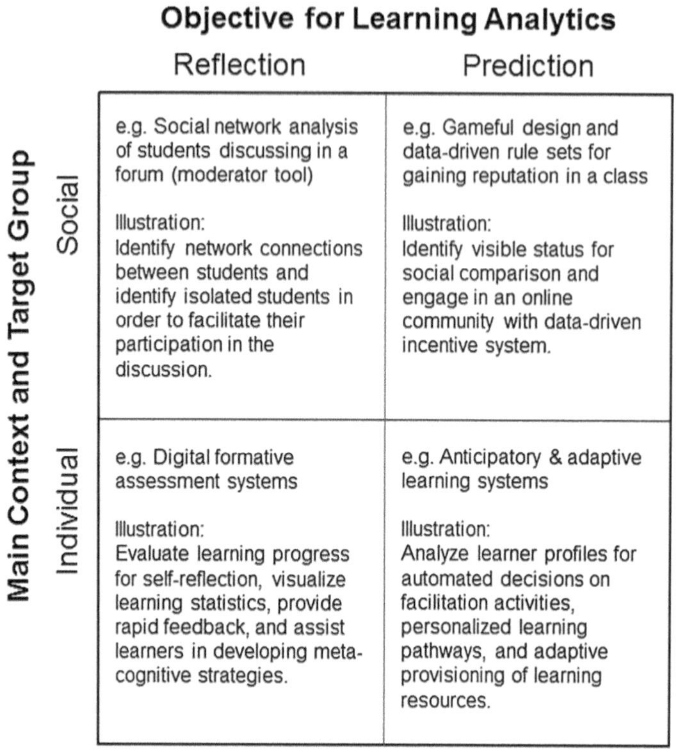

Fig. 3 Generic strategies for approaches to learning analytics

in LA is oriented towards supporting and determining individual achievement, for example by analyzing the data generated through summative assessments. Buckingham Shum and Ferguson (Buckingham Shum and Ferguson, 2012) have argued, that "new skills and ideas are not solely individual achievements, but are developed, carried forward, and passed on through interaction and collaboration". In consequence, LA in social systems (e.g. in the context of a classroom in school) "must account for connected and distributed interaction activity". Buckingham Shum & Ferguson, therefore, propose social learning analytics as a domain in its own right (Buckingham Shum and Ferguson, 2012).

Similar, gamification or gameful design for learning is considered as an on own domain (Deterding, Dixon, Khaled & Nacke, 2011) using LA in social systems, for example to provide visible status and progress, social comparison and reputation (e.g. with badges).

The focus on individual learners is focused on the goal of personalization and individualization. In order to provide pedagogically valuable feedback, assessment systems have to become intelligent and connected with higher order learning skills. Adaptive learning systems (individual and prediction) represent an own, quite new research field based on interactive machine learning.

In the following sections, we will illustrate how this matrix framework can be translated into specific use cases:

- Social learning analytics for reflection
- Individual learning analytics for reflection
- Social learning analytics for prediction
- Individual learning analytics for prediction and prescription

Use case 1: Social learning analytics for reflection

The first use case relates to conducting a social network analysis of students discussing in a forum, for example using the SNAPP tool developed by Dawson et al. (Dawson, 2008; MacFayden & Dawson, 2010). This implies a shift in attention away from summative assessment of individuals towards learning analytics of social activity (Buckingham Shum & Ferguson 2012, p. 5). Here, it is relevant to distinguish between social analytics sui generi (e.g., social networks analysis or discourse analytics) from socialized analytics that are based in personal analytics while also being relevant in a social learning context (e.g., analytics of user generated content, analytics of personal dispositions or analytics of contexts such as mobile computing and the networking opportunities related to this) (Buckingham Shum & Ferguson, 2012, p. 10–11).

The following example exemplifies the first type of social analytics sui generis (Table 3).

Use case 2: Individual learning analytics for reflection

This use case is about LA with a focus on reflection at the individual level—for example about assessment results. As Evans (2013) found out in a thematic analysis of the research evidence on assessment feedback in higher education (over 460 articles from a time span of 12 years), effective online formative assessment can enhance learner engagement during a semester class. Focused interventions (e.g., self-checking feedback sheets, mini assessments) can make a difference to student learning outcomes as long as their value for the learning process is made explicit to and is accepted by students and lecturers. The development of self-assessment skills requires appropriate scaffolding on the part of the lecturer working with the students to achieve co-regulation (Evans, 2013) (Table 4).

Use case 3: Social analytics for prediction

The more environments for working and learning are becoming digital, the more data is generated in the course of working and learning: accessing web pages, working on short knowledge tests, posting in an online forum, commenting on a forum post, etc. (Manouselis et al., 2010). Until recently, the availability of such data for analysis has been mostly confined to what is going on inside a particular learning management system (LMS). With the development of the xAPI specification for transfer of interaction data, a much wider range of data from both inside and outside an LMS can be made available for analysis (Berking et al., 2014).

Table 3 Exemplary detailing of use case 1

Dimension	Exemplification
Objective	Reflection: Analyze student interactions in a forum discussion, identify network connections between students, and identify isolated students as a prerequisite for remedial action (aimed at helping these students to create links to others)
Digital competences required/to be developed	Interpretation: Do teachers/facilitators have the necessary competences to interpret and act upon the information available? Critical thinking: Are teachers/facilitators able to critically evaluate the data basis (e.g., missing data) when interpreting and/or devising a path of corrective action?
Contribution to fundamental principles of the digital agenda (Helbing et al., 2017)	— support informational self-determination and participation; — improve transparency in order to achieve greater trust in strategies for teaching/facilitation; — support social and economic diversity (i.e. success by diverse students); — improve interoperability and collaborative opportunities; — create digital assistants and coordination tools for the teacher; — support collective intelligence on the basis of visualizations of contributions and interactions.
Constraints	Privacy: Is the analysis in accordance with privacy arrangements and are the students properly informed? Ethics: What are the dangers of abuse/misguided use of the data? Norms: Are there legal data protection or IPR issues related to this kind of use of student data? Time scale: Is the analysis post-hoc or just-in-time? Will students still be able to benefit from the analytics outcome?

These developments help to enable gamified learning designs (Berkling & Thomas, 2013). By this, we refer to the use of game design elements in non-game contexts (Deterding et al., 2011, p. 10). Frequently, this takes the form of awarding points and badges for individual learning activities (e.g. posting in a discussion forum) and displaying top performers (or rather point generators) on leaderboards (Deterding et al., 2011; Mak, 2013). While there is some evidence that gamified designs (can) lead to higher student engagement and improved learning (Dicheva

Table 4 Exemplary detailing of use case 2

Dimension	Exemplification
Objective	Reflection: Evaluate objective and subjective assessments; Identify knowledge gaps in order to support improved learning strategies (e.g., preparation for an exam); Provide opportunities for active learning during/after lectures in order to evaluate the impact of teaching.
Digital competences required/to be developed	Students: self-assessment competences; metacognitive learning strategies. Teachers: scaffolding competences (help students to interpret the data).
Contribution to fundamental principles of the digital agenda (Helbing et al., 2017)	— increasingly decentralize the function of information systems; — support informational self-determination and participation; — improve transparency in order to achieve greater trust in strategies for teaching/facilitation; — reduce the distortion and pollution of information; — enable user-controlled information filters; — create digital assistants (for students); — promote responsible behavior.
Constraints	Privacy: Is anonymity (hiding of student names) required for effective self-assessment? Ethics: Is the potential for misinterpreting data hindering the scaffolding process by teachers? Norms: Is social comparison inducing motivation or demotivation in students? Time scale. Should the analyses be carried out in-class or outside of class (trade-off with time required for teaching time)?

et al., 2015, p. 83), the opportunity to engage in a more systematic motivation design that also includes choices, social integration, team assignments as well as characters and stories is often missed (Seufert et al., 2017b; Sailer et al., 2013).

The following use case focuses on gamified learning designs (Table 5).

Use case 4: Individual analytics for prediction and prescription

More than 30 years ago, Leonard Bloom demonstrated that individual tuition leads to a 2-Sigma performance improvement in tests compared to standard expository teaching techniques in classrooms with about 30 learners (Bloom, 1984). The idea of individualized tuition for large numbers of learners is currently pursued in the context of research and development of adaptive or intelligent tutorial platforms (Romero et al., 2008) which in turn is based on advances in artificial intelligence

Table 5 Exemplary detailing of use case 3

Dimension	Exemplification
Objective	The LA application based on a data-driven rule system and a gameful design provides an incentive system for different types of learners in order to increase engagement and activity in learning in general. Predict which learners will respond to incentives by displaying more desired behaviors (e.g., engagement/activity in the course).
Contribution to fundamental principles of the digital agenda (Helbing et al., 2017)	— improve transparency in order to achieve greater trust in strategies for teaching/facilitation (on the part of teachers/facilitators); — improve collaborative opportunities (through targeting students at risk and—hopefully—retaining them in class); — create digital assistants and coordination tools (for teachers/facilitators).
Digital competences required/to be developed	Students: Readiness for (more) autonomy in learning and for self-regulation based on system feedback; ability to navigate gamified environments; ability to interpret dashboard information. Learning designers: Realistic estimates of ability and motivation of learners when creating a gamified learning design. Teachers/Facilitators: Ability to interpret (visualizations of) levels of student activity.
Constraints	Privacy: What are relevant authentication & data security issues when points earned for gamified activities are feed into final grades? Ethics: What are dangers of abuse/misguided use of a data-driven rule system? Norms: Course gamification could be misused for selling old designs in new terminology, for example, by renaming assignments to quests and scores to experience points, without contributing to the students' learning goals. Time scale: What is the overall dramaturgy of the design and how much time is required for different phases (e.g. onboarding, scaffolding, mastery)?

and cognitive computing (Verbert et al., 2012). Adaptive learning systems aim at supporting the development of conceptual structures in learners rather than merely supporting the (repetitive) solution of problems as was the case in prior generations of so-called intelligent tutorial systems. Adaptive Learning Systems closely track student activities and student performance and, based on machine learning algorithms and predictive models, provide students with adequate learning pathways and adaptive learning resources (Butz, Sigaud & Gerard, 2003). However, more substantial empirical research is needed to investigate, in particular, the appropriateness of such algorithms in disciplines other than the typical mastery learning subjects (e.g. biology, mathematics, and information science) and the effectiveness for reaching higher learning outcomes.

The following use case focuses on adaptive learning designs (Table 6).

6 Conclusion and Outlook

In this chapter, we started out taking a wider perspective on big learning data and learning analytics. Against a backdrop of alternative scenarios for a second machine age and the possibilities of software obliterating management as a profession and a field for education, we have pursued the issue of what it means to be competent in digital learning—specifically in the use of big learning data and learning analytics. We have taken note of scenarios for the use of AI that may lead from "programming computers to programming people". And we have pointed out how it is important for humans to be in the loop and to provide judgment when it comes to working with algorithms and AI-systems. We have pointed out that in collaborating with powerful information systems and intelligent machines we need to focus on our core competences as humans: critical thinking, empathy, and creativity/capability for innovation. And we have alerted to a set of principles that should guide how we design and work with information systems—such as big data and analytics systems in education.

The discussion on big data in education is mostly focused on the potential of learning analytics to increase the efficiency and effectiveness of educational processes. A classic case is the endeavor to identify and support students at risk in order to reduce dropout rates. Accordingly, prediction is in focus while the potential for supporting reflection on learning is neglected. We proposed the concept of 'reflective practitioner' as a guiding normative principle for both educators and (continuous) learners. And we pointed out that in the context of a general shift from "old work/old learning" to "new work/new learning" learners—as reflective practitioners—need to take over more responsibility in managing the process of learning. Building on both these concepts, 'reflective practitioner' and 'new work/new learning', we provided a rough overview on what competences are required when developing learning analytics for reflection and prediction at different levels of cognitive processes.

In a next step we proposed a 2 × 2 matrix for learning analytics, differentiating 'reflection' and 'prediction' as relevant objectives and also the use in 'individual'

Table 6 Exemplary detailing of use case 4

Dimension	Exemplification
Objective	Prediction based on student model/learner profiles and prescription of next learning activities in order to facilitate comprehension and retention. Achieve learning outcomes more efficiently (and possibly also outcomes at higher cognitive levels) through continuous analysis and guidance in the learning processes.
Contribution to fundamental principles of the digital agenda (Helbing et al., 2017)	— improve transparency in order to achieve greater trust in strategies for teaching/facilitation (on the part of both learners and teachers); — support collective intelligence.
Digital competences required/to be developed	Students: basic understanding of how such systems work and acceptance of permanent monitoring as well as suggestions by system; Learning designers/institutions: deep understanding of how such systems model the domain, the students and the tutoring process and where they differ in order to select/configure appropriate solutions;
Constraints	Problems may be caused by poor models. Sensitivity, spurious correlations, meaningless patterns, noise and classification errors (all very common problems in Big Data analytics) Data manipulation. Privacy: What data are generated in closely monitoring students' activities and who has access to these in what manner? Ethics and norms: Is there a risk that students guided by such systems will develop less metacognitive abilities regarding monitoring and planning their own learning?

and 'social' learning. The four fields set apart in this matrix we have subsequently illustrated through four use cases: (1) social learning analytics for reflection; (2) individual learning analytics for reflection; (3) social learning analytics for prediction; (4) individual learning analytics for prediction and prescription. For each use case, we have set out the objective, the digital competences required, the contribution to principles of designing/working with information systems, and, last but not least, relevant constraints.

When it comes to supporting learners as reflective practitioners through analytics, it is not only important to enable them in their reflection on the different cognitive process dimensions we have pointed out (remembering, understanding, applying, etc.)—and the implications for their own study behaviors and strategies. As developed at the beginning of this chapter, it is also important to alert learners to larger issues related to machine learning, augmentation, and autonomy. Via small "nudges"—but on massive scale—we as citizens (and learners) are steered towards healthier, safer, and more environmentally friendly behavior in many domains: when selecting a menu as well as when driving cars (Helbing, 2017). Learners, i.e. all of us, need to be aware of the possible impact such nudging may have on our acting as reflective practitioners. Big learning data and learning analytics should help us find the way to our own (learning) goals. This is the support that learners should expect.

In order to deal with these issues, future research should focus on empirical evaluation methods of learning analytics tools (Ali et al., 2012; Scheffel, Drachsler, Stoyanov & Specht, 2014) and on competence models for digital learning (Dawson & Siemens, 2014). The LA taxonomy proposed in this paper provides a (small) starting point for modeling required skills and attitudes as the needed implementation requirements to guarantee successful exploitation of learning analytics. The conceptual framework can be further elaborated with the application of the four different use cases by adjusting and integrating partial theories for the competence development of students (e.g. mapping multiliteracies to learning analytics techniques and applications (Dawson & Siemens, 2014), Student Tuning Model as a continual cycle in which students plan, monitor, and adjust their learning activities (and their understanding of the learning activities) as they engage with LA (Wise et al., 2016).

References

Abdous, M., He, W., & Yen, C.-J. (2012). Using data mining for predicting relationships between online question theme and final grade. *Educational Technology & Society, 15*(3), 77–88.

Ali, L., Hatala, M., Gasevic, D., & Jovanovic, J. (2012). A qualitative evaluation of evolution of a learning analytics tool. *Computers & Education, 58*(1), 470–489.

Anderson, L., & Krathwohl, D. A. (2001). *Taxonomy for learning, teaching and assessing: A revision of Bloom's taxonomy of educational objectives*. New York: Longman.

Berking, P., Foreman, S., Haag, J., & Wiggins, C. (2014). *The experience API—Liberating learning design*. Report, eLearning Guild.

Berkling, K., & Thomas, C. (2013). Gamification of a software engineering course and a detailed analysis of the factors that led to its failure. In M. E. Auer & D. Guralnick (Eds.), *Proceedings of International Conference on Interactive Collaborative Learning* (pp. 525–530). https://doi.org/10.1109/icl.2013.6644642.

Bloom, B. S. (1984). The 2 sigma problem: The search for methods of group instruction as effective as one-to-one tutoring. *Educational Researcher, 13*(6), 4–16.

Buckingham Shum, S., & Ferguson, R. (2012). Social learning analytics. *Educational Technology & Society, 15*(3), 3–26.

Butz, M.V., Sigaud, O. & Gerard, P. (2003). Internal models and anticipations in adaptive learning systems. In M.V. Butz, O. Sigaud, & P. Gerard (Eds.), *Anticipatory behavior in adaptive learning systems*. Volume 2684 of the series Lecture Notes in Computer Science (pp 86–109). Berlin: Springer.

Dawson, S. (2008). A study of the relationship between student social networks and sense of community. *Educational Technology & Society, 11*(3), 224–238.

Dawson, S., & Siemens, G. (2014). Analytics to literacies: The development of a learning analytics framework for multiliteracies assessment. *The International Review of Research in Open and*

Distributed Learning, 15(4). Retrieved from http://www.irrodl.org/index.php/irrodl/article/view/1878/3006.
Dehnbostel, P. (Ed.). (2003). *Perspektiven moderner Berufsbildung. E-Learning, didaktische Innovationen, modellhafte Entwicklungen*. Bielefeld: Bertelsmann.
Deterding, S., Dixon, D., Khaled, R. & Nacke, L. (2011). From Game Design Elements to Gamefulness. In Academic MindTrek 2011, ACM Digital Library. ACM Special Interest Group on Computer-Human Interaction. ACM Special Interest Group on Multimedia (Eds.), *Proceedings of the 15th International Academic MindTrek Conference Envisioning Future Media Environments*. Defining "Gamification" (pp. 9–15). New York, NY: ACM.
Dicheva, D., Dichev, C., Agre, G., & Angelova, G. (2015). Gamification in education: A systematic mapping study. *Educational Technology & Society, 18*(3), 75–88.
Dyckhoff, A. L., Zielke, D., Bültmann, M., Chatti, M. A., & Schroeder, U. (2012). Design and implementation of a learning analytics toolkit for teachers. *Educational Technology & Society, 15*(3), 58–76.
European Union (2006). Recommendation of the European Parliament and of the Council of 18 December 2006 on key competences for lifelong learning (2006/962/EC). Retrieved from http://eur-lex.europa.eu/legal-content/EN/TXT/?uri=celex%3A32006H0962.
Evans, C. (2013). Making sense of assessment feedback in higher education. *Review of Educational Research, 83,* 70–120.
Gaviria, F., Glahn, C., Drachsler, H., Specht, M., & Gesa, R. F. (2011). Activity-based learner-models for learner monitoring and recommendations in Moodle. In C. D. Kloos et al. (Eds.), *Proceedings of the 6th European Conference on Technology-Enhanced Learning* (pp. 111–124). Berlin: Springer.
Greller, W., & Drachsler, H. (2012). Translating learning into numbers: A generic framework for learning analytics. *Educational Technology & Society, 15*(3), 42–57.
Helbing, D. (2015). *Thinking ahead: Essays on big data, digital revolution, and participatory market society*. Dordrecht: Springer.
Helbing, D. (2017). From remote-controlled to self-controlled citizens. *The European Physical Journal Topics, 226,* 313–320.
Helbing, D., Frey, B. S., Gigerenzer, G., Hafen, E., Hagner, M., Hofstetter, Y., van den Hoven, J., Zicari, R. V., & Zwitter, A. (2017). *Will Democracy survive Big Data and Artificial Intelligence?* Retrieved from https://www.scientificamerican.com/article/will-democracy-survive-big-data-and-artificial-intelligence/.
Holzinger, A. (2016). Interactive machine learning for health informatics: when do we need the human-in-the-loop? *Brain Informatics, 3*(2), 119–131. https://doi.org/10.1007/s40708-016-0042-6.
Kelly, N., Thompson, K., & Yeoman, P. (2015). Theory-led design of instruments and representations in learning analytics: Developing a novel tool for orchestration of online collaborative learning. *Journal of Learning Analytics, 2*(2), 14–43. http://dx.doi.org/10.18608/jla.2015.22.3.
MacFayden, L. P., & Dawson, S. (2010). Mining LMS data to develop an "early warning system" for educators: A proof of concept. *Computer & Education, 54*(2), 588–599.
Mak, H. W. (2013). *The gamification of college lectures at the University of Michigan*. Retrieved from http://www.gamification.co/2013/02/08/the-gamification-of-college-lectures-at-the-university-of-michigan/.
Manouselis, N., Drachsler, H., Vuorikari, R., Hummel, H., & Koper, R. (2010). Recommender systems in technology enhanced learning. In P. B. Kantor, F. Ricci, L. Rokach, & B. Shapira (Eds.), *Recommender systems handbook* (pp. 387–415). Berlin: Springer.
OECD (2016). *Skills for a digital world. 2016 Ministerial Meeting on the digital economy*. Background Report. OECD Publishing (OECD Digital Economy Papers, 250).
Pariser, E. (2011). *The filter bubble. What the internet is hiding from you*. Penguin Books.
Pasquale, F. (2015). *The Black Box Society: The secret algorithms that control money and information*. Harvard: Harvard University Press.

Rahwan, I. (2016). *Society-in-the-Loop—Programming the Algorithmic Social Contract.* Blogpost retrieved from https://medium.com/mit-media-lab/society-in-the-loop-54ffd71cd802#.bydlhcygm.
Romero, C., Ventura, S. Espejo, P. G., & Hervs, C. (2008). Data mining algorithms to classify students. In R. de Baker, T. Barnes, J. Beck (Eds), *Proceedings of the 1st International Conference on Educational Data Mining* (pp. 8–17). Retrieved from http://www.educationaldatamining.org/EDM2008/uploads/proc/1_Romero_3.pdf.
Sailer, M., Hense, J., Mandl, H. & Klevers, M. (2013). Psychological Perspectives on Motivation through Gamification. *Interaction Design and Architecture(s) Journal, 19*, 28–37.
Scheffel, M., Drachsler, H., Stoyanov, S., & Specht, M. (2014). Quality indicators for learning analytics. *Journal of Educational Technology & Society, 17*(4), 117–132.
Schön, D. A. (1983). *The reflective practitioner. How professionals think in action.* London: Temple Smith.
Seufert, S. (2013). *Bildungsmanagement: Einführung für Studium und Praxis.* Stuttgart: Schäffer Poeschel.
Seufert, S. (2017). *Digital competences. Position paper for the Swiss Sciences and Innovation Council.* St.Gallen: University of St.Gallen.
Seufert, S., & Diesner, I. (2010). Wie Lernen im Unternehmen funktioniert. *Harvard Business Manager,* August 2–5, 2010.
Seufert, S., Meier, C., Schneider, C., Schuchmann, D., Krapf, J. (2017a). Geschäftsmodelle für inner- und überbetriebliche Bildungsanbieter in einer zunehmend digitalisierten Welt. In: Erpenbeck/Sauter (Eds.), Handbuch Kompetenzentwicklung im Netz. Bausteine einer neuen Lernwelt. Stuttgart: Schäffer-Poeschel, pp. 429–447.
Seufert, S., Preisig, L., Krapf, J., & Meier, C. (2017b). *Von Gamification zum systematischen Motivationsdesign mit kollaborativen und spielerischen Gestaltungselementen. Konzeption und Anwendungsbeispiele* (scil Arbeitsberichte No. 27). St.Gallen: Institut für Wirtschaftspädagogik/scil.
Seufert, S. & Vey, K. (2016). Hochschulbildung 2030. Humboldt im digitalen Zeitalter. *Neue Züricher Zeitung*, September 9, 2016.
Siemens, G. (2011). *Learning analytics: A foundation for informed change in higher education.* Retrieved from http://www.slideshare.net/gsiemens/learning-analytics-educause.
Siemens, G., & Gasevic, D. (2012). Guest editorial—Learning and knowledge analytics. *Educational Technology & Society, 15*(3), 1–2.
Schulz von Thun, F. (n.d.). *Six tools for clear communication.* Available via http://www.schulz-von-thun.de/index.php?article_id=172.
Stanford History Education Group. (2016). *Evaluating information: The cornerstone of civic online reasoning.* Executive Summary. Retrieved from https://sheg.stanford.edu/upload/V3LessonPlans/Executive%20Summary%2011.21.16.pdf.
Thaler, R. H., & Sunstein, C. R. (2008). *Improving decisions about heath, wealth and happiness.* Yale: Yale University Press.
Verbert, K., Manouselis, N., Drachsler, H., & Duval, E. (2012). Dataset-driven research to support learning and knowledge analytics. *Educational Technology & Society, 15*(3), 133–148.
Wise, A. F., Vytasek, J. M., Hausknecht, S., & Zhao, Y. (2016). Developing learning analytics design knowledge in the "middle space": The student tuning model and align design framework for learning analytics use. *Online Learning, 20*(2). Retrieved from https://olj.onlinelearningconsortium.org/index.php/olj/article/view/783.

Towards Big Data in Education: The Case at the Open University of the Netherlands

Hubert Vogten and Rob Koper

1 Introduction

When reviewing technology developments over the past centuries a pattern emerges: the rate of these developments is not evenly spread over time, but rather, there seem to be pivotal moments in time when some key developments and discoveries accelerate and fuel a whole range of derived advancements. Some examples of this flywheel effect are the harnessing of steam power, the introduction of electrical power, the discovery of the transistor or the visionary work on user interfaces by Engelbart and English (1968) and his team.

We argue that we have reached such a pivotal moment in time again, although this time the field is data science. Data science is the emerging intersection of various disciplines such as social science, statistics, and information and computer science. The internet, social networks, new devices such as mobile devices and more recently the internet of things are responsible for an explosion of digital data, which is increasing exponentially each year. Some forecast predict we will produce and consume 40 Zetta bytes by 2020 (Gantz and Reinsel 2012). Data science is all about making sense of these vast amounts of partly unstructured data, so-called 'big data'. There have been three key developments, which are intertwined, that spurred on the data science field.

First, there is the rise of cloud computing, which makes data storage increasingly cheap and ubiquitous while at the same time it provides us with cheap, on-demand and virtually endless processing power. Cloud computing is also a double-bladed knife, as it not only is the backbone for services that are the source of the big data

H. Vogten (✉) · R. Koper
Open University of the Netherlands, Valkenburgerweg 177, 6419 AT Heerlen, Netherlands
e-mail: hubert.vogten@ou.nl

R. Koper
e-mail: rob.koper@ou.nl

J. M. Spector et al. (eds.), *Frontiers of Cyberlearning*, Lecture Notes in Educational Technology, https://doi.org/10.1007/978-981-13-0650-1_7

in the first place, but it also provides the computing resources, processing and storage, needed for the data science services themselves. Secondly, there are the recent advances and developments in distributed computing technologies. Google's paper on their MapReduce algorithm (Jeffrey and Sanjay 2008), resulted in a whole range of distributed software systems, libraries and services with the common denominator that they scale very well and therefore are very suitable for processing big data. Thirdly, there have been impressive advancements in field of machine learning. In fact, to such a degree that nowadays artificial intelligence and machine learning are considered synonymous. Especially deep learning, which in fact builds on the relative old idea of neural networks reaching back as far as the 1950s with the Perceptron project (Rosenblatt 1958), has shown great promise because large amounts of data combined with ample processing power made this old idea viable albeit with some essential twists on the original idea.

All these developments, glued together via the internet, provide the necessary means to do 'clever stuff' with these big data or phrased more eloquently, they enable the development of smart services. These smart services will affect all of our society and hence also education. The idea of educational smart services is not entirely new. Educational datamining or learning analytics have been around for a while. However, in practice, the data are primarily stemming from the learning management system and are relative limited. Solutions often use traditional and proven technologies, such as learning record stores that depend on relational databases. This approach may be appropriate for now but is in our view is too limited for the next generation of smart services, as relevant data continues to grow exponentially and are not restricted to the LMS. We can expect that data will not merely be the result of human interactions but also will be generated by smart devices such as wearables and the internet of things. Research carried out at OUNL on the relation between some biometric variables and learning effectiveness, showed that traditional learning record stores could not cope with the large data streams produced in the experiment (Di Mitri et al. 2016)

The Open University of the Netherlands (OUNL) launched in 2016 a new project called 'Data Sponge' (DS) with the ambition to research and develop an enterprise level big data infrastructure for OUNL that will enable and stimulate the development of educational smart services. OUNL is in a relative good position to do so, as in 2015 OUNL completed a major step in restructuring their educational model (Schlussmans et al. 2016), moving from a guided self-study model for distance education towards an activated learning model for distance education. This model change was accompanied by the introduction of a complete new learning management system (LMS) (Koper 2014; Vogten and Koper 2014). The combination of this new educational model and new LMS was also a major step towards a fully digital university and as a result, OUNL has access to a fair amount data. Several departments at OUNL are already making use of these data: the data warehouse of OUNL captures data from various administrative systems mainly to produce information for the management; faculties use the LMS which incorporates a proprietary data store to monitor student's and tutor's progress; the Welten Institute research center has developed an infrastructure for learning analytics that captures biometric data using Google services. What becomes clear from this is that these efforts are dispersed and therefore are not as effective as they could be. Furthermore, these initiatives are bounded by their respective departments and as a result, data is only sparsely available throughout the wider organization. In other words, OUNL has no "single integrated version of the truth" with respect to their data.

DS should overcome typical obstructions when trying to get hold of the dispersed data across various source systems and departments. DS has the ambition to be the single integrated version of the 'truth' for researchers, developers of smart services and OUNL's management. As a consequence, DS should collect as much data as possible even though these data may be not used yet. One could argue that it makes no sense to store these unused data as they can be retrieved later from their respective source systems. This is a faulty assumption however, as we have to be aware that the vast majority of today's databases reflect designs from decades ago, when memory and disks were very small and very expensive. Databases could simply not afford to keep track of a so-called change log. Rather, these databases typically only contain the last known state of an entity, which is the result of consecutively applying all incoming changes. As a consequence, if we don't take any measures, the history of these changes is lost forever. This change log can be essential when developing new smart services. Therefore, we need an infrastructure that keeps track of all these changes, for a variety of data sources.

Furthermore, some event data are currently not stored in any of OUNL's systems but are still very relevant when developing smart services. Examples are mouse clicks, browsing behavior, biometric data etc. DS should be capable to capture these fine-grained event data as well, which will not only result in large amounts of data, but will also affect the throughput requirements and characteristics of DS. The DS architecture should be capable to deal with the backpressure arising from sudden bursts of vast amounts of incoming data.

These immutable event and changelog data resemble journal entries in a ledger for the enterprise. Obviously, as these data are immutable, the amount of data will therefore only grow and therefore DS should be capable of dealing with a very large ledger. Such a ledger for the whole enterprise is also known as an Enterprise Data Lake. This ledger can be suitable for some statistical analytics, but most likely, it is not very suitable for most smart services to be used directly. The ledger data have to be transformed into different, more suitable formats, sub-selections and aggregations for an effective processing by most smart services. The prompt transformation of the event data in the ledger is an essential requirement for DS. The term 'prompt' is relevant here as some of the smart services may have to provide virtual instantaneous feedback, using the most recent data, while others are much more lenient and are perfectly fine working with data that is maybe a couple of days old. DS must be suited for both real-time and more batch oriented smart services. The resulting transformed data of this transformation that can be queried by the smart services is called the data factory.

Obviously, development of such smart services is an ongoing process. New smart services will be developed while existing smart services have to be maintained because, for example, the provided data formats have changed as a result of alterations in one of the source systems. Furthermore, it must be possible to repair bugs in the data transformations without losing any data as a result. The DS architecture should have provisions for updating existing and adding new smart services without the risk of losing any data or producing incorrect results.

In addition, DS should facilitate the discovery and the development of new smart services. For it is crucial that data analysts can get a good understanding of the nature of the available data so they can develop new hypothesis and questions that could be answered via new smart services. It should also be possible to develop prototypes validating these assumptions in a very agile way. These are typically functions of a Data Lab. The DS architecture must provide the required agility to support this functionality as well.

Figure 1 depicts a high-level view on the resulting DS architecture. OUNL has partnered with SURFsara, which will provide the infrastructure for DS, through its high performance computing cloud platform (SURFsara, 2017). In the remainder of this chapter we will derive the main none functional requirements of DS and see how we can meet these requirements. Finally, we will describe the resulting DS architecture in more detail.

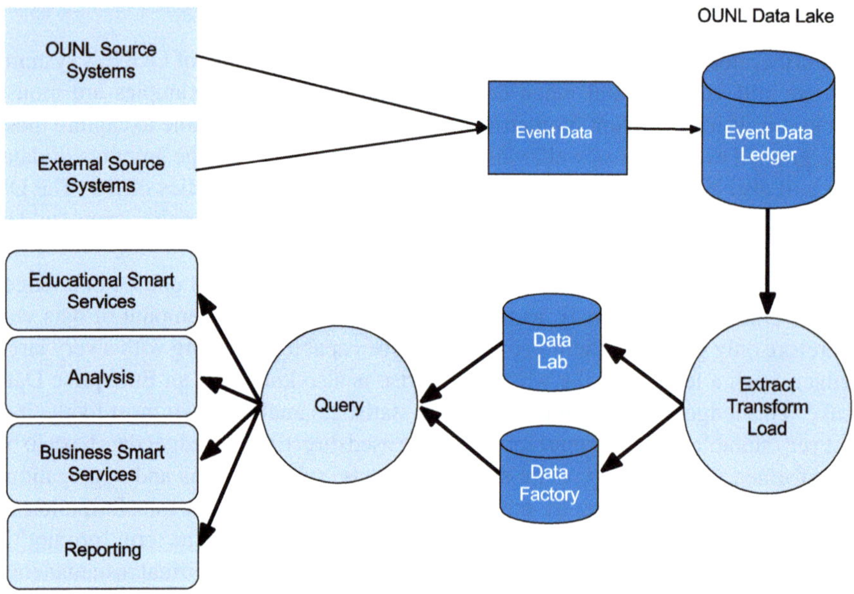

Fig. 1 High level data sponge architecture

2 Data Sponge Requirements

From the discussion in the previous sections, we can derive a set of non-functional requirements which DS and its underlying architecture has to meet. We define four major requirements: *scalability*, *availability*, *reliability* and *flexibility*.

Scalability is the term we use to describe a system's ability to cope with increased load. Load can be parametrized by the size of the data and the amount of data packages. We shall define 'coping' as being able to deliver similar performance even when the load metrics change. Performance can be measured by throughput, that is: how much data can be processed on average within a certain time period. This is a good indicator for the extent that the data are up to date. For near real-time systems, such as online systems, latency is a very important performance indicator. We define latency as the time it takes from the start of the request until the delivery of the requested data. DS must guarantee scalability of both aspects: DS performance should not deter when more, potentially much more, data is produced. DS latency should not deter when data load increases.

Availability will be rather intuitively defined as the ratio of the total time DS is operational during a given interval to the length of that interval. High availability of DS is of utmost importance as downtime would lead not only to inaccurate data for various smart services, but also to a potential permanent loss of data as incoming data cannot be processed. This is especially the case when these data are not stored by any other source system of OUNL or are exclusively fed into DS. The architecture of DS should take into account that disturbances, such as hardware failures, will not affect its availability.

Reliability is the measure of how far we can trust the data in DS to be correct and up to date. There is an obvious relationship with scalability and availability. However, a scalable and highly available DS does not in itself guarantee that data are correct. We must expect incoming data to be erroneous from time to time for example due to human error. The DS architecture is considered reliable when it provides means to correct such errors once they have been detected.

Flexibility is a measure to what extent DS can handle changes in the system. Data fed into DS will change over time as the source systems evolve. This not only applies for new data types, but also for changes in existing data types. Similarly, smart services may require different data types as the services evolve over time. DS should be able to cope with these changes, without compromising availability and reliability.

In the next sections we will discusses different architectures that can meet these requirements and we look in more detail at the proposed architecture for DS. We will address each requirement in more detail in the next section and discuss how these requirements influence the architectural choices. Finally, we will present a high-level overview of the DS architecture.

3 Consequences for Data Sponge Architecture

The DS architecture must meet the scalability, reliability, availability, and flexibility requirements. The first requirement, scalability, will affect the DS architecture most. A major decision is what type technology stack we will use to meet the scalability requirement, which for a large part determines the DS architecture. One option is to use, what we will call 'traditional' technologies, which typically include a relational database and one or more application and/or web servers. Such a three-tiered approach is very well understood as it is applied in numerous systems over last decades. An ACID compliant database (Haerder and Reuter, 1983), usual SQL compatible, is essential in this type architecture, as the upper layers very much depend on the transactions typically provided by these database management systems. This type of architecture typically will scale well up to a certain point, when the underlying database system becomes too slow. For incoming data, it will cause backpressure issues and as a consequence eventually could lead to permanent data loss. This typically occurs when the amount of input data is greater than the system can handle for a prolonged period of time. Another consequence is that database latency will be high and this could also lead to a potentially unacceptable increase in overall system latency, simply because the data cannot be retrieved in due time. Both situations, backpressure on the input data and high latency in the data throughput are obviously undesirable. We could fix such a situation by upgrading the underlying database hardware, which is known as vertical scaling. Vertical scaling only goes so far as what the best hardware has to offer, while at the same time hardware costs increase exponentially when squeezing the last bit of performance out the server hardware. However, there are alternative approaches that could help alleviate the database bottleneck. Probably the first step would be to shard the database, which basically is dividing the database into partitions which are hosted on different database servers. But there is a high price to pay when sharding a relational database. A lot of the logic behind this sharding has to be handled by the application layer and ordinary operational tasks such as backing up, schema changes become much more difficult. An example of the increased complexity introduced by sharding of the database is the multi write problem. As data will be distributed over multiple database servers, the application becomes responsible for the data integration, meaning it must keep the databases up to date with the correct data. This data integration problem is complex and race conditions can lead to faulty data which is very hard to detect and correct. In other words, we have lost the benefits of having an ACID compliant database. Alternatively, we could also introduce additional data caches and alternative storages to increases data throughput. However, such architecture will become very complex very quickly, which is ultimately very difficult to manage, maintain and understand. In conclusion, using a 'traditional' three-tier approach has the advantage that the underlying technologies are very well understood and have proven to work well. Nevertheless, at a certain point the underlying database technology will not scale anymore without additional measures, which in turn will quickly lead to an architecture that is very complex, messy and very difficult to maintain.

An alternative to these 'traditional' technologies are distributed data systems, which are relative new and received a lot of attention when Google published their paper 'MapReduce: Simplified Data Processing on Large Clusters'. Since, an explosion of environments has emerged including many NoSQL databases and numerous variations on the original MapReduce data processing model. What these applications have in common is the way they approach scalability. Rather than relying on more powerful computer hardware to address scaling as is typical in vertical scaling, they are built around the concept of horizontal scaling. Horizontal scaling is achieved by adding additional computing resources to a cluster of connected nodes which allows the nodes in the cluster to work in parallel at the same tasks. The processing and data load is spread amongst the available nodes in the cluster by one or more supervisor nodes. This approach, theoretically, should scale limitless as long as additional computing resources are available. Cloud computing fits very nicely into this model as it provides the means to increase and decrease the number of computing resources in the cluster as needed.

Distributed data systems, having horizontal scalability in their DNA, are very well suited to process large amounts of heterogeneous data. However, this does not also imply that they are automatically suitable for real-time applications typically having low latencies. For example, many MapReduce implementations are rather batch oriented and therefore have not the required low latencies for near real-time processing of data. We will discuss two different approaches that will address this latency problem of batch oriented distributed data processing frameworks. The first approach is known as the 'Lambda architecture' which we will discuss next.

4 The Lambda Architecture in a Nutshell

In 'Big Data: Principles and best practices of scalable realtime data systems' (Marz and Warren, 2015) Marz and Warren describe an architecture that they dubbed "Lambda Architecture'. This architecture not only addresses the issue of meeting the low latencies requirements with batch oriented distributed data processing frameworks such as Hadoop, but also addresses the reliability and flexibility requirements.

This architecture is made up by three distinct layers: a batch layer, a speed layer and finally a serving layer. The serving layer combines the outcomes of the batch layer and speed layer into multiple up to date views on the input data. Up to date means that the latency of the serving layer is sufficiently low so data in the views can act as input for real-time systems. Figure 2 depicts a high-level overview of the Lambda architecture.

The batch layer uses an immutable master data set as input to re-compute, on regular intervals, the data in views of the batch layer. This processing of the data may take minutes or even hours. Clearly, the computed batch views are out of date by the time this processing has been completed as under while new data has been pouring into the master data set. For this reason, the architecture also includes the speed layer. The speed layer is responsible for calculating exactly the same views as

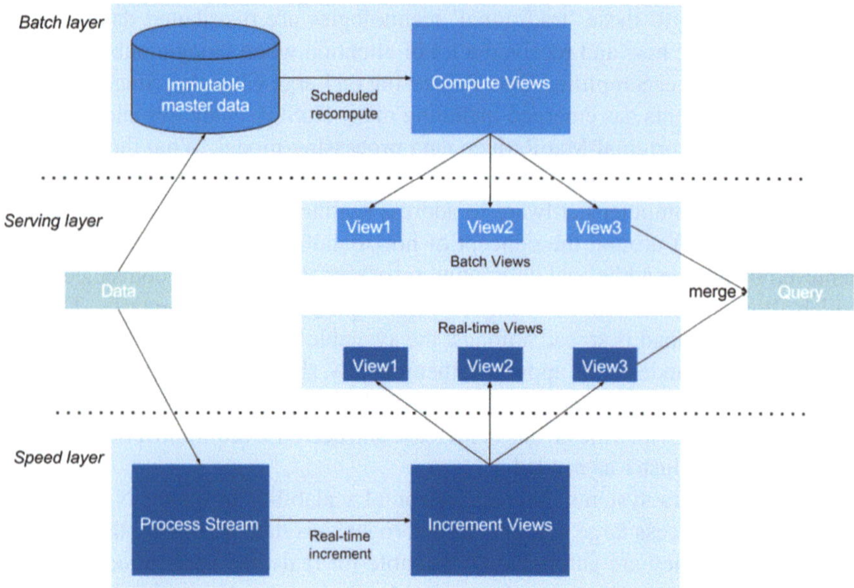

Fig. 2 The lambda architecture

the batch layer does, but with the distinction that the serving layer only processes the input data that is not already processed by the batch layer. Because the batch layer regularly catches up with the speed layer, the amount of data to be processed by the speed layer at any given moment in time is fairly limited. This limited data set can easily be processed with sufficiently low latencies. The speed layer can use a variety of sub-architectures such as micro batch jobs, micro batched streams, or single item streams.

Finally, the serving layer is responsible for merging the outcomes of the batch views and the real-time views into up-to-date views on the input data. The Lambda architecture solves two major problems. First, it provides the low latencies required by near real-time applications, whilst at the same time allows the use of batch oriented distributed technologies such MapReduce to do the majority of the data processing. But maybe as important, the architecture introduces the necessary resilience against faults in the data processing which could be caused for example by changing requirements, modified data formats, or programming errors. The key to this resilience is keeping the original input data in an immutable data store. This ensures that no original data is lost and each view can be recomputed at any time. Updating both the programming for the batch and speed layer with the necessary changes and or fixes, followed by the reprocessing of all input data in the master dataset will return the system in a valid and correct state again. This meets our reliability and flexibility requirement as it allows us to deal with faults and changed requirements.

Although this architecture solves the low-latency demands of our scalability requirement, it also introduces additional complexity. First, we need to synchronize the speed layer with the batch on regular intervals, by unloading data from the speed layer once the batch layer views have been updated. Secondly, and more importantly, the speed layer does use a different technology stack from the batch layer and as a consequence, the programming code of the batch layer cannot directly be reused in the speed layer. Having two code bases increases the likelihood of interpretation differences and programming errors, while maintenance efforts are at least doubled because every piece of code has to be programmed twice.

The architecture and technologies used in the speed layer differs depending on whether the real-time views are updated synchronously or asynchronously. In case the speed layer views are updated synchronously, the updating process is stopped until all processing has been completed. In most cases, this is undesirable, and an asynchronous approach is therefore preferred in which a stream processor acts as buffer avoiding backpressure in the data providers. The data provider will continue immediately after the data is queued by the stream processor. This way, peaks and sudden bursts of data can be easily accommodated. There are many stream processing frameworks available, but in combination with big data processing Apache Kafka (Kreps et al., 2011) is a very popular choice. Kafka provides a unified, high-throughput, low-latency platform for handling real-time data feeds. The persistent multi-subscriber message queue is built as a distributed transaction log. These features make Kafka an appealing choice as streaming framework for the speed layer.

Interestingly, it is the main architect of Kafka, Jay Kreps who questions the Lambda architecture (Kreps, 2014a) and proposes an alternative architecture exploiting the unique properties of Kafka, while maintaining the resilience offered by the Lambda architecture.

5 The Kappa Architecture, in a Nutshell

Jay Krepps argues in 'I Heart Logs' (Kreps, 2014b) that streaming micro services using Kafka's distributed persistent messagebus, could replace the batch layer of the Lambda architecture. By doing so, one of the main drawbacks of the Lambda architecture, the need to maintain two different application environments for the batch and speed layer, can be overcome. This approach is dubbed 'Kappa architecture' with an obvious wink to the 'Lambda Architecture'. Kreps recognizes that one of the strong points of the Lambda architecture is it resilience to cope with changes and bugs by exploiting its immutable master data set. The proposed 'Kappa' architecture also provides this resilience, albeit in a slightly different and more implicit fashion, by using Kafka's unique persistent multi-subscriber message streams.

Figure 3 depicts the 'Kappa architecture' based on Kafka. It becomes immediately obvious that the batch layer has disappeared in this architecture. A stream processing framework converts all input data, persisted through Kafka input topics into the required views. This approach very much resembles a speed layer of the Lambda

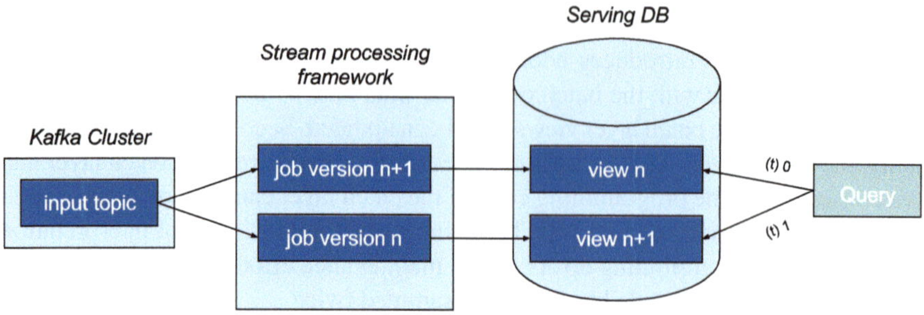

Fig. 3 The 'Kappa' architecture

architecture that is tuned for asynchronous data processing. However, in the case of the Kappa architecture, all input data will be processed by the stream infrastructure and not only the most recent data as it is the case with the Lambda architecture.

But how does this architecture achieve the resilience of the Lambda architecture? To answer this question we have to look a little closer at the Kafka architecture. Kafka is a distributed messaging system, a real-time stream processor and distributed data store in one closely integrated package. Kafka retains messages, by topic, as an immutable log. The retention period can be configured by topic and may be indefinite. Each topic can have multiple independent subscribers, meaning that each subscriber is receiving all messages of the topic. Each subscriber maintains a pointer to the last read message, which is simply the index of the last processed message by that subscriber. The collection of immutable topic logs very much resembles the immutable master data set of the Lambda architecture. Therefore, if we must recalculate our output views as a result of programming errors or perhaps emerging requirements, we can feed the complete topic log again to the stream processing system by simply resetting the last read index of the relevant topic subscribers. While this reprocessing is taking place, which may take many hours, the system would be producing out of date, albeit correct, data. Depending on the type of defect being fixed, it could be preferable to serve more up to date, but less correct, data as long as the reprocessing has not yet had time to catch up. It therefore makes sense not to overwrite the existing output views right away, but instead rename the updated stream processes and the resulting output views by adding a version number to them. This way the old views and the new corrected views coexists for a period of time. Once the new streams are up to date, the consumers of the old views can be configured to start using the latest versions of the output views containing the corrected data. Because both versions of the stream processes and resulting views are constantly being updated with the latest input, there is no immediate pressure to switch all consumers simultaneously, which is essential in real life situations where a centralized release management of various sub-systems is at best undesirable and more likely unrealistic. Once all consumers have been adapted and configured to use the latest versions of the streams and views, we can delete the old version with its corresponding data and thereby free the used computing resources. This way the Kappa architecture achieves a similar resilience against erroneous data and programming bugs as the Lambda architecture. Hence, the Kappa architecture also meets the reliability and flexibility criteria of DS.

In the previous section, we did not address another major difference between the two architectures that has to do with scalability. Although both architectures can use a distributed message broker such as Kafka, the scalability demands of this message broker are very different in the Lambda architecture compared to the Kappa architecture. The Lambda architecture has a message broker in the speed layer, if it has one at all. This speed layer only processes data not yet processed by the batch layer and therefore the required low latency is relative easily achieved when compared to the Kappa architecture where the message broker is responsible for processing all incoming data. In other words, the Kappa architecture depends much more on the scalability of the message broker compared to the Lambda architecture. Is Kafka up to this task? Because Kafka is a distributed message broker, it will allow vertical scaling by adding additional nodes to the cluster. Kafka is also a persistent message broker. The persistence of the message streams is achieved via a distributed NoSQL key/value store, which implementation can be changed via configuration. This store will scale vertically as well. In fact, the developers of Kafka claim that the system is capable of handling millions of message per second in a properly configured Kafka cluster with very low latencies. This should be ample to meet the scalability requirement of DS. This leaves the availability requirement which we will discuss next.

Kafka addresses the availability requirement by introducing a failover mechanism for each topic in the Kafka cluster. A Kafka topic is split into one or more partitions, and each partition is responsible for processing a shard of the total message stream. The distribution is determined by the hash value of a unique message key. The partitions themselves are distributed as evenly as possible over the available Kafka nodes in the cluster. Each partition is replicated across a configurable number of Kafka nodes for fault tolerance and each partition has one node which acts as the 'leader' and zero or more nodes which act as 'followers'. The leader handles all read and write requests for the partition while the followers passively replicate the leader. If the leader fails, one of the followers will automatically become the new leader. Each node acts as a leader for some of its partitions and as follower for others, so the load and risks are well balanced within the cluster guaranteeing the availability of the services provided by the cluster should one or more nodes in the cluster fail. In case of a catastrophic failure where none of the replicas are available two alternative recovery scenarios are available. Either wait for a synchronized replica to come back to life and choose this replica as the leader or alternatively choose the first replica that comes back to life, as the leader, which is not necessarily fully synchronized. This is a tradeoff between availability and reliability. Kafka can be configured either way, but by default, reliability is sacrificed over availability.

So when properly configured we may conclude that Kafka also meets the reliability requirement of DS and thereby meets all four requirements. This combined with the advantages of the reduced complexity through a single technology stack makes is an appealing choice for DS. However, the message broker is only one, although very important, part of overall Kappa architecture. The stream processing system is the other part and it must meet the scalability, availability, flexibility, and reliability requirements as well.

6 The Stream Processing System

We didn't pay much attention to the stream processing system so far, but it is an essential component of the Kappa architecture. The stream processing system is focused around so-called micro-services, which are responsible for small parts of the transformation of the data, very similar to pipelines known from Unix (Kleppmann and Kreps, 2015). There are various implementations of these stream processing frameworks such as Apache Storm, Apache Samza, Spark Streams, and more recently Kafka Streams (KS). Having a native stream processing framework integrated in Kafka makes an interesting proposition for DS, as this reduces the learning curve and ensures optimal integration. Next, we will have a more detailed look at KS and review how KS meets our requirements.

Kafka stream processing applications are ordinary Java applications that can be run everywhere without any special requirements. For packing and deployment, KS relies on external specialized tools such as Puppet, Docker, Mesos, Kubernetes, or even YARN. Therefore, KS does not rely on a proprietary deployment manager. From a deployment perspective, a Kafka stream is just another service that may have some local state on disk, which is just a cache that can be recreated at any time if it is lost or if the streaming application is moved to another node. Kafka will partition and balance the load over the running instances of the streaming application. This partitioning is what enables data locality, scalability, high performance, and fault tolerance.

So KS meets the scalability and availability requirements of DS, given it has been be properly configured. How do KS meet our reliability and flexibility requirements? To answer this question, we must have a closer look at a concept known as 'Stream Table Duality'. We have seen that Kafka threats messages as an immutable changelog. This changelog would therefore only be growing, which could become problematic. To keep the changelog manageable, Kafka has a feature called log compaction. Log compaction determines the most recent version of a changelog entry for every key and discards all other changelog entries for that key. The compacted changelog effectively can be regarded as a traditional state table. KS uses this duality of the changelog to the fullest by interpreting a stream as a changelog of a table and tables as a changelog of a stream.

Stream as Table: A stream can be considered a changelog of a table, where each data record in the stream captures a state change of the table. A stream is thus a table in disguise, and it can be easily turned into a 'real' table by replaying the changelog from beginning to end to reconstruct the table.

Table as Stream: A table can be considered a snapshot, at a point in time, of the latest value for each key in a stream. A table is thus a stream in disguise, and it can be easily turned into a 'real' stream by iterating over each key-value entry in the table.

Because of this duality, the Kafka message broker can used to replicate the local state stores across nodes in the cluster for fault tolerance. It also provides a mechanism to correct mistakes, as the streaming applications also maintain an index to the last processed changelog entry. Recalculating results is a matter of deleting some intermediate topics and resetting the corresponding indexes. The framework will handle the rest automatically and after some time it takes to catch up, the results will be up to date again. So probably not unsurprisingly, KS fits well in the Kappa architecture and meets the reliability and flexibility requirements of DS.

7 Cold Start Problem, CDC to the Rescue

Now that we have determined a basic architecture and corresponding implementation framework for DS that meets our global requirements, we focus on something we will call the cold start problem. The cold start problem refers to initial lack of data that can directly be fed into DS. In an ideal world, all of OUNL's source systems would be extended with triggers, event listeners, and so forth that would provide DS with all event data from these systems. However, this is not very realistic, as this would require a tremendous effort. More realistically, the required modifications will be implemented as these source systems develop over a prolonged period of time. This process could take years to fully complete. How can we survive this data drought in the meantime?

The most practical and least invasive approach is to develop applications that monitor changes in the databases of the source systems and thus in effect creating a simulated change log on these databases. The advantage of this approach is that the source systems do not have to be affected by this at all, while some of the most relevant data becomes available for DS straight away with a minimum of effort. This approach is also known as Change Data Capture (CDC).

How we monitor DB changes very much depends on the available database technologies and the characteristics of the data involved. For example, some database management systems have out of the box support for an actual changelog, which is also used for replicating the databases for backup purposes. In these cases developing a proprietary change listener feeding directly into DS is a realistic approach. If the used database systems do not have support changelogs other scenarios are possible as well. If data is not very volatile and relative limited in size, such as student course registrations for example, it is possible to create a batch job that determines the delta of the table values on a daily basis and sends its results to DS.

Obviously, CDC cannot capture data that is not stored in any of the databases and this approach will eventually miss relevant data. So besides implementing CDC, efforts must go towards capturing event data in the various systems as well. However, by establishing a basic DS infrastructure solely based on CDC data, we can showcase

DS and make a more informed case to emphasize the importance to make changes to various source systems to capture the missing data.

The Confluent platform extends Kafka with a number of very useful additions among which there is a framework for implementing our CDC requirements, called Kafka Connect (KC). KC defines two basic interfaces: source connectors which are producers that feed Kafka with new data and sink connectors which are consumers that export data from Kafka to various other formats and systems. With this framework, it is possible to develop proprietary connectors. However, the Confluent platform also ships a number of standard connectors, among which is a JDBC source and sink connector. These KC connectors can be configured to work in stand-alone or in distributed mode. Distributed mode obviously is targeted at scalability and availability. Whether this is a requirement depends very much on the characteristics of the data, such a volume and volatility. DS will make use of these connectors to overcome the cold start problem by implementing a CDC solution for some of OUNL's most essential source systems.

8 Data Formats and Schemas

The format and semantics of data will change over time as systems continue to develop. This is a major challenge for any data transformation process and therefore also for DS. Semantic changes can be very hard to track and failure to do so can lead to erroneous and unpredictable results in downstream consumers. Unfortunately, besides very tight change management procedures, there is very little in terms of technology that can be offered to overcome this situation. However, there are some solutions that can help to keep track of changes in the data formats used.

Various standards have evolved that allow the formal definition of data structures in a programming language independent manner. Up until recent years XML and more specifically XML DTD's and XML schema's where the representations of choice. More recently, JSON has become very popular and is replacing XML as format of choice. While XML schemas or XML DTDs allow to formal definition of the data structures, JSON does not have any possibility to define data structures out of the box. Furthermore, both formats are very verbose and therefore not very suitable when processing and streaming large amounts of data. To overcome this issue several data language and format independent serialization frameworks have emerged. Probably the best-known ones are Apache AVRO, Apache Thrift and Protocol Buffers. These frameworks provide ways to compact rich data structures into an efficient binary format and describe the rich data structures by some sort of schema. Schemas not only play an important role in the definition of the data structures, but also in the evolution of these data structures. When applications evolve, the data structures change and thereby the schemas must evolve as well. Merely detecting that data structures have changed is useful by itself as it can trigger an alert that producers and consumers are not compatible anymore. However, by designing these schemas cleverly, we can achieve compatibility between older and newer versions of these data structures.

Schemas can be backward compatible, meaning that the consumers using the latest version of the schema can process data from producers using an older version. This can, for example, be achieved by defining default values for data elements that are added in the new version of the schema. Forward compatibility is achieved when a consumer using an older schema version can still process data from a producer that uses a newer schema version. This can be achieved by simply ignoring data elements introduced by the newer schema. Forward compatibility is very important when data is changed upstream and the downstream consumers can't be updated simultaneously. Forward compatibility helps to avoid the need of a big bang release of the entire stack of stream processing applications. In addition, schemas can also be both forward and backward compatible at the same time, which is obviously the most flexible situation. Figure 4 depicts the four cases of producer and consumer compatibility or the lack of it.

Kafka does not support any of the aforementioned serialization frameworks out of the box. However, Kafka supports some basic stream serializers and de-serializers (SERDE), which can be extended. The Confluent platform extends Kafka s standard SERDEs with an Apache AVRO SERDE. In addition, the Confluent platform also provides a schema registry that allows the versioned storage of AVRO schemas.

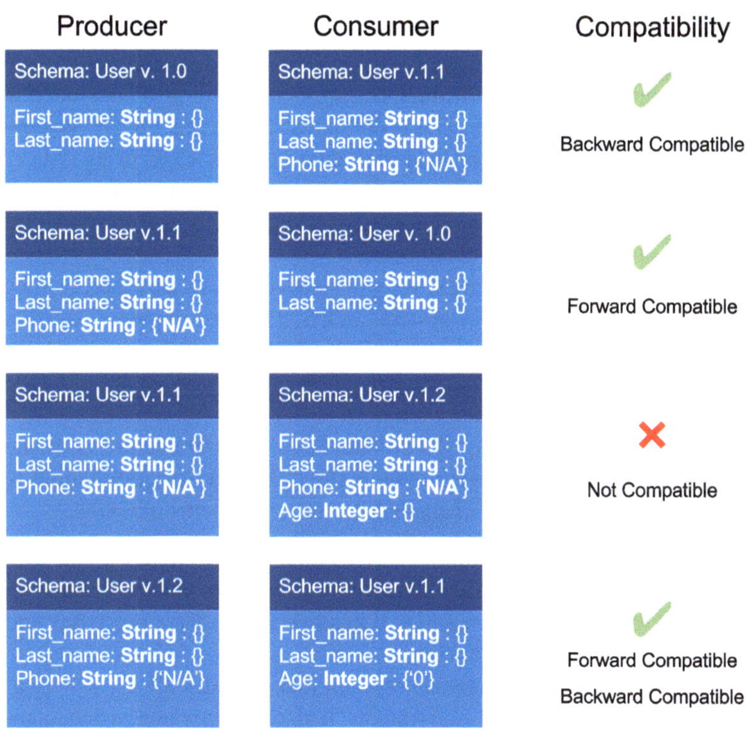

Fig. 4 Schema evolution and compatibility

This allows the efficient serialization and deserialization of message data into their appropriate formats, while also guaranteeing data compatibility between producer and consumer. Incompatible data automatically trigger an error.

Schema compatibility and more specific forward schema compatibility is essential component to satisfy our flexibility and reliability requirements. The data structures in the source systems will evolve over time, and the downstream processing applications should regardless be able to keep performing their task correctly. This allows for a gradual upgrade of the downstream applications enabling them to start benefiting from the new schema.

9 Data Sponge Architecture

In the previous sections, we discussed the general requirements DS has to meet concerning scalability, availability, reliability, flexibility. We saw that the distributed data systems can overcome scalability issues of more traditional multi-tier systems. The low-latency issue, a scalability requirement for near real-time systems can be overcome by incorporating a distributed streaming server into our architecture. We reviewed two architectural approaches to overcome the low-latency issue and concluded that the Kappa architecture using a Kafka only solution will meet our DS requirements. We argued that sticking to a single framework solution is enticing as it reduces the learning curve and simplifies operations. We also concluded that DS is facing a cold start problem and that is not realistic to expect OUNL systems to be adapted on the short term so they feed their data into DS. CDC using data connectors can help overcome this cold start problem in a fairly elegant manner. Finally, we reviewed schemas and schema evolvement and compatibility as a means to guarantee data correctness for producer and consumers.

For the first implementation of DS we will restrict ourselves by merely integrating the most crucial of OUNL source systems in DS. This first implementation will act as a proof of concept and will be a technical validator and pioneering platform on the one hand and a means for generating awareness of the importance of data science within OUNL on the other hand.

Figure 5 depicts the resulting DS architecture. The architecture is divided into two distinct layers. The first layer contains the CDC infrastructure which is using Kafka Connect to keep track of changes three source systems of OUNL:

- Student Administration: the administrative system of OUNL known as SPIL is the source for student enrollments, course registrations, and student grades.
- yOUlearn: OUNLs proprietary LMS. It handles all in course processes and interactions between tutors and students;
- IDM: OUNLs identity management system and provides all users with a single identity across various OUNL subsystems. It also incorporates an access manager handling the log-in and log-out to the OUNL.

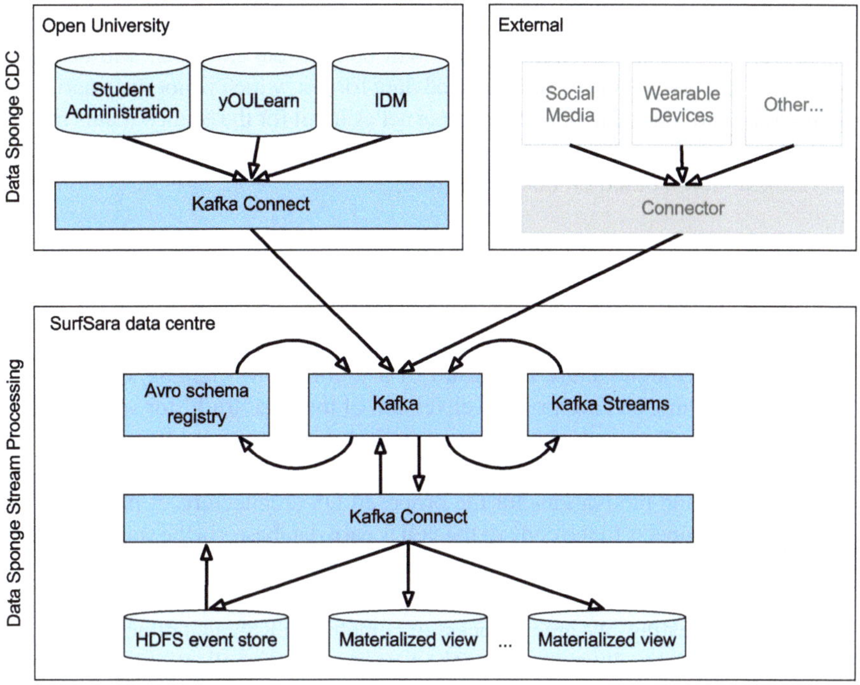

Fig. 5 The data sponge architecture

Integration of these three systems should provide DS with a first solid data set data that can be for some interesting analyses. At a later stage, other systems can be included in the CDC layer as well. The connectors will be hosted by OUNL itself as the required hardware for running these connectors is fairly limited and available. Another part of the first layer is handling user data stemming from external systems and devices such as social networks and wearables. These systems will be connected through their proprietary connectors. Although these external systems are important, they will be out of scope for the first implementation iteration of DS.

The second layer of the architecture is formed by the stream processing framework at which's core is Kafka with some of the Confluent extensions. The Kafka messaging component is the hub via which all other components communicate. The Kafka message broker cluster is extended with a cluster of nodes that run the Kafka stream processing jobs. Both clusters will be hosted by SURFsara as part of their Big Data Services. An Avro schema registry acts as schema service for the various data formats used. After the necessary processing of the incoming data, the results are exported to views that act as inputs for the smart services. These views are referenced as 'materialized views' because they contain data from several sources that are combined into denormalized data storage. A materialized view might also contain aggregates or data stemming from some business logic. The consumer of a materialized view determines which data should be available and the stream processing framework will be responsible for a continuous, low latency, delivery of these data to that view. A special materialized view will be an event store that will basically capture all input events into a standardized data format, which is not necessarily the original format of data. This event store can act as input for the event streams in case of cataclysmic failure of the total system. In theory, we should be able to rebuild all materialized views, based on this event store.

9.1 Next Steps

The proposed DS architecture is a result of a journey investigating various solutions for establishing an enterprise level version of the data 'truth' for various target groups at OUNL. Practical experience so far is limited to a set of prototypes that have shown the feasibility of various platforms. In this chapter, we have presented the background and motivations for the proposed DS architecture. A prototype has been built that connects to the copy of the yOULearn database via the standard JDBC source connector. This resulting input stream has been processed by a stream processing service that does some very basic joins and counts. However, the proof of the pudding is in the eating. We are in process of launching a Kafka/Confluent cluster on the SURFsara big data infrastructure. The first streaming applications will process some basic data from OUNL's source systems via Kafka connector, similar to the prototype and will produce some basic materialized views. We intent to use the data from the materialized view to construct an appealing info graphic of all learning and teaching activities that are happening at OUNL. This graphic will be projected on the OUNL's information screens present in several buildings for all passing staff, students and visitors to see. This serves a twofold purpose. First, for the first time in OUNL's history, it will provide a feeling of activity at OUNL campus, that otherwise is a somewhat desolate environment characterized by a total lack of students. Remember that OUNL is a distance teaching university and students do not reside on the campus. The secondary goal is raising awareness of the importance and relevance of the DS project within OUNL itself.

Real life experience will tell if the proposed architecture is up to the task, or whether new insights will lead to adaptations. The whole data science field is still very in turmoil at the moment as generally accepted practices are just start to come into place. Time will tell.

References

Di Mitri, D., Scheffel, M., Drachsler, H., Börner, D., Ternier, S., & Specht, M. (2016). Learning pulse: Using wearable biosensors and learning analytics to investigate and predict learning success in self-regulated learning. In *Proceedings of the First International Workshop on Learning Analytics Across Physical and Digital Spaces* (pp. 34–39). CEUR.

Engelbart, D., & English, W. (1968). A research center for augmenting human intellect. *Proceedings of the December 9–11, 1968*. http://dl.acm.org/citation.cfm?id=1476645. Accessed 4 May 2017.

Gantz, J., & Reinsel, D. (2012). The digital universe in 2020: Big data, bigger digital shadows, and biggest growth in the far east. *IDC iView: IDC Analyze the future*. https://www.emc-technology.com/collateral/analyst-reports/idc-the-digital-universe-in-2020.pdf. Accessed 4 May 2017.

Haerder, T., & Reuter, A. (1983). Principles of transaction-oriented database recovery. *ACM Computing Surveys (CSUR)*. http://dl.acm.org/citation.cfm?id=291. Accessed 4 May 2017.

Jeffrey, D., & Sanjay, G. (2008). MapReduce: simplified data processing on large clusters. *Communications of the ACM*.

Kleppmann, M., & Kreps, J. (2015). Kafka, Samza and the Unix Philosophy of Distributed Data. *IEEE Data Engineering Bulletin*, 1–11. https://www.cl.cam.ac.uk/research/dtg/www/files/publications/public/mk428/streamproc.pdf.

Koper, R. (2014). Towards a more effective model for distance education. *eleed*, (10). https://eleed.campussource.de/archive/10/4010.

Kreps, J. (2014a). Questioning the Lambda Architecture. *O'Reilly*. https://www.oreilly.com/ideas/questioning-the-lambda-architecture.

Kreps, J. (2014b). *I Heart Logs: Event Data, Stream Processing, and Data Integration*. O'Reilly Media. https://books.google.nl/books?hl=en&lr=&id=gdiYBAAAQBAJ&oi=fnd&pg=PR3&dq=I+heart+logs,+I+Heart+Logs,+Event+Data,+Stream+Processing,+and+Data+Integration&ots=3wV748ShbL&sig=-GnFj2Rq7vuy-1hBamtw3NF0izo. Accessed 4 May 2017.

Kreps, J., Narkhede, N., & Rao, J. (2011). Kafka: A distributed messaging system for log processing. *Proceedings of the NetDB*. http://people.csail.mit.edu/matei/courses/2015/6.S897/readings/kafka.pdf. Accessed 4 May 2017.

Marz, N., & Warren, J. (2015). *Big data: Principles and best practices of scalable realtime data systems* (1st ed.). Greenwich: Manning Publications Co. http://dl.acm.org/citation.cfm?id=2717065. Accessed 4 May 2017.

Rosenblatt, F. (1958). The perceptron: A probabilistic model for information storage and organization in the brain. *Psychological Review*. http://psycnet.apa.org/journals/rev/65/6/386/. Accessed 4 May 2017.

Schlussmans, K., Van den Munckhof, R., & Nielissen, R. (2016). Active online education: A new educational approach at the Open University of the Netherlands. In *The Online, Open and Flexible Higher Education Conference* (pp. 19–21). Rome.

SURFsara. (2017). Big Data Services. https://www.surf.nl/en/services-and-products/big-data-services/index.html. Accessed 4 May 2017.

Vogten, H., & Koper, R. (2014). Towards a new generation of learning management systems. In *Proceedings of the 6th International Conference on Computer Supported Education* (Vol. 1, pp. 513–519). Barcelona: CSEDU. https://doi.org/10.5220/0004955805140519.

Learning Analytics in Practice: Providing E-Learning Researchers and Practitioners with Activity Data

J. Minguillón, J. Conesa, M. E. Rodríguez and F. Santanach

Abstract In this chapter, we describe a practical solution for providing all researchers and practitioners in an online university with a unified learning analytics database (LA-DB) containing evidence-based activity data. Our goal is to seamlessly capture all relevant data generated within a virtual learning environment, using a very simple learning record store containing only a few tables, trying to overcome the typical problems in such a huge and complex scenario, namely data fragmentation, duplicity, inconsistencies, and lack of standardization across different data sources currently used by the university, without interfering with current information systems and procedures. In order to do so, some technological and organizational changes to promote a "data culture" within the institution have been considered. The system, implemented entirely using cloud services, allows researchers and practitioners to pose and answer questions using a simple activity-driven data model, combining data from three different levels of analysis, ranging from session-based (short-term) to institutional (long-term). Available data includes navigation, interaction, communication, and assessment, as well as high-level indicators that aggregate and summarize learner activity. Finally, we also present some preliminary actions taken for fighting early dropout as an institutional project using the proposed infrastructure and gathered data.

Keywords Learning analytics · Learning record store · Higher education
Activity-driven data model · Evidence-based data

J. Minguillón (✉) · J. Conesa · M. E. Rodríguez · F. Santanach
Universitat Oberta de Catalunya, Rambla Poblenou 156, 08018 Barcelona, Spain
e-mail: jminguillona@uoc.edu

J. Conesa
e-mail: jconesac@uoc.edu

M. E. Rodríguez
e-mail: mrodriguezgo@uoc.edu

F. Santanach
e-mail: fsantanach@uoc.edu

J. M. Spector et al. (eds.), *Frontiers of Cyberlearning*, Lecture Notes in Educational Technology, https://doi.org/10.1007/978-981-13-0650-1_8

1 Introduction

Nowadays, most educational institutions use online/web platforms as a tool, providing learners with additional support and extending the traditional teaching process, generating plenty of research data from very different perspectives (Oncu & Cakir, 2011). This is especially true in higher education, as predicted a long time ago by Taylor (1999). In some cases, some of these universities are even completely virtual/online, with reduced or no face-to-face interaction at all (Sangrà, 2002). It is important to note, however, that massive e-learning adoption does not turn online higher education into a commodity (Chau, 2010), literally avoiding "technology-enhanced non-learning" (Kinchin, 2012). Therefore, there is a real need to evaluate the use of e-learning platforms and tools in order to really understand their impact on teaching/learning processes (Kirkwood & Price, 2013).

The use of virtual learning environments (VLE) to support teaching and learning processes involves the automatic capturing and gathering of all the activities done by students and teachers. The amount of available data waiting to be analyzed is larger than ever, surpassing the analytical capabilities of any educational institution. Nevertheless, the simple existence of available data does not imply success in decision-making, as some authors have pointed out, especially if such data are not analyzed according to an institutional strategic plan (Macfadyen & Dawson, 2012).

Currently, VLEs are very complex and integrate a wide range of systems with different underlying technologies, such as communication tools, virtual libraries, digital repositories, social networks, Web 2.0 tools, and so on. In some cases, other administrative tasks (enrollment, secretary's office, etc.) are also part of the VLE, forming integrated but independent modules. Although VLE users seamlessly navigate through these different information systems and tools, this is not the case from the perspective of the data captured and gathered in each one of them. On the contrary, several problems such as fragmentation, duplication, and different identifiers and non-standardized vocabularies are typical, thus making it very difficult to analyze such data as a whole and to fully exploit it (Guitart & Conesa, 2016). Furthermore, these questions can be raised from an educational perspective as well, trying to find answers that might improve teaching and learning processes from a pedagogical point of view.

Therefore, there is a genuine need to organize all data sources into a single analytical data store that contains only the relevant data properly described and aggregated, in order to make analytical work easier for all the different stakeholders within the VLE. By doing this, the stakeholders will only need to worry about carrying out the analytical process and be able to forget about the process of gathering and preprocessing the required data, thus promoting the adoption of learning analytics strategies within the institution.

According to Siemens and Gasevic (2012), learning analytics is defined as "the measurement, collection, analysis and reporting of data about learners and their contexts, for purposes of understanding and optimizing learning and the environments in which it occurs. [...] High expectations exist for learning analytics to provide new insights into educational practices and ways to improve teaching, learning, and decision-making". Learning analytics has its roots in educational data mining (Romero & Ventura, 2007; Peña-Ayala, 2014) and intelligent tutoring systems (Anderson, Boyle, & Reiser, 1985), but the importance of this renewed research field is demonstrated by the enormous attention that it has received recently, as well as the existence of several conferences and journals devoted to this topic (Siemens, 2013; Selwyn, 2015; Guitart & Conesa, 2016).

Following the framework described by Greller and Drachsler (2012), in this chapter we describe a practical solution for implementing learning analytics in an online university. Starting with an abstract data model that captures all evidence-based data within the institutional VLE, we describe how such data are gathered and stored, the technical details behind the implementation used to manage such data and the organizational changes needed to provide researchers and practitioners with ready-to-use data.

2 Capturing Data in Virtual Learning Environments

There are several approaches to capturing and gathering data in a VLE. In (Santos et al., 2015) the authors compare several specifications, with xAPI (Del Blanco, Serrano, Freire, Martínez-Ortiz, & Fernández-Manjón, 2013) and IMS Caliper (Sakurai, 2014) being the most relevant among them. These systems try to capture the interactions between entities in a VLE (learners, courses, degrees, etc.) as they are generated, following a "noun, verb, object" triplet, also called a statement. This is a shift from the traditional relational database paradigm (Atzeni et al., 2013), which stores data from each one of the entities separately, to a non-relational model.

All the statements generated within a VLE are stored in what is called the learning record store (LRS), which contains all the data on evidence of activity that are considered to be relevant for learning analytics purposes (Berking, 2015). Currently, the LRS improves the VLE by extending tracking and record keeping capabilities, gathering evidence data. Due to the intrinsic nature of statements representing such evidence data, the adoption and use of non-relational databases is more than justified, especially in large VLEs that encompass very diverse services.

2.1 Data Sources in VLEs

As stated, VLEs are complex scenarios where different tools, services and resources coexist, (hopefully) providing learners and teachers with the appropriate spaces for interacting with each other. Due to its rapid development, technology has become a commodity that supports different educational processes such as searching for information, reading and annotating course materials, participating in debates and discussions, and so on. In fact, the technology underlying a VLE is not a relevant factor with respect to successful e-learning (Sun, Tsai, Finger, Chen, & Yeh, 2008), although it obviously influences learners' experience of the VLE. On the contrary, bad technology choices may lead to the opposite effect (Kinchin, 2012), especially when very different tools are integrated without any supporting framework. In this case, when VLEs are just a collection of poorly integrated tools, data gathering and management can be very difficult and time-consuming.

Therefore, it is important to use data models that do not depend on the underlying technology, capturing all evidence-based data considered relevant for learning analytics purposes, following a user (learner) centered design approach. Among others, we are interested in capturing (at least) the following data:

- Admission and pre-enrollment data: before enrolling on a degree course, potential learners browse the institutional website, searching for information about different degrees, requirements, and so on. In some cases, they use traditional channels such as phone calls or visit one of the admission desks. In this case, it might be interesting to store data related to all this interaction, as it may reveal interesting information about learners' expectations and goals.
- Learner data: those potential learners that ask for a specific degree need to provide basic information about them in order to become enrolled students. This includes age, gender, residence, previous academic background, and so on. All this data can be used to build an initial profile of the learner that will evolve with time.
- Enrollment data: once the potential learner enrolls on a degree course, some decisions need to be taken, mainly the number of courses or subjects taken during that semester and which ones, based on certain (optional) recommendations and constraints, which may differ depending on institutional policies.
- Navigational and interaction data: during the academic semester, learners are expected to periodically connect to the VLE and interact with other learners, teachers, resources, and other services such as the Digital Library, for instance, according to the syllabus and teaching plans of the different courses they are enrolled on.
- Assessment data: as part of their learning process, learners will be asked to perform certain learning activities, obtaining marks that will be used for their final assessment.
- Survey data: learners are invited to participate in institutional surveys about the quality of Virtual Campus services, as well as other surveys oriented to gathering data about pilot experiences or research projects.
- Other data: finally, some innovation and research projects generate their own data that is also captured to measure both learners' engagement and performance. For instance, an intelligent tutoring system for helping learners to solve exercises step-by-step in a course about Logic, providing automated and personalized feedback.

Typically, each one of these data sources may be supported by a different technology, use different data formats, and even different vocabularies and identifiers for describing the same entities (i.e., learner identification before and after enrollment). Therefore, it is necessary to think of these data sources as processes that generate evidence, rather than as databases or information systems (Guitart & Conesa, 2016).

This abstraction between the current technological solutions used within the VLE and the data stored in the LRS can be exploited beyond the traditional relational database model, thus simplifying the LRS itself.

2.2 *Storing Evidence-Based Data*

Relational databases have been the predominant paradigm for information systems and data management for more than thirty years. Concepts such as data warehouse, data mart, and OLAP (online analytical processing) have become very popular (Kimball & Ross, 2011). During this time, alternative proposals have appeared and ultimately have failed or been condemned to niche markets. This was the case with object-oriented databases, which at the end of the last century tried to improve relational databases' lack of semantic expressiveness and solve impedance mismatch problems.

In recent years, as more and more kinds of data from different sources have become available, the ways to manage and access data have evolved rapidly (Guitart & Conesa, 2016). This situation has fostered the development of non-relational database technologies referred to as NoSQL databases. These databases address two different issues. Firstly, in terms of implementation, NoSQL databases are horizontally scalable, distributed and, for the most part, open source (Atzeni et al., 2013). Another implementation aspect to consider when comparing NoSQL and relational databases is the consistency and the availability of the data they provide. Usually, NoSQL databases promote availability over consistency, so they may be particularly useful in distributed and critical systems, such as in the management of health record systems at country level (Moore, Qassem, & Xhafa, 2014). Secondly, at data model level, being schema-less is one of the main reasons for the interest in NoSQL databases. NoSQL databases can deal with a wide range of data structures (structured, semi-structured and unstructured), thereby offering increased flexibility. Furthermore, the data schema definition (if any) can be implicitly provided at the time of data insertion, and it can vary between individuals belonging to the same entity, i.e., all sorts of data structures can be stored without prior definition (Cattell, 2011). Therefore, NoSQL databases can be the underlying technology for implementing an LRS (Berking, 2015).

It is important to note that the relational world has also evolved, especially where performance is a major concern. Classical relational database management systems, originally conceived for OLTP (online transactional processing) applications, have failed when used in OLAP environments. This has given rise to the need for developing independent database engines, i.e., data warehouse products that gather and integrate data from multiple operational databases, and allow complex ad hoc queries to be executed, for example, for business intelligence purposes (Stonebraker & Cetintemel, 2005), beyond traditional reporting.

The proposal described in this chapter falls within the context of an OLAP system and, therefore, the best systems to store and manage the analytical data stores are not classical relational databases, but data warehouse products and NoSQL databases. The abstract data model presented in Sect. 3 is implemented in a NoSQL database; specifically, we have chosen Amazon DynamoDB. It was conceived originally as a key-value NoSQL database (DeCandia et al., 2007), although it has evolved into a document-oriented database that allows the storage of JSON-formatted documents, which is the format we use to store the data coming from tracking API web services. We found a document-oriented NoSQL database suitable for our needs, as our data are semi-structured and the documents to be stored may have different structures depending on the service they represent. We need to capture massive data sets produced within the UOC Virtual Campus (the institutional VLE described in the next section). DynamoDB is, therefore, a convenient choice since it facilitates horizontal scalability and distributed processing through its integration with the Hadoop ecosystem (White, 2012), which is also used as part of the institution's technological infrastructure based on Amazon Web Services.

3 UOC Abstract Data Model

Since its inception in 1994 as a purely online university, the Universitat Oberta de Catalunya (UOC) has been able to position itself among the leading universities of the Catalan and Spanish university systems. Most of the students at the UOC (currently more than 60,000) are adults who have a profile that would be hard to fit into the traditional university system. In the UOC, they have found an opportunity to start or continue their higher education degrees in a very innovative environment (Sangrà, 2002). The intensive use of ICT for both the teaching/learning processes and management allows researchers and practitioners to obtain data about what takes place within the UOC Virtual Campus, which is continuously being improved based on such findings, as part of the institutional strategic plan.

As a completely online university, most of the interactions between learners, teachers, and managers occur within the UOC's Virtual Campus (Mor, Minguillón, & Carbó, 2006). This is, however, distributed among many different services and tools. Currently, a huge OLAP based on relational databases is used to store all the relevant information needed for administrative purposes, while all user interaction with the VLE is partially stored in different servers with the corresponding databases and/or log files. Learning analytics has been a reality at the UOC since its inception (Mor et al., 2006; Romero & Ventura, 2007), but important barriers regarding access to the UOC's data have kept researchers and practitioners from developing its full potential. As part of the institutional strategic plan, a new approach to capturing, storing, and providing e-learning researchers and practitioners with data has been developed to promote a culture of data/evidence-based decision-making.

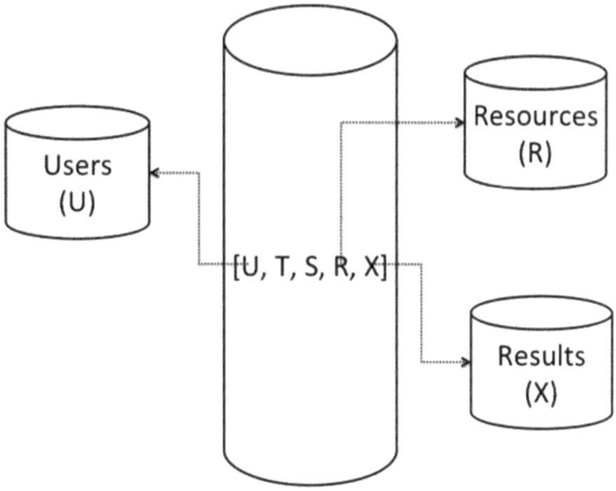

Fig. 1 Star model used to describe users, resources and results

3.1 *Evidence-Based Data Gathering*

Using an activity-driven data model (van Barneveld, Arnold, & Campbell, 2012), an analytical data store with a reduced set of tables has been created. All the activity in the Virtual Campus considered to be relevant for learning analytics purposes is stored as a 5-tuple, as follows:

```
[U(D), T, S, R, X]
```

This states that "user U (optionally, using device D) at moment T applies service S on resource R with result X". It is an extension of the "actor verb object" model, including a timestamp (T) and the result (X) of applying the verb (S) on the specified object (R). All these tuples are stored in a single table which acts as the principal one in the LRS (Del Blanco et al., 2013; Berking, 2015), while other tables (in a traditional relational sense) are used for storing data about users (U), resources (R), and results (X), following a star schema (Kimball & Ross, 2011), as shown in Fig. 1. These 5-tuples are polymorphic, as the service S completely determines the structure of the other parameters, as well as their semantics. In fact, depending on the level of analysis (micro, meso or macro, as defined in the following section), the other parameters can also have different granularity (Santos et al., 2015).

3.2 *Three-Level Data Analysis*

When students interact with the VLE they may have different goals in mind, taking into account temporal restrictions. Pursuing a degree is a long-term goal (spanning several years) decomposed into a sequence of mid-term goals (i.e., academic semesters or courses, spanning a few weeks or months) which are performed through a sequence of short-term actions (i.e., learning activities, spanning a few minutes or a few hours).

Integrating these temporal scales into a single continuum is not easy as, in order to succeed, learners need to take different temporal resolutions into account (Barbera et al., 2015). In order to do so, we use a three-level framework (Mor, Garreta-Domingo, Minguillón, & Lewis, 2007) that identifies the data generated at each level, as well as the kind of questions that can be posed at each level, which determines the data needed for learning analytics:

- Session level (short-term/micro): What do learners do when they connect to the Virtual Campus? This level captures the way users navigate with particular goals in mind, for example, how users use the e-mail service or how they access the proposed resources and exercises or an intelligent tutoring system. At this level, the learner's short-term navigational behavior is studied. For instance, we record when learners log into and log out from the Virtual Campus, generating 5-tuples as follows:

  [1234, 2015 − 10 − 29 08:08:08, USER_LOG_IN, Ø, Ø]

  ...

  [1234, 2015 − 10 − 29 08:18:28, USER_LOG_OUT, Ø, Ø]

  In this example, student `1234` (which is an anonymized version of the student's personal ID) logs into and logs out from the virtual campus, spending a total of 10 min and 20 s. Each one of the actions performed by the learner is also stored in the LRS using the same format.
- Course level (mid-term/meso): What does the learner do during a course (or academic semester)? This level tries to join all the single user sessions together in a continuous flow during a longer period of time, limited to an academic semester or course. This mid-term navigation behavior will be useful in validating hypotheses about the relationships of user actions and the results, which are related to the way learning resources are organized; assessment and feedback; assessment; and so on. For instance, if the same learner replies to a message (`mID1`) in a forum with another message (`mID2`):

  [1234, 2015 − 10 − 29 08:09:10, USER_MESSAGE_RESPONSE, mID1, mID2]

  Notice that this tuple contains neither the replied message nor the new one, as both `mID1` and `mID2` are just pointers to the database storing the messages. In the LRS we are only interested in storing the fact (i.e., the evidence) that the learner has replied to a message. If further content analysis needs to be performed, messages can be reached through `mID1` and `mID2`.
- Institutional level (long-term/macro): What do learners do from the time of enrollment until they finish (or drop out of) the degree? Finally, this level can be considered a long-term navigational behavior analysis. In this case, the main interest is to analyze how students evolve from the beginning of a degree until success-

fully completing it (or, less successfully, dropping out). This includes the study of several stages in the student life cycle: first contact and university access, first and following registrations, etc. For instance, the number and types of subjects in which our learner is enrolled for the current semester would be as follows:

```
[1234, 2015/1, ENROLLMENT_USER_NUMSUBJECT, Ø, 3]
[1234, 2015/1, ENROLLMENT_USER_SUBJECT, cID1, 1]
[1234, 2015/1, ENROLLMENT_USER_SUBJECT, cID2, 1]
[1234, 2015/1, ENROLLMENT_USER_SUBJECT, cID3, 2]
```

In this case the learner is enrolled on three different courses (`cID1` and `cID2` for the first time and `cID3` for the second time). Notice that both services are entangled: the number of courses enrolled on must be equal to the number of tuples describing each course for a given semester. In fact, the service named "`ENROLLMENT_USER_NUMSUBJECT`" acts as an indicator, summarizing the fact that the student is enrolled in that semester.

All data are, in fact, generated at the session level, that is, when the learner performs a specific action within the VLE. Nevertheless, depending on their intrinsic temporal nature and semantics they are considered to be part of the corresponding level of analysis, as shown in Fig. 2. The three levels of analysis are nested (Mor et al., 2007), but every piece of data gathered at each level can always be described using a unique 5-tuple, by specifying the action or service S that determines both its syntax and semantics. According to the semantics of service S, user U always identifies unique users across all the institutional systems, although it can also be used to identify user groups if necessary; T is usually a timestamp but in some cases it can also be used to describe a semester using UOC nomenclature; R is always an identifier pointing to a resource that uniquely describes it (when needed; otherwise, Ø); and X is completely open—it can be anything (except content), depending on both service S and resource R. Each level poses different research questions[1] that need different data in order to be answered.

3.3 Available Services

The LRS can be seen as a dictionary of services (shown in Table 1) which can be used to extract specific information about learners and their activities. These services are organized according to their level of analysis (long-, mid- or short-term):

- Long-term services: admission, including all the information the potential learners provide about themselves, the number of degrees that the potential learners request information about, the different channels used by the potential learners and, finally, an internal label generated by the admission department about the learners' level of

[1] http://researchmap.pilots.elearnlab.org/

Table 1 List of available services

Service
CLASSROOM_INSTRUCTOR_USER
CLASSROOM_SUBJECT_USER
CLASSROOM_USER_ACCESS
CLASSROOM_USER_ACTIVITY_ASSESSED
CLASSROOM_USER_ACTIVITY_RESOURCE_ACCESS
CLASSROOM_USER_ACTIVITY_SUBMIT
CLASSROOM_USER_ACTIVITY_VIEW
CLASSROOM_USER_CONTINOUSASSESSMENT_GRADE
CLASSROOM_USER_FINALEXAM_GRADED
CLASSROOM_USER_FINALEXAM_PRESENTED
CLASSROOM_USER_FOLLOWS_CONTINOUSASSESSMENT
CLASSROOM_USER_GRADE
CLASSROOM_USER_LIBRARYMATERIALS_ACCESS
CLASSROOM_USER_LIBRARYMATERIALS_RESOURCE_ACCESS
CLASSROOM_USER_LTI_TOOL_ACCESS
CLASSROOM_USER_PASSED
CLASSROOM_USER_SUBJECT_PERFOMANCE
CLASSROOM_USER_SURVEY_FILLED
CLASSROOM_USER_TEACHINGPLAN_VIEW
CLASSROOM_USER_TOOL_ACCESS
ENROLLMENT_USER_CONTINUES
ENROLLMENT_USER_NUMSUBJECT
ENROLLMENT_USER_RECOGNIZED
ENROLLMENT_USER_RECORD
ENROLLMENT_USER_SEMESTER
ENROLLMENT_USER_SUBJECT
STUDIES_USER_GRADUATED
USER_LOG_IN
USER_LOG_OUT
USER_MESSAGE_READ
USER_MESSAGE_RESPONSE
USER_MESSAGE_WRITE
USER_PLAN_PROGRESS
USER_PREVIOUS_STUDIES
USER_TUTOR_ASSIGNED
USER_TUTOR_FOLLOWS

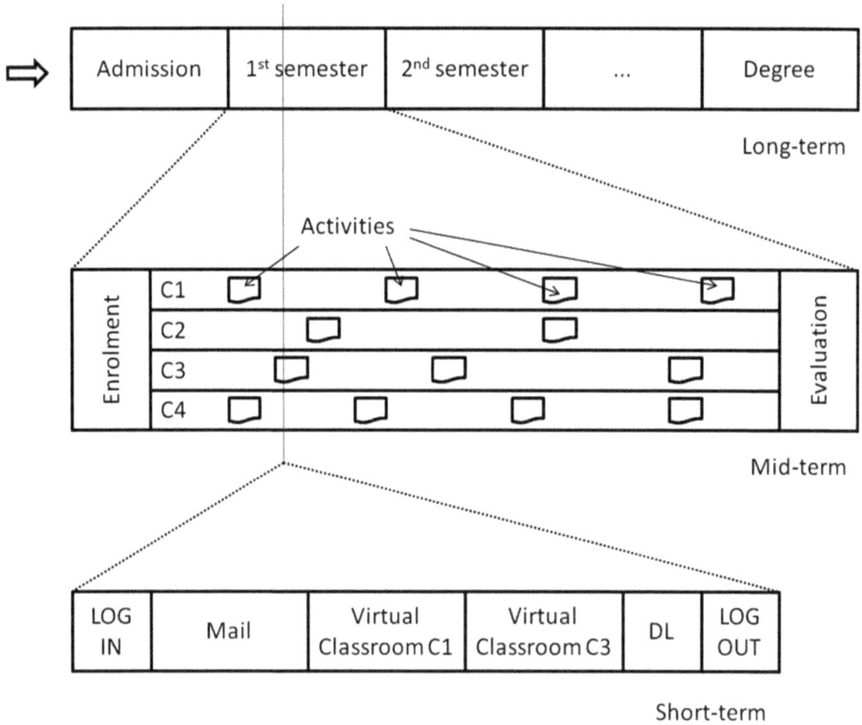

Fig. 2 Three-level framework for learning analytics at the UOC

conviction regarding their decision; mentoring, including interaction between the learners and their mentor (writing, replying to, or reading messages in the virtual classroom designed for mentoring), and whether the learner follows the mentor's recommendations for enrollment or not; and finally, whether they obtain a degree.

- Mid-term services: enrollment, including the number and typology of courses the learner enrolls on, and assessment, including all the marks obtained by the learner during the semester (i.e., continuous assessment) and in the final exams.
- Short-term services: log into and log out from the virtual learning environment; accessing campus-wide spaces such as the digital library, secretary's office or other learners' administrative support offices; all the interaction with the designed spaces (mailbox, virtual classroom, forums and other communication spaces, resources and activities, etc.).

The dictionary of services is made available to all e-learning researchers and practitioners as a public internal document which can be used as a guide for requesting data. Each service S includes a detailed description, its syntax and semantics for parameters U, T, R, and X, an example of use and the possible relationships with other related services. As new services are added every semester, information about data availability is also included.

4 LA-DB: Learning Record Store Implementation

As stated, the aim of a learning analytics database (LA-DB) at the UOC is to cover the learners' entire relationship with the institution, from the first time that a learner asks for information (even before their first enrollment) to the end of the degree, according to the three aforementioned levels. The LA-DB is not supposed to replace the institutional data warehouse, but to complement it. In fact, the LA-DB was designed bearing in mind that it could not interfere with current systems and processes carried out by the different university departments and areas. Therefore, data are still generated and managed in their places of origin, which are responsible for data quality and availability. In this sense, any change in the data source needs to be communicated to the LA-DB office, in order to update all the ETL (extract-transform-load) processes that feed the LRS.

In pursuit of comprehensiveness, several different sources of information (previously described in Sect. 2.1) have been considered. In general, these sources can be divided into two types: (1) those related to the VLE and other learning spaces (LMS or equivalent), containing evidence-based data that has to be transferred to the LA-DB every day; and (2) data warehouse systems, containing data coming from management systems (CRM, ERP, etc.), which includes data about enrollment, accreditation, assessment, student curriculum, and so on. Usually, data from this second type of source is transferred to the LA-DB just once a semester. The first type is mostly related to the short-term level, while the second is related to mid-term and long-term levels. Figure 3 summarizes the internal structure of the LA-DB and the main services offered through it.

Regarding the first type, the UOC's VLE contains learning spaces that already include a xAPI implementation (i.e., using the TinCan API) (Del Blanco et al., 2013). This collects (using JSON-formatted structures) most of the data from the virtual classroom, such as resource/tool access, downloading and uploading of learning activities, study plan access, and feedback from the instructor, as well as some specific data from specific resources, like forums (that is, who reads, writes and replies to messages). In these learning spaces, login and logout events, among others, are also gathered. These data are temporarily stored in a MongoDB database (because it is the database used by the TinCan API implementation) and automatically transferred daily to the LA-DB through an ETL process.

For the second type, the process has been intentionally more manual. Since the data warehouse information is used by certain people to perform and improve management processes, we have asked (once a semester) the people in charge of such processes for their data in the same format as that used for their management purposes. These data have then been adapted manually to perform an ETL that includes all data changes as well as any new data since the last upload to the LA-DB. Using this approach, the quality of data, semantics and potential upgrades has been guaranteed.

In both cases, during the ETL processes the data are anonymized (Drachsler et al., 2015). This anonymization process consists of removing/obfuscating all the personal data and changing all the internal IDs to a new one called LA-ID. As a result, the LA-

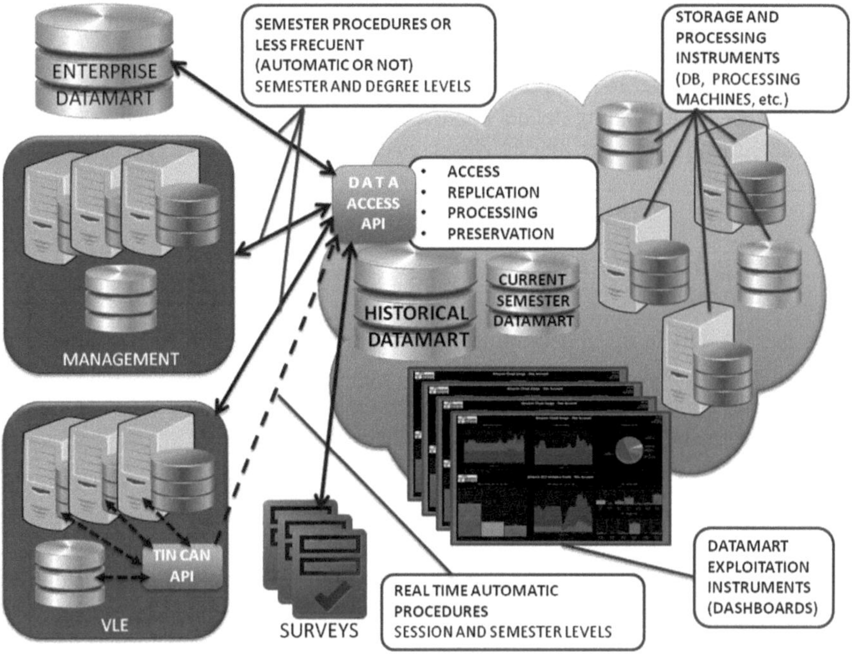

Fig. 3 LA-DB internal structure and main services

ID/internal IDs' equivalence tables are stored at the UOC, at the appropriate security level, and under the responsibility of the UOC's Chief Security Officer (CSO). Thus, the anonymized LA-DB can be safely stored in the cloud in order to be accessed and exploited as an e-learning research and QA database for all interested researchers and practitioners.

4.1 LRS Storage

The LA-DB cloud infrastructure is based on Amazon Web Service (AWS) and composed of an Amazon DynamoDB, a NoSQL database service with seamless scalability that automatically spreads the data and traffic over a sufficient number of servers to handle both the request capacity and the amount of data stored. The infrastructure is completed by an Amazon S3 store service which acts as a repository for all of the LA-DB query results. DynamoDB provides out-of-the-box Amazon Elastic MapReduce (Amazon EMR) integration, allowing the use of Apache Hadoop and Hive engines as a powerful toolbox for managing, analyzing, and even monetizing the data stored in the LA-DB.

The internal LA-DB structure is based on Ralph Kimball's star schema approach (Kimball & Ross, 2011), where there is a fact table that contains all of the aforementioned values or statements, and a set of dimension tables referenced by "facts". Therefore, in the 5-tuple structure described in Sect. 3, the "fact" is service S and the other parameters refer to the specific dimension tables describing users U, resources R and results X, containing details about each dimension element such as user profiles, subject and curricular hierarchy, semester structure, resource types, and so on.

4.2 Using Multiple LRSs

Once the LA-DB is up and running, it stores all the Virtual Campus activity as previously described. Nevertheless, to improve both performance and data quality, the LA-DB is conceptually split into three different LRSs according to their temporal span (analogously to the levels described in Sect. 3.1):

- Historical level: it contains all historical data from previous semesters (not including the current semester), that is, all evidence-based data that is not supposed to change or that can be manually changed for very specific or rare requests.
- Current semester level: it contains all the data that is generated during the current semester. Most learning analytics initiatives can be implemented using data from this LRS. The dictionary of services is the same as in the historical level, as described in Sect. 3.3.
- Application level: it contains only data for a given application or service that needs to use the LA-DB for a very specific purpose, such as an intelligent tutoring system, for instance. Several applications at this level can co-exist at the same time, each of them efficiently writing and reading 5-tuples in a "private" LRS, even using private dictionaries of services, if needed. This is a typical scenario for pilot initiatives that need to be tested during one or two semesters before becoming part of the Virtual Campus.

At the end of an academic semester, once the current semester-level LRS is considered to be stable (with respect to the data it contains), it is dumped onto the historical one. Application-level LRSs can decide whether they want to keep the data from one semester to the next and/or also be dumped onto the historical LRS.

On top of these LRSs, there is an access layer that provides access to all LRS data organized by academic semesters and services. In fact, most analyses only need a very small fraction of the total LRS or they are focused on a specific period of time and/or cohort. This layer allows researchers and practitioners to obtain data for a specific subset of services within a period of time (typically one semester). Requested data are dumped to several CSV files, one for each service and/or semester, which can easily be manipulated by researchers and practitioners in order to further analyze them. This is the most basic access level for LRS data, hiding the technical details needed to exploit it.

4.3 *Indicators as Activity Summary*

An interesting possibility offered by the LA-DB is that the most popular requests from researchers and practitioners can be stored as new services, summarizing or aggregating a specific subset of data. Although this may pose consistency problems if the underlying "raw" data changes, it simplifies the usage of the LA-DB for most practitioners, who are neither experts nor willing to query a database. Indicators are created according to the following criteria:

- Indicators that describe a complex aspect about learners regarding their interaction or academic performance. For instance, for a given semester, the accumulated number of semesters, courses, and credits the learner has previously enrolled on. Or, according to the learner's navigation profile, the accumulated number of connections and days connected to the VLE, updated every week, as follows:

```
[1234, 2015/1, DAYSCONNECTED, W, N]
```

Here W represents the relative number of the week in the current academic semester ("2015/1" or Fall 2015 according to the UOC's nomenclature) and N is the total of days the learner has connected to the VLE.

- Indicators that summarize a concept about the teaching/learning process from an institutional perspective. For instance, once the enrollment process has finished and data can be considered to be stable, a 5-tuple containing the total number of students can be generated, as follows:

```
[Ø, 2015/1, TOTALUOCENROLLMENT, Ø, N]
```

Here N is the total of learners enrolled in the "2015/1" semester. Analogously, the total number of enrolled course credits could also be stored using another service S, for instance. Therefore, for a given semester, the total number of learners can be retrieved with a single query using this service.

In fact, this is the first step towards providing the UOC's researchers and practitioners with indicators that can be used to answer typical questions in a VLE, such as dropout rates, usage of learning resources, learner satisfaction, and so on. On top of these indicators, several dashboards addressing different issues (i.e., engagement or retention) can easily be designed (Verbert et al., 2014). As part of the institutional strategy, several indicators and dashboards are being developed within internal innovation projects, namely UOC INDEX.[2]

[2]https://www.uoc.edu/portal/en/elearncenter/innovacio/projectes/fitxes-projectes/projecte-10.html

5 LA-DB as an Institutional Service

There are many possible uses of the LA-DB, but the main one is to provide data for innovation and research purposes. As described in Sect. 3, the UOC is a completely online university using e-learning as the basis for its educational model (Sangrà, 2002). The innovation and improvement of its model as well as the ability to promote applied research in e-learning within the institution are key processes that make the UOC a unique laboratory. Therefore, the ability to collect and gather data from the teaching and learning processes to validate innovation projects and foster applied research in the field of e-learning is crucial (Macfadyen & Dawson, 2012).

In order to promote innovation and applied research projects, a data extraction service from the LA-DB has been set up. This service is open to all faculty staff that would like to improve their courses by applying innovation, as well as to researchers in the field of e-learning and technology-enhanced learning. Currently, faculty or researchers can request specific data by using a simple form, which initiates an internal procedure that starts with a meeting between them and the UOC's LA-DB team. During the meeting, all aspects regarding data collection (including privacy and ethical issues, which are mandatory) have to be defined and planned. The LA-DB team provides support to faculty and researchers throughout the process of setting up all the experiments or data collection instruments, in addition to related issues such as surveys, student consent, and agreements. The LA-DB team also performs the task of sending all the queries to the LA-DB using the appropriate tools (Hadoop, Hive, and so). Finally, all extracted data are merged and combined and then made available to the faculty and researchers, usually as a collection of CSV files ready to be analyzed and visualized using several tools including Tableau, Splunk or R.

5.1 *Current Status*

In 2008, like many other European universities, the UOC adopted the directives defined by the European Higher Education Area[3] (EHEA), also known as the Bologna Process. New degrees based on competence acquisition and development were designed, focusing on activities rather than on traditional content, raising the importance of gathering evidence-based data. Currently, LA-DB contains enrollment and assessment data for all the students enrolled on those EHEA degrees and, since 2014, all the additional data described in Sect. 3.3, which was not easily accessible before.

The LRS currently contains around 300,000,000 records, which represents more than 400 GB of data. Each semester, around 12 GB of data are added to the LRS. Since 2014, the LRS has been gathering data from 60,000 different VLE users (mostly students, but also teachers, managers, and support staff) and their interaction with

[3]http://www.ehea.info/

more than 6500 virtual classrooms, generating around 600,000 pieces of evidence using the 5-tuple format every day.

5.2 Limitations

Although LA-DB is under continuous development, it is also already in production, providing some e-learning researchers and practitioners at the UOC with evidence-based data. Nevertheless, in order to become a basic tool which is part of the institutional infrastructure, some barriers must be addressed and overcome:

- Organizational: LA-DB depends on data which is generated in different departments, so any change in the source needs to be transferred to the LRS, taking into account all the possible changes (missing data, different semantics, etc.). On the other hand, if it is to be successful, LA-DB cannot itself become a bottleneck for addressing all the UOC data requests, it is necessary to provide simple mechanisms for retrieving data, indicators, and even automated dashboards.
- Technological: although it is not a problem yet, in the near future the LRS will need to handle around 10^9–10^{10} records, which will push the underlying database to its limit. Although LA-DB uses scalable cloud services, it will also have to fulfill the requirements defined by the institutional technology strategic plan, which may establish some security and efficiency requirements for the ETL processes.
- Cultural: finally, it is necessary to spread awareness of the possibilities of LA-DB among all UOC researchers and practitioners, including training regarding the current data dictionary and helping them to formulate the right questions; detecting new possible data requirements for addressing new problems.

5.3 Case Study: Fighting Early Dropout

From an institutional perspective, the LRS is the cornerstone of several projects addressing very important issues, such as understanding and fighting early dropout, for instance (Grau-Valldosera & Minguillón, 2014). Each semester (enrollment at the UOC takes place twice a year), almost 30% of the students first enrolled on an official degree the previous semester take a break, that is, they do not enroll on any course during the second semester of the degree they initiated. Only around 10% of these students return after such a break, that is, the immense majority become early dropouts. Therefore, taking a break in the second semester is a very probable sign of dropping out. Systems are therefore needed that rapidly detect those students at risk, in order to apply the necessary corrective measures and reduce these high dropout rates. This is a typical scenario for the use of learning analytics within a higher education institution (Freitas et al., 2015), combining gathered data with institutional know-how about all the processes involved during such a short period (i.e., one academic semester). Currently, the LRS can provide the following data for analyzing the causes of dropout:

- Before enrollment: learner profile, including age, gender, previous academic background, admission procedure, and so on.
- Enrollment data: number and type of courses.
- Navigational and interaction data during the academic semester.
- Academic performance: continuous and final assessment.
- Answers to the institutional survey.
- Decision taken about enrolling or taking a break in the second semester.

Notice that the available data about learners is incremental in time. Before the semester starts, we only have the learner's profile and admission procedure available. Once learners have enrolled on one or more courses, they start the academic semester, following the proposed activities and interacting with other users, resources and services within the VLE. They obtain marks and final assessments for each one of their activities and courses and, optionally, they may provide answers to the institutional survey. Finally, they decide whether to take a break or not during the following semester. Our goal is to predict this fact as soon as possible, based on the gathered data, and for this purpose we built several models using all the available data at a given moment. Preliminary experiments are consistent with the results of Freitas et al. (2015) and show that:

- Model 1 (learner profile only, before enrollment): no predictive power, as no variable or combination of variables explains early dropout. Nevertheless, some profiles show minor tendencies towards dropout, i.e., students that already have a degree are more likely to drop out than those that come to continue previous unfinished studies, so they might need additional counseling. Students that are less confident during the admission process and have more doubts about which degree they want to start are also more likely to drop out, also needing additional mentoring.
- Model 2 (enrollment data, before the semester starts): no predictive power, as no combination of courses is crucial for determining early dropout. Nevertheless, some course combinations yield poor academic results and should be avoided during the enrollment process. This fact has also resulted in interesting actions, as some course calendars have been redesigned in order to minimize overlapping among the most popular courses taken in combination.
- Model 3 (navigational and interaction data, during the semester): experiments show that there are six different navigational profiles according to the number of days per week a student connects to the VLE. There are four profiles ranging from very high (7 days/week) to low (1–2 days/week) VLE usage and two additional interesting profiles: those that start connecting 3–4 days/week, then fall to 1–2 days/week after a few weeks, and finally not connecting at all after approximately the eighth week; and those connecting only 1–2 days/week during the first three or four weeks, and disappearing after the fourth week. Learners falling into these two last clusters are most likely to fail and drop out.

- Model 4 (assessment data, once the semester has finished): high predictive power, as students that fail in every course they are taking are those most likely to take a break and to actually drop out. Using a backwards reasoning process, the main proxy indicator of dropping out is not passing any course, which is directly related to not following the proposed continuous assessment, and this can easily be detected through the analysis of the navigational profile.

Following the ideas described by Greller and Drachsler (2012), the simple fact of gathering and organizing all this data serves two purposes: first, to revise current processes and data sources, detecting omissions and inconsistencies; and second, to convert all the institutional know-how about dropout (as both researchers and practitioners) into a complex model, including asking the right questions and finding the possible answers. Furthermore, even preliminary analyses reveal interesting patterns and give rise to new questions, as well as new data requirements for addressing such questions. Without this know-how and the proper alignment with the institutional strategic plan, it is impossible to address dropout as the complex, multi-faceted problem that it is (Macfadyen & Dawson, 2012). Nevertheless, this effort provides partial results in the form of knowledge about learners, courses, assessment processes, etc. This knowledge can be used to rethink and redesign some of the institutional procedures (i.e., enrollment or admission), in order to correct the detected hindrances and improve learners' experiences from the very beginning.

6 Conclusions

Although both traditional bricks-and-mortar universities and online/distance ones have been using virtual learning environments for some years now, it has only been recently that such institutions have seriously considered the opportunities that the analysis of such huge amounts of data brings. Learning analytics is the new framework for turning questions related to teaching and learning processes into new tools and dashboards that help learners, teachers, and managers to better perform and understand their tasks within an educational institution.

In this chapter, we have presented a practical implementation of a learning record store named LA-DB, inspired by the xAPI specification for gathering evidence-based data. Our proposal defines all the relevant learner activity within the institutional VLE as a 5-tuple that describes who applies which service on which resource and when, with an optional result for such an action. We have shown that this abstract model can be used to represent all the relevant learner activity within the VLE at different levels of analysis, ranging from session-based (short-term) to institutional (long-term), covering the entire learner life cycle from the very beginning. As a summary, system implementation is based on a set of ETLs (extract-transform-load process) gathering data from different sources. There are two main kinds of sources: the learning environment source (LMS, educational resources, etc.) and the management environment sources (SIS, ERP, and other institutional processes). Data from the

VLE are gathered through a Tin Can API engine and collected as a set of statements in MongoDB. Every day, an ETL processes and stores those data (anonymized) in the LRS. Management data are generated at different paces (e.g., semester by semester), so ETL processes are executed every time that such data are generated. LA-DB is based on a classic star schema and has been implemented using cloud AWS infrastructure with DynamoDB and an additional layer of CSV files stored in an S3 server. AWS allows us to provide ad hoc infrastructure for processing data, from simple sets of CSV files that can be processed with Tableau, for instance, to complex data sets analyzed through Hadoop, Redshift, and other tools.

Data from all the academic semesters since the adoption of the EHEA in 2008 are already available on the LA-DB, although its real usage is still limited, mainly because of the lack of a user-friendly interface for making queries and extracting slices of data for analysis purposes. Only users competent in database management can use it now, which is not the case with most of the UOC's e-learning researchers and practitioners. As an ongoing institutional project, we are now promoting the usage of the LA-DB among those researchers and practitioners, in order to foster bottom-up innovation and applied research projects that boost the UOC's educational model and improve our understanding of teaching and learning processes. The intention is also to help learners and teachers to fully develop their potential as part of the UOC community. As part of the institutional strategy, a guided procedure for obtaining data in a simple format such as CSV has been established, and all issues related to data privacy and ethics have been taken care of. Several top-down institutional projects such as fighting early dropout have also recently been started using data from the LRS.

Current and future work in this field involves the acquisition of more evidence related to learner activity, its definition as new services using the 5-tuple model and the implementation of the ETL processes needed to feed the institutional LRS. Providing e-learning researchers and practitioners with pre-defined indicators is also another important task that is currently under development through institutional innovation projects. Once this has been accomplished we will be able to build better dashboards that could be seamlessly integrated into the institutional VLE, hopefully helping all its stakeholders (learners, teachers, and managers) to achieve their particular educational goals. We expect LA-DB to boost the UOC's potential in learning analytics, promoting research and best practices in complex educational issues such as dropout, engagement and automated feedback.

Acknowledgements This work has been partially supported by the Generalitat de Catalunya (Government of Catalonia) ref. 2014 SGR 1271.

References

Anderson, J. R., Boyle, C. F., & Reiser, B. J. (1985). Intelligent tutoring systems. *Science (Washington), 228*(4698), 456–462.

Atzeni, P., Jensen, C. S., Orsi, G., Ram, S., Tanca, L., & Torlone, R. (2013). The relational model is dead, SQL is dead, and I don't feel so good myself. *ACM SIGMOD Record, 42*(2), 64–68.

Barbera, E., Gros, B., & Kirschner, P. A. (2015). Paradox of time in research on educational technology. *Time & Society, 24*(1), 96–108.

Berking, P. (2015). *Choosing a learning record store (LRS).*

Cattell, R. (2011). Scalable SQL and NoSQL data stores. *ACM SIGMOD Record, 39*(4), 12–27.

Chau, P. (2010). Online higher education commodity. *Journal of Computing in Higher Education, 22*(3), 177–191.

Del Blanco, Á., Serrano, Á., Freire, M., Martínez-Ortiz, I., & Fernández-Manjón, B. (2013, March). E-Learning standards and learning analytics. Can data collection be improved by using standard data models? In *Global Engineering Education Conference (EDUCON), 2013 IEEE* (pp. 1255–1261). IEEE.

DeCandia, G., Hastorun, D., Jampani, M., Kakulapati, G., Lakshman, A., Pilchin, A., et al. (2007). Dynamo: Amazon's highly available key-value store. *ACM SIGOPS operating systems review, 41*(6), 205–220.

Drachsler, H., Hoel, T., Scheffel, M., Kismihók, G., Berg, A., Ferguson, R., & Manderveld, J. (2015, March). Ethical and privacy issues in the application of learning analytics. In *Proceedings of the Fifth International Conference on Learning Analytics and Knowledge* (pp. 390–391). ACM.

Freitas, S., Gibson, D., Du Plessis, C., Halloran, P., Williams, E., Ambrose, M., et al. (2015). Foundations of dynamic learning analytics: Using university student data to increase retention. *British Journal of Educational Technology, 46*(6), 1175–1188.

Grau-Valldosera, J., & Minguillón, J. (2014). Rethinking dropout in online higher education: The case of the Universitat Oberta de Catalunya. *The International Review of Research in Open and Distributed Learning, 15*(1).

Greller, W., & Drachsler, H. (2012). Translating learning into numbers: A generic framework for learning analytics. *Educational technology & society, 15*(3), 42–57.

Guitart, I. & Conesa, J. (2016). Creating University Analytical Information Systems: A grand challenge for information systems research. In *Formative assessment, learning data analytics and gamification* (pp. 167–186), Cambridge: Academic Press.

Kimball, R., & Ross, M. (2011). *The data warehouse toolkit: The complete guide to dimensional modeling*. New York: Wiley.

Kinchin, I. (2012). Avoiding technology-enhanced non-learning. *British Journal of Educational Technology, 43*(2), E43–E48.

Kirkwood, A., & Price, L. (2013). Missing: Evidence of a scholarly approach to teaching and learning with technology in higher education. *Teaching in Higher Education, 18*(3), 327–337.

Macfadyen, L. P., & Dawson, S. (2012). Numbers are not enough. Why e-learning analytics failed to inform an institutional strategic plan. *Educational Technology & Society, 15*(3), 149–163.

Moore, P., Qassem, T., & Xhafa, F. (2014, November). 'NoSQL' and electronic patient record systems: Opportunities and challenges. In *Proceedings of the Ninth International Conference on P2P, Parallel, Grid, Cloud and Internet Computing (3PGCIC), 2014* (pp. 300–307). IEEE.

Mor, E., Garreta-Domingo, M., Minguillón, J., & Lewis, S. (2007, July). A three-level approach for analyzing user behavior in ongoing relationships. In *International Conference on Human-Computer Interaction* (pp. 971–980). Berlin: Springer.

Mor, E., Minguillón, J., & Carbó, J. M. (2006). Analysis of user navigational behavior for e-learning personalization. *Data Mining in E-Learning (Advances in Management Information), 4,* 227–243.

Oncu, S., & Cakir, H. (2011). Research in online learning environments: Priorities and methodologies. *Computers & Education, 57*(1), 1098–1108.

Peña-Ayala, A. (2014). Educational data mining: A survey and a data mining-based analysis of recent works. *Expert Systems with Applications, 41*(4), 1432–1462.

Romero, C., & Ventura, S. (2007). Educational data mining: A survey from 1995 to 2005. *Expert Systems with Applications, 33*(1), 135–146.
Sakurai, Y. (2014, June). The value improvement in education service by grasping the value acceptance state with ICT utilized education environment. In *International Conference on Human Interface and the Management of Information* (pp. 90–98). Berlin: Springer.
Sangrà, A. (2002). A new learning model for the information and knowledge society: The case of the Universitat Oberta de Catalunya (UOC), Spain. *The International Review of Research in Open and Distributed Learning, 2*(2).
Santos, J. L., Verbert, K., Klerkx, J., Duval, E., Charleer, S., & Ternier, S. (2015). Tracking data in open learning environments. *Journal of Universal Computer Science, 21*(7), 976–996.
Selwyn, N. (2015). Data entry: Towards the critical study of digital data and education. *Learning, Media and Technology, 40*(1), 64–82.
Siemens, G., & Gasevic, D. (2012). Guest editorial-learning and knowledge analytics. *Educational Technology & Society, 15*(3), 1–2.
Siemens, G. (2013). Learning analytics: The emergence of a discipline. *American Behavioral Scientist, 57*(10), 1380–1400.
Stonebraker, M., & Cetintemel, U. (2005, April). "One size fits all": An idea whose time has come and gone. In *21st International Conference on Data Engineering, 2005. ICDE 2005. Proceedings* (pp. 2–11). IEEE.
Sun, P. C., Tsai, R. J., Finger, G., Chen, Y. Y., & Yeh, D. (2008). What drives a successful e-Learning? An empirical investigation of the critical factors influencing learner satisfaction. *Computers & Education, 50*(4), 1183–1202.
Taylor, J. C. (1999, June). Distance education: The fifth generation. In *Proceedings of the 19th ICDE World Conference on Open Learning and Distance Education.*
van Barneveld, A., Arnold, K. E., & Campbell, J. P. (2012). Analytics in higher education: Establishing a common language. *EDUCAUSE Learning Initiative, 1*(1), l–ll.
Verbert, K., Govaerts, S., Duval, E., Santos, J. L., Van Assche, F., Parra, G., et al. (2014). Learning dashboards: An overview and future research opportunities. *Personal and Ubiquitous Computing, 18*(6), 1499–1514.
White, T. (2012). *Hadoop: The definitive guide.* O'Reilly Media, Inc.

Julià Minguillón received his Ph.D. degree in Computer Engineering from the Universitat Autònoma de Barcelona (UAB) in 2002. Since 2001, he has been an associate professor at the Faculty of Computer Science, Multimedia and Telecommunications of the Universitat Oberta de Catalunya (UOC). He is a member of the LAIKA research group. His research interests include the design, development, and analysis of technology-enhanced learning solutions related to personalization and adaptive learning, the analysis of user behavior in virtual learning environments, and the development of institutional learning analytics strategies. He has led the conceptualization of the UOC Learning Record Store described in this chapter as well as a special interest group in dropout, which serves as a framework for several institutional innovation projects related to better understanding, explaining and fighting early dropout from a data-driven perspective.

Jordi Conesa is an associate professor of information systems at the Universitat Oberta de Catalunya (UOC) and a member of the SmartLearn research group. He received his Ph.D. in software engineering from the Universitat Politècnica de Catalunya—BarcelonaTech (UPC). His research interests concern the areas of conceptual modeling, ontologies, semantic web, knowledge-based systems analytics, and e-learning. His long-term goal is to develop methodologies and tools to use ontologies effectively in several application domains, such as conceptual modeling, software engineering, and e-learning. He has authored more than 50 research papers, participated in several research projects, including EU FP7, CICYT and AVANZA funded projects, and contributed to the organization of various international conferences.

M. Elena Rodríguez received her BSc and Ph.D. degrees in Computer Science from the Universitat Politècnica de Catalunya – BarcelonaTech (UPC) and the University of Alcalá, respectively. Since June 2001, she has been a lecturer at the Faculty of Computer Science, Multimedia and Telecommunications of the Universitat Oberta de Catalunya (UOC) with a tenure position. She has participated in several national and international research projects devoted to the development of technology that applies the Semantic Web to e-learning specifications and standards. Her current research interests deal with knowledge representation with particular application in technology-enhanced learning and assessment within the Teking research group (eLearn Center, UOC). From a teaching perspective, she coordinates undergraduate and master's degree database courses.

Francesc Santanach has a Bachelor's degree in Computer Engineering from the Universitat Politècnica de Catalunya – BarcelonaTech (UPC). He currently works in the eLearn Center, the e-learning research and innovation center of the Universitat Oberta de Catalunya (UOC). He is in charge of the e-learning laboratory at the UOC, providing the infrastructure and the set of instruments needed for experimentation in real classrooms. He is also in charge of the learning analytics infrastructure, providing a data analytics service for research and innovation projects at the UOC. He runs national and international projects in the field of learning technologies, learning resources, learning standards, interoperability and learning analytics. Previously, he was responsible for the design and technical architecture of the UOC's Virtual Campus, and for the interoperability and integration of e-learning solutions and educational resources. He has also been a researcher in the field of e-learning, author of learning materials and instructor at the UOC.

Using Apache Spark for Modeling Student Behavior at Scale

Nicholas Lewkow and Jacqueline Feild

Abstract This chapter is an introduction to parallel processing with education data. As the amount of education data continues to grow, new methods for processing this data efficiently are required. This chapter gives a history of popular parallel computing frameworks and discusses problem types that are easily mapped to these frameworks. Following that, an example machine-learning problem is described and a single-threaded and parallel pipeline using Apache Spark are compared. We hope this information can be used by other practitioners looking to utilize Apache Spark to expand their models to include more students and more data.

Keywords Apache Spark · Machine learning · Predictive model · Big data

1 Introduction

The amount of data being collected by online systems continues to increase, and the domain of education is no exception. Digital textbooks and assignments capture a wide range of student and instructor interactions every day, clicker systems provide data on classroom attendance and engagement, and the amount of background data collected by student information systems continues to grow. In addition to traditional academic institutions, the first massively open online course (MOOC) appeared in 2011 (Pappano, 2012) and an estimated 58 million students were enrolled in a MOOC in 2016 alone (Shah, 2016).

Increasingly, all of this data is being used to build predictive models that can aid with student interventions and increase student retention. The large amount of data available allows for better predictive models, since most models require a lot of

N. Lewkow (✉) · J. Feild
McGraw-Hill Education, 281 Summer Street, Boston, MA 02210, USA
e-mail: nicholas.lewkow@mheducation.com

J. Feild
e-mail: jacqueline.feild@mheducation.com

J. M. Spector et al. (eds.), *Frontiers of Cyberlearning*, Lecture Notes in Educational Technology, https://doi.org/10.1007/978-981-13-0650-1_9

training examples to increase accuracy. At the same time, this large amount of data also means that these models can be computationally expensive to build and test.

Fortunately, when working with educational data, problems are often data parallel, meaning that computation for an assignment, section, or even a student, is independent from computation for other assignments, sections, or students. This allows for computations to easily be done in parallel on different CPU cores or even on different machines altogether, with the final results being aggregated from the different machines at the end of the computation. For example, to compute the average grade for each student in the class, the data for each student can be sent to different CPUs to calculate the average grade separately, without any data interactions between students.

Working with large data sets (e.g. those that don't fit in memory on a laptop) requires re-thinking how data-structures and algorithms work in parallel. Traditionally, this has been done with code from very low-level libraries such as openMPI, which is very time consuming to write and debug. Luckily, recently developed frameworks like Apache Hadoop and Apache Spark offer easier methods for writing parallel algorithms. Apache Spark has gained popularity over Hadoop recently because it is easy to use and offers APIs in several popular programming languages. Additionally, Apache Spark has an extensive set of parallel APIs that are useful for building predictive models. These include functions for creating and cleaning features, as well as functions for training and testing different supervised and unsupervised machine learning models.

This chapter provides the history of some popular parallel computing frameworks and a discussion of what types of problems in the domain of education these frameworks might work well for. It also provides an example predictive modeling pipeline and the details of how this model was built and tested in parallel. A similar pipeline can be followed by practitioners looking to use parallel programming to expand their existing or future models to handle growing data sets.

2 Background on Parallel Computing

For decades, parallel computing was limited to extremely specialized problems done by scientists and researchers working on expensive, custom supercomputers. In 2003, Google released a whitepaper describing a new type of distributed computing (Ghemawat, Gobioff, & Leung, 2003). The system described in the Google whitepaper outlined a new path forward for parallel computing, using fault tolerant data structures on large commodity hardware clusters. This allowed for large computing clusters to be built with off-the-shelf hardware, resulting in extremely cheap computation compared to custom hardware. It also allowed for horizontal scalability, in that a cluster could be doubled by doubling the number of commodity nodes in the cluster. The fault tolerant data structures ensured that if a node in the cluster failed, the computation could recover and proceed forward.

The main ideas summarized in the Google whitepaper revolve around the concept of map-reduce computations performed on worker nodes and controlled by a driver node. The user interacts with the driver node which in turn sends computation instructions to the worker nodes. In the map-reduce paradigm, data can be thought of as always residing in a vector which is distributed among the workers nodes, with operations being mapped to all elements in parallel, and aggregations being done to reduce results from all elements. As an example, we can imagine having a collection of random numbers residing in a vector-like data structure. A map operation is one that performs the same function to every element in the vector. If we wished to multiply every number in our vector by 2, we could perform a map operation. In contrast, a reduce operation performs aggregations on a vector. If we wished to sum all of the random numbers in our vector, we would perform a reduce operation. The combination of the map and reduce operations are used as the building blocks for parallel algorithms in the map-reduce paradigm.

In 2006, the open source Apache foundation created the Hadoop project, which is based on the Google whitepaper. Hadoop provided a high-level set of APIs for map-reduce parallel computing and was built on top of the Hadoop Distributed File System (HDFS) which allowed for reading and writing data in parallel to a file system in a fault tolerant fashion. A typical workflow for using Hadoop might be the worker nodes reading a data set in parallel from HDFS, performing a set of maps and reduces, and writing the results in parallel back to HDFS. In 2008, Hadoop set a new world record by using 910 worker nodes to sort 1 TB of data in 209 s (O'Malley, 2008).

Following from the successes of Hadoop, Apache Spark was created in 2009 at the UC Berkeley AMPLab and was made open source in 2010. Apache Spark followed a lot of the same concepts that Hadoop pioneered such as implementing resilient, distributed data structures and performing map-reduce operations. The major advancement in Apache Spark came from the use of in-memory data structures which allowed for a huge increase in performance. In a 2014 performance test, Apache Spark sorted 100 TB of data in 23 min (Xin, 2014). This same sort on Hadoop took 3 times slower and required 10 times more machines. In addition to performance, Apache Spark has several useful packages in addition to map-reduce such as libraries for machine learning, graph analysis, and a SQL interface. All of these packages extend the functionality of Apache Spark while maintaining the high performance and speed of computation. Apache Spark is currently the most widely used parallel framework for working with big data on commodity hardware or using cloud-computing services such as Amazon Web Services. Additionally, Apache Spark has APIs in several commonly used languages such as Scala, Java, Python, SQL, and R.

3 When to Use Parallel Computing

Parallel computing is an important tool for reducing computation time for large problems, but it is important to know when it is the right solution. The most common reasons to need parallelization are working with more data than will fit in memory on a single machine and performing computationally expensive calculations (e.g. performing sentiment analysis on an essay for each student which may take several minutes for a standard paragraph of text).

When data fits in memory on a single machine, standard tools like Python Pandas or R may be fast enough in practice. They might be desirable over a framework like Spark because they don't require learning a new tool, and may have more sophisticated statistics and machine learning packages available. On the other hand, these tools are only fast when data fits in memory, so if data volume increases past this limit, code will have to be entirely re-written for computation to remain tractable.

Even if a data set fits in memory on a single machine, it may still make sense to use parallel computation if the calculations are computationally expensive. Take as an example the scenario where you want to perform sentiment analysis on student essays. If this process takes one minute per student essay, the analysis for a class of 100 students will take over an hour and a half to finish. If instead you use Apache Spark to parallelize this computation, the analysis could be done in as little as one minute as essays for all of the students could be worked on in parallel.

When you do have a lot of data or computationally expensive calculations, there are a number of problem types that Apache Spark works well for. These include problems that are naturally data parallel in some way (e.g. computing the same thing for a large number of students), and problems where the computation can be divided into pieces that can be computed independently without interactions. There are many examples of data parallel problems in education, since education data is naturally grouped by categories like student, class, or university. Any time a calculation is repeated for all members of a particular category, that problem is naturally data parallel. An example of this includes computing assignment submission statistics for every course in a discipline. Each set of statistics can be computed independently by different machines without needing any information about other courses in the discipline. Another example is doing sentiment analysis on discussion forum posts for every student in a course. Each student's discussion forum posts can be analyzed independently, without needing any information about other students' posts.

4 An Example Predictive Model Pipeline Using Parallel Computing

In this section, we provide a toy model pipeline and show what it looks like as a single-threaded and parallel pipeline. Specifically, we will look at the problem of predicting course dropout from assignment submission data. Providing a way for instructors to easily identify students at-risk of dropping out is useful for those teaching online courses or courses with a large number of students, as it allows time for intervention before students actually drop out of the class and can help increase retention rates which is a common goal for most higher-ed institutions.

This problem is an instance of binary classification and given historical behavioral data, we want to label students as either at-risk or not which is represented as either a 0 or 1. There are many existing machine-learning techniques for modeling this type of problem. Some of the most well known include logistic regression, decision trees, random forests, SVMs and naive Bayes. We chose to use logistic regression for this example because it has a number of desirable properties. First, the output of a logistic regression model is a number between zero and one representing the confidence of the class label, instead of a hard classification label that only describes whether a student is at risk of dropping out or not. This allows for a more granular comparison of the predictions. This output can also be thresholded to find the binary class label. Additionally, logistic regression computes weights for each feature, so it is possible to understand how important each feature is to the model. It is also possible to express how important each feature is to a prediction, which can help provide actionable interventions for dropout risk.

The data used in this example is assignment submission data. For each assignment, it includes assignment due date and type (e.g. homework, quiz, etc.) and for each submission it includes start time, submit time, time spent, score and attempt number. Using this data, we derived four model features. They include:

- Average Grade
- Average time spent on the assignment relative to class average
- Percent assignments submitted
- Submission time relative to due date

These features are all time invariant, meaning that they don't depend on what day or week of the semester it is. This is important, because we want to create one classifier that can be used at any point in the semester.

4.1 A Single-Threaded Feature Generation Pipeline

Building and testing our logistic regression model requires a set of labeled feature vectors. In order to simulate how this classifier would be used during the semester, we generated one feature vector per student per week. This simulates making a prediction once a week for the entire semester. To generate feature vectors for week one, we used only the submission data for assignments due through week one. To generate feature vectors for week two, we used only the submission data for assignments through week two and we continued this pattern through the end of the semester.

Since some of the features require calculating a value for a student relative to the entire class (e.g. time spent on assignment relative to the class average), computing features requires the data for all students in a section at one time. Because of this, one workflow we used was to pull all of the data for one section, compute feature vectors for all students in that section, then pull all of the data for the next section, compute feature vectors for all students, and repeat for all sections. This is shown in Fig. 1. The result is a final list of all feature vectors from all students in all sections.

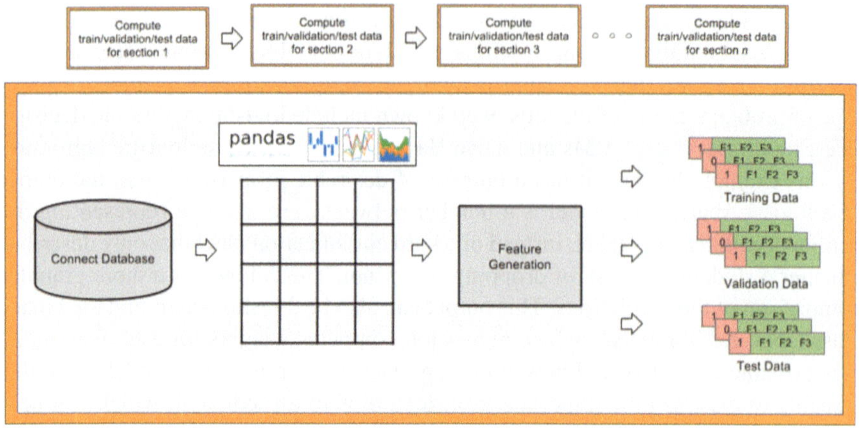

Fig. 1 Single-threaded pipeline

This workflow worked well for a small number of sections, but our full data set has around 300,000 sections. This means that to generate training/validation/testing data using all sections would take 20 days. This makes it apparent that in order to run experiments in a reasonable amount of time, a parallel solution is necessary.

4.2 A Parallel Feature Generation Pipeline

Fortunately, this problem is data parallel and thus lends itself nicely to a parallel solution with Apache Spark. In the above workflow, we repeated work for each section by computing feature vectors for each. In contrast, we used the map-reduce framework of Apache Spark to compute the feature vectors for each section in parallel on multiple cores at the same time. To do this we used the same function from the single-threaded pipeline that took a section id as an argument and computed all of the feature vectors for all students in that section. We used a Spark map operation to call this function on all section ids in parallel. The result is a final list of all feature vectors from all students in all sections, just like the single-threaded workflow. This is shown in Fig. 2. An analysis of the speedup achieved using this solution is in the following section.

4.3 Speed-Up Analysis

To understand the speedup gained from using Apache Spark and adding additional worker nodes in order to compute feature vectors in parallel, we ran experiments where we varied the number of worker nodes in the Spark cluster and recorded the

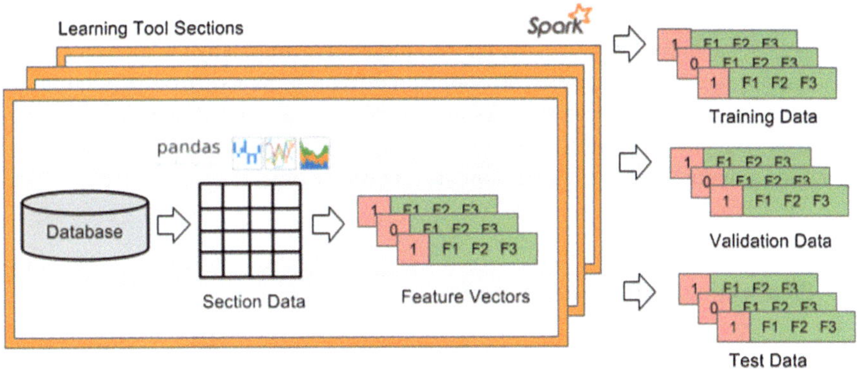

Fig. 2 Parallel pipeline

computation times. Figure 3 shows the speedup resulting from use of a singular worker node up to 20 worker nodes.

Here, parallel speedup is defined as

$$S_n = \frac{t_1}{t_n}$$

where S_n is the parallel speedup, t_1 is the time for the computation on 1 worker node and t_n is the time for computation on n worker nodes. This calculation can be thought of as the time saved on a computation by using n workers in parallel.

Figure 3 shows this parallelization process created a speedup of 15× when using 20 worker nodes. This measured speedup can be compared to linear speedup which is the theoretical best speedup that you can achieve in which doubling the number

Fig. 3 Parallel speedup achieved using Apache Spark to generate student feature vectors. Each worker node consisted of 4 CPUs and 30.5 GB of memory

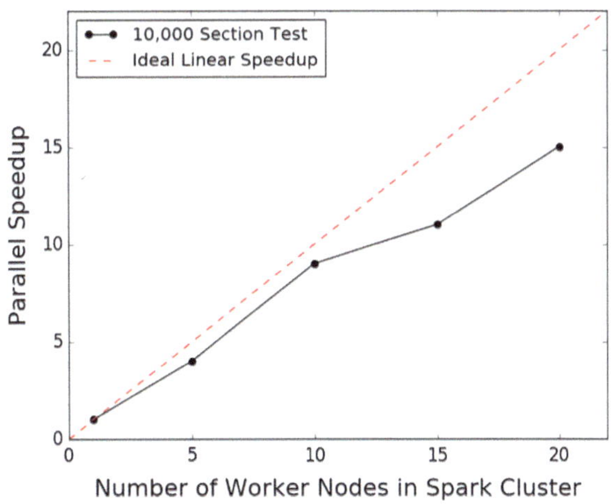

of worker nodes reduces the computation time by half. The reason linear speedup of $20\times$ was not achieved was because the computation is limited by the uneven number of semester weeks and number of students between sections. If every section had the same number of semester weeks and students, exact linear speedup would be expected. Despite the limitations, this shows that this speedup is essential for this computing feature vectors in a reasonable amount of time.

5 Discussion and Conclusions

As the amount of education data being collected continues to grow, frameworks like Apache Spark are becoming important tools to enable parallel computation on big data. Fortunately, the structure of educational data makes it a good candidate for parallel computation and this chapter described how to map several common problem types to the Apache Spark framework. We have analyzed an example machine-learning problem using a single-threaded pipeline and a parallel pipeline and compared the speedup provided by using Apache Spark. We hope this information and example problem help other practitioners get started learning to process large amounts of education data using Apache Spark.

References

Ghemawat, S., Gobioff, H., & Leung, S. (2003). The Google file system. In *ACM SIGOPS operating systems review* (Vol. 37, No. 5). ACM.

O'Malley, O. (2008). Tera2byte sort on Apache Hadoop. http://sortbenchmark.org. Cited October 31, 2017.

Pappano, L. (2012). The year of the MOOC. *The New York Times*. http://www.nytimes.com/2012/11/04/education/edlife/massive-open-online-courses-are-multiplying-at-a-rapid-pace.html. Cited October 31, 2017.

Shah, D. (2016). By the numbers: MOOCS in 2016. In *Class central*. https://www.class-central.com/report/mooc-stats-2016. Cited October 31, 2017.

Xin, R. (2014). Apache spark the fastest open source engine for sorting a petabyte. In *Databricks engineering blog*. https://databricks.com/blog/2014/10/10/spark-petabyte-sort.html. Cited October 31, 2017.

Nicholas Lewkow has a background in computational physics and high performance computing. He has been a data scientist at McGraw-Hill Education since 2014.

Jacqueline Feild has a background in computer science and computer vision. She has been a data scientist at McGraw-Hill Education since 2014.

Towards a Cloud-Based Big Data Infrastructure for Higher Education Institutions

Stefaan Ternier, Maren Scheffel and Hendrik Drachsler

Abstract This chapter reports about experiences gained in developing a learning analytics infrastructure for an ecosystem of different MOOC providers in Europe. These efforts originated in the European project ECO that aimed to develop a single-entry portal for various MOOC providers by developing shared technologies for these providers and distributing these technologies to the individual MOOC platforms of the project partners. The chapter presents a big data infrastructure that is able to handle learning activities from various sources and shows how the work in ECO led to a standardised approach for capturing learning analytics data according to the xAPI specification and storing them into cloud-based big data storage. The chapter begins with a definition of big data in higher education and thereafter describes the practical experiences gained from developing the learning analytics infrastructure.

Keywords Cloud storage · Real time feedback · xAPI interfaces · Visualisation · Dashboard · Learning analytics

1 Introduction to Big Data in HEI

Discussing 'big data in higher education' often manifests itself as a discussion about 'learning analytics in the higher education domain'. The actual research activities in

S. Ternier (✉) · M. Scheffel · H. Drachsler
Welten Institute, Open University of the Netherlands, Valkenburgerweg 177, 6419 AT Heerlen, The Netherlands
e-mail: stefaan.ternier@ou.nl

M. Scheffel
e-mail: maren.scheffel@ou.nl

H. Drachsler
e-mail: drachsler@dipf.de

H. Drachsler
German Institute of International Educational Research (DIPF), Goethe University Frankfurt, Schloßstraße 29, 60486 Frankfurt Am Main, Germany

J. M. Spector et al. (eds.), *Frontiers of Cyberlearning*, Lecture Notes in Educational Technology, https://doi.org/10.1007/978-981-13-0650-1_10

the field of learning analytics are similar to those in other big data-related research disciplines, e.g. in business or commerce. The term learning analytics matured to a commonly used key phrase encompassing the central aspects of learning and educational systems that are crucial for the whole big data process chain of harvesting, pre-processing, and analysing learning data in order to model, visualise and predict the different states of an educational situation (Greller & Drachsler, 2012). Learning analytics research also involves many other factors related to dealing with big data such as instructional design, ethics and privacy as well as policy-making. In that sense learning analytics is more diverse than its sister community of educational data mining, which is bound closer to the central tasks of predictive model testing in educational contexts (Berland, Baker, & Bilkstein, 2014).

One could say that the term learning analytics already provides some relevant context variables for the application of data science within the educational field, for instances: (1) learning analytics should be about learning and should support the learning process, e.g. with feedback systems, (2) certain aspects of learning like motivation, learning goals, learning activities or assessment results should be taken into account when providing outcomes of data science to learners, and (3) educational datasets are often much smaller than data sets in many other disciplines like health, finance or physics.

Due to this last point, it is thus somewhat questionable whether learning analytics (and educational data mining) do indeed belong to the broader research field of big data where it is quite common that data sets do not simply fit into an ordinary relational database. However, the definition of big data having to be big in terms of bytes is a rather simplistic one. A more informed definition of big data is based on six 'V', namely: (1) volume, (2) variety, (3) velocity, (4) veracity, (5) validity, and finally (6) volatility. Those "V's" can be used to identify whether a data set can be considered as one involving the challenges of big data research. In the next few sections we will shortly introduce these V-characteristics of big data and explain their specific role and meaning for education and learning analytics.

1.1 Volume

The simplest characteristic of big data is indeed volume, i.e. the pure size of data as it is generated at big data companies like Google or at research facilities like CERN's Large Hadron Collider (LHC). Data from particle collisions at the LHC reaches the realms of tens of petabytes per year (one petabyte equals 1000 terabytes). Storing, analysing and processing this amount of data have always been a major challenge in the past that stimulated the need for better performing data infrastructures. And these days even more data is being produced by machines as well as humans in social networks and other online environments, thus increasing the amount of data to a massive scale.

In the educational field, though, this is not the case. In most cases, the data of a middle-range university with about 20,000 students can still be stored on a storage device with the capacity of 100 GB and is thus nowhere near the amounts of data that Google or any other data-intensive organisation produces. However, with the rise of digital systems and devices in education, the volume of data generated by educational institutions will increase and thus turn the educational domain into a big data discipline in terms of volume more and more.

1.2 Variety

Variety in terms of big data refers to the many sources and types of data available. Those can roughly be split into structured and unstructured data. On a more detailed level, these days' data types can be very diverse as especially educational data ranges from texts, videos, images and all sorts of files over a user's interaction with those resources to mobile devices, cameras, bio signals such as heart rate, eye-tracking information, and data from various other sensors that are involved in the educational process. Thus, data is becoming more and more multimodal and heterogeneous (Di Mitri et al., 2017; Pijeira-Díaz, Drachsler, Järvelä, & Kirschner, 2016). This variety of data creates major challenges for storing the data, cleaning the data, mining and analysing data.

Multimodal data is a challenge for big data research in general, but it is an even bigger challenge for the educational sector as there is no standardised approach so far to deal with this kind of data. However, especially the educational sector is taking advantage of a plethora of media that results in multimodal data types that demand an analytics process that is able to handle the variety of data that is being produced.

1.3 Velocity

In terms of big data, velocity is the pace at which data flows in from resources to a data infrastructure. Thus, it specifically refers to the continuity and speed of a data stream with different varieties and volumes that hit a big data infrastructure. Apart from the challenge of keeping a big data infrastructure alive given the continuous and massive streams of data, another challenge of data velocity is to provide—as far as possible—real-time information and feedback about this massive data stream. Real-time feedback is a challenging objective that one can only try to get close to. However, fast an analysis might be, there is usually always some kind of gap between the data collection and the provision of information or feedback from a system to the user.

The velocity of the data flow can thus influence the size of this time gap and needs to be taken into consideration as real-time information is an expensive good, i.e. various valuable services are conceivable if real-time analysis and feedback were possible. In the educational domain, for instance, a student analytics dashboard (Verbert, Duval, Klerkx, Govaerts, & Santos, 2013) could be updated once every night only. The calculation of scores and the prediction of success for every student, however, should be provided shortly after an assessment in order to support teachers and students in their processes in a valuable and meaningful way.

1.4 Veracity

Big data veracity refers to the biases and noise in data. Most researchers indicate that data veracity is an even bigger challenge than volume and velocity. Making a proper selection of the right data needed to answer the right question or solve the right problem is always a challenge that—if done correctly—can strongly contribute to solving the challenges of volume and velocity. Selecting the right data for a particular information need from a noisy big data set can not only decrease the volume of data that needs to be harvested, but also its velocity. Yet, very often the handling of data is conducted the other way around, i.e. instead of first formulating a question that needs to be answered and then harvesting the data needed to answer that question, huge amounts of data are collected and then analysed to identify patterns with no clear goal in mind.

When scoping out a big data strategy, it needs to be taken care of keeping the data clean to prevent 'dirty' or 'noisy' data from accumulating in the system. To ensure data veracity, contextual knowledge about the domain that big data research is applied to is needed. Taking advantage of the above mentioned context variables that learning analytics entails is thus vital to overcome the veracity challenge in order to provide meaningful insights for the right target groups.

1.5 Validity

Similar to big data veracity is the issue of validity that refers to the correctness and accuracy of the data in terms of intended use. An important difference between validity and veracity is that validity does not focus on the presence or absence of noise in the data, i.e. on the cleanliness or purity of the data, but on the contentual and contextual correctness for the given situation, i.e. whether the right data was selected to make the right analyses for a specific information need. Validity is a very common concept within scientific research in general but also in educational sciences in particular as the validity of any instrument or measurement needs to be tested before it can be rolled out in the field. For example, the validity of assessment or survey items are often tested using item response theory, factor analysis or similar approaches.

1.6 Volatility

Big data volatility refers to the length of time that data is valid for and thus the duration of its storage. Even though the term big data usually refers to vast amounts of collected information, there is a need to delete some data at a certain point in time as storing all data ever generated is simply not possible. Therefore, the concept of data degradation is becoming increasingly popular in big data research as it enables the gradual removal of data in those cases where data neither is of current use nor deemed valuable for future use anymore.

In the educational field, the data degradation aspect of volatility is also strongly related to data privacy and data access. As described in the DELICATE checklist (Drachsler & Greller, 2016), those handling data from and about others are—at least within the European Union—required by European law, i.e. the General Data Protection Regulation coming into effect in 2018, to clearly state which data is being stored and how long it will be stored. A data subject, i.e. the person whose data is being collected and stored, has the right to always get access to this data and can also demand for this data to be deleted if it is of no purpose for the data subject anymore.

Keeping this informed definition of big data in education in mind, it is now time to look at some practical experiences with learning analytics standards and technologies. While Sect. 2 describes the xAPI specification used for activity data collected from various learning environments, Sect. 3 reports on experiences gathered in the application of big data cloud solutions.

2 A Specification for Learning Data

2.1 ECO—A Big Data Project in Higher Education

In early 2014, the Open University of the Netherlands received funding from the European Commission to develop a learning analytics infrastructure in the context of the ECO project (Brouns et al., 2014). Goal of the ECO project (Elearning Communication Open-Data)[1] was to develop a single-entry portal for various MOOC (massive open online course) providers. It aimed to increase awareness about the advantages of open online education in Europe and to develop shared technologies for different MOOC providers. By first pushing technologies to individual MOOC platforms within the consortium, these technologies could be developed and tested in pilots before being transferred to all project partners and then Europe at large as described by the MOLAC innovation cycle (Drachsler & Kalz, 2016).

One of the tasks within the ECO project was to build an infrastructure that was able to consume the learners' activity data from the different MOOC providers and to combine them into one learning analytics output. Integrating the different MOOC

[1] http://project.ecolearning.eu/.

platforms into the ECO project's infrastructure, however, was a complex task especially with regards to the information available about the courses' design and structure from each MOOC provider as well as the learners' activity data needed for any form of learning analytics; that is (1) the data collected by the different providers varied and was thus not homogeneous, and (2) the database schemas used by the different providers to store the data about the learners' activities varied and were not homogeneous.

The problem of every MOOC provider using their own logging and monitoring system was solved within the ECO project by letting each provider use their proprietary methodology as long as they also provided the data to the ECO platform according to a designated xAPI specification. A central learning record store (LRS) architecture to store xAPI statements about the learners' activities in the different MOOCs was established that allowed the analysis of the collected data with one learning analytics engine across the different providers. This ECO learning analytics web service displays visualisations of these data analyses on a dashboard within the ECO platform to learners as well as instructors. The collected data include static data from the courses, e.g. course schedule, learning tasks, as well as dynamic data about the learners' actions within the course, e.g. navigation through the course website, interaction with learning resources, etc.

2.2 *Harmonising Data Extraction Using xAPI*

The xAPI specification[2] can be used to log actions a learner performs in an online learning environment. An xAPI statement takes the form of actor-verb-object to describe such an action and thus registers who performs which activity with which object at what time and in which context. Next to the context object, where additional information about an action such as the name of a course or a specific forum discussion can be stored, xAPI statements can also include result objects where outcomes, such as quiz scores or entered text can be captured.[3]

For the ECO project an overview of all events that can take place in any of the involved courses was created that included the xAPI statement for each of these events in order ensure a shared and standardised way to store learning activities among the different MOOC providers. These events are visualised in Fig. 1.

By stimulating the joint collection of xAPI-conform data within the ECO project's LRS, the aim was to also contribute to the definition of a xAPI specification that is used beyond the ECO project. The results of these efforts have led to an inter-project and inter-institutional specification of xAPI statements (Berg, Scheffel, Drachsler, Ternier, & Specht, 2016). This Dutch xAPI specification for learning activities (DSLA) is available as a github repository[4] where the complete statement for each

[2]See https://experienceapi.com and https://github.com/adlnet/xAPI-Spec.

[3]Detailed examples are available at https://experienceapi.com/statements-101/.

[4]https://github.com/TrustedLA/xAPI-Dutch-Spec/.

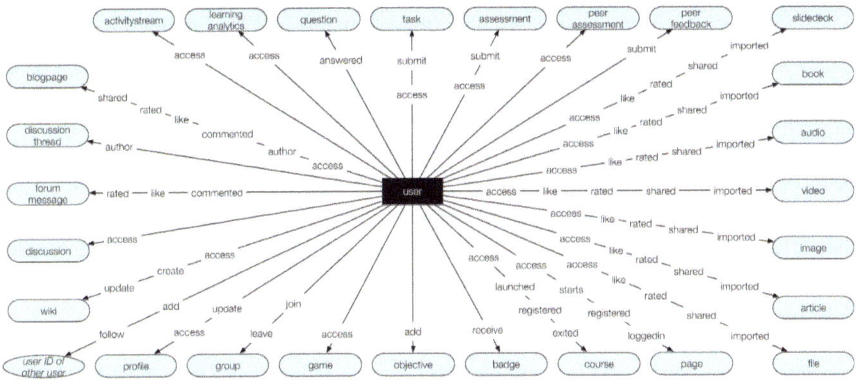

Fig. 1 Overview of learner activities in MOOCs of the ECO project

event is given in JSON format. A deliberate effort was made to stay within known verb usage. It needs to be stressed that the list of events does not claim to be complete but that it is an alignment of various xAPI-related projects that used the statements from the ECO project as its basis as it represents the most traditional events of online learning.

2.3 *Advantages and Disadvantages of Using xAPI*

The cleaning and mangling of data has been a significant if not the most significant cost to analytics projects (Dasu & Johnson, 2003). The xAPI standard ensures that data is recorded in a known and machine-readable format and securely and centrally stored in a LRS that is queryable through web services. The use of standard web services increases the pool of developers who can create analytic applications. Applying xAPI methodology across an organisation enables the building of a consistent analytics infrastructure. In doing so, the efforts of an institution's IT support to maintain different data approaches and to couple the full range of applications to a central data repository can be decreased.

Increasing adoption[5] of the xAPI standard across the educational sector delivers an opportunity for plug and play analytics services. If vendors uniformly adopt the standard then analytic services such as student dashboards (Jivet, Scheffel, Drachsler, & Specht, 2017) and student retention systems are more easily decoupled from specific applications. In summary, the use of xAPI potentially decreases security risks, increases the consistency of data, increases the pool of potential developers by leveraging well-known approaches (JSON, web services) and decouples data sources from analytics services.

[5] https://experienceapi.com/adopters/.

The most challenging issues when it comes to using xAPI is the freedom of choice when designing xAPI statements. Anyone can on demand define statements and related vocabulary. This will work for an isolated solution; however, this approach generates considerable issues once the barriers between data silos are broken down and xAPI datasets are combined. The interoperability issue is not a new one and has been described for other standards such as IMS LD (Koper & Olivier, 2004) and SCORM (Qu & Nejdl, 2002) long before the xAPI approach came up. Nevertheless, the call for a more standardised approach to collecting data that increases the insights one could gain out of standardised data is still valid and becomes even more urgent with the learner activity-based data collection (Drachsler et al., 2010).

Apart from the Dutch specification for learning activities, there are some other contemporary sources of xAPI recipes. One source of information is the xAPI vocabulary and profile index.[6] The primary recipe library is advertised on the ADLnet website.[7] However, since October 2015 the documented recipes have been limited in extent to a number of contexts (attendance, bookmarklet, checklist, open badges, SCORM to tincan, tags, video, virtual patient activities). A second set of recipes that expand coverage to support cMOOCs (Kitto, Cross, Waters, & Lupton, 2015) are also available via a Github repository.[8] And finally, Jisc has also made their xAPI recipes available.[9]

Although these sources are suggestive and act as sources of guidance there is currently no clearly authoritative one source of truth. The lack of authoritative guidance in selecting verbs and other metadata terms generates a huge inconsistency between single statements of different providers and institutions. For instance, the interaction of a learner with a video could be tracked as (A) 'Learner A *played* the *movie* How to cook good xAPI', or as (B) 'Learner B *watched* the *video* How to cook good xAPI'. Both statements express the same experience in a slightly different semantic manner. Therefore, xAPI promotes the use of recipes to standardise the expression of experiences, as there are often multiple plausible paths to defining that a learner has interacted with an object. The xAPI community as a whole thus relies on its members to publicise and deliver recipes, i.e. those working with xAPI in the educational domain need to share their recipes in order for events to be recorded in a standardised way.

An alternative albeit commercial approach to the xAPI specification, IMS Global's Caliper Analytics,[10] tries to overcome this challenge by directly providing predefined recipes for processes of a learner such as user registration, user login, user logout, user assessment, etc. The learning traces that consist of a chain of single activities of a learner are nested in a predefined recipe containing specific metadata verbs and parameters. The Caliper consortium therefore chose to follow a more guided

---

[6]http://xapi.vocab.pub.

[7]https://experienceapi.com/recipes/.

[8]https://github.com/kirstykitto/CLRecipe.

[9]https://github.com/jiscdev/xapi.

[10]https://www.imsglobal.org/activity/caliper.

approach by having the core consortium define the recipes and then later rolling those out its members.

3 An Infrastructure for Learning Data in the Cloud

In a traditional physical deployment setting, an institute is responsible for acquiring software and hardware to implement a big data solution. With cloud computing, these resources are made available through a network. Hardware, software and data are made available on demand. Generally, cloud applications come in three layers:

1. Software as a service (Saas) solutions offer an application to the customer, e.g. email, project management, customer relationship management, etc. The service provider offers readily usable applications to their customers who can then often adapt and configure the software's settings to their needs.
2. Platform as a service (PaaS) often comprises standardised services, e.g. access management, data storage, database management, identity management, etc. The service provider maintains the framework and infrastructure but often offers facilities for development in languages like Python, .NET or Java. PaaS customers do not get direct access to the operating system but operate with the definition of the provided platform.
3. Infrastructure as a service (IaaS) introduces the most flexibility to the customer but also requires more maintenance work on the customer side. Infrastructures such as servers, networks and data storage facilities are offered to the customer who has complete freedom in how to use the hardware.

Cloud-based computing has significant advantages over traditional physical deployments. Big data solutions require data mining, a process that can be very resource-intensive for shorter periods of time. Rather than having to acquire expensive hardware, cloud providers enable horizontal and vertical scaling for these short periods of time, i.e. when the data mining process takes place, more servers are temporarily allocated (horizontal scaling) or the amount of processor cores and/or ram memory is increased (vertical scaling). This gives big data customers almost unlimited access to resources that would otherwise be very expensive to acquire.

In Europe cloud infrastructures from big providers such as Google or Amazon are often seen as not being a 'safe harbour' for the storage of data (Drachsler & Greller, 2016) as they are suspected of using the stored data for their own purposes. On the other hand, a local installation of cloud services in a university's IT system is also a big risk, as local installations require a continuously high maintenance effort that also brings certain security issues with it.

3.1 Big Data Storage in ECO

Originally, the goal of ECO was to be able to host more than 1000 MOOCs by the end of the project. Although only 60k users were reached in the end, the storage was of course planned and set up with the project goal numbers in mind. Taking into account that one xAPI record takes on average only 2 kB of memory, it was estimated that the used learning record store required query access for 1 billion xAPI records.

In the beginning of the ECO project, an open source learning record store solution was installed locally on a server at the university. However, after inserting 100k records, both the query as well as the indexation service of the used LRS got very slow. The indexation service often took more than 1 s to ingest a new record. Moving the learning record store to an IaaS server improved the situation slightly, i.e. creating new indexes on the underlying MongoDB infrastructure was better but the throughput was still not satisfactory and not scalable for the data expected in the ECO project.

Based on these first lessons learned, the learning record store was migrated to a two-layered PaaS solution, where unlimited access was provided to both query and storage facilities. In this solution, access to the underlying data management infrastructure was no longer available, so in the case of slow responses it would be impossible to optimise the service by creating indexes.

The first layer of the infrastructure comprises a facts table that is merely responsible for accepting and storing facts according to the xAPI format (see Fig. 2). Upon submission, facts are assigned a globally unique identifier and are stored as JSON records. Hence, records for every possible xAPI application profile can be stored in this table. The table is future-proof as records can easily be extended.

The xAPI facts table is implemented as a schemaless NoSQL store that can store hierarchically structured xAPI data. This PaaS technology allows fast and scalable storage of data. Data access is, however, limited. Data can be retrieved through the GUID and through simple queries, e.g. by asking to retrieve all records that were submitted between two timestamps. SQL techniques like joining tables, creating subqueries or other techniques that require instant access to all data are not possible.

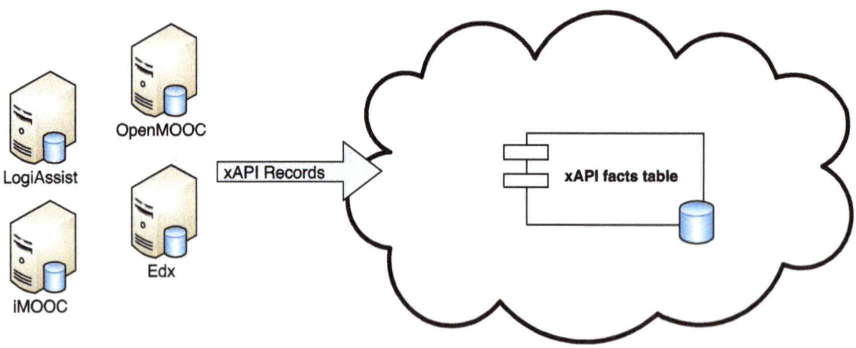

Fig. 2 Data flow from different MOOC providers to the xAPI facts table

These more advanced techniques have become especially relevant when implementing a user dashboard that benefits from the second layer of this architecture. Here a search index has been implemented on a PaaS relational database that allows for SQL queries (see Fig. 3). This component's only responsibility is to allow for fast queries and data updates. Deleting or altering records is not possible as this operation comes at the expense of slower queries.

One might argue that updating and deleting from the query table is an important feature. Throughout the project's runtime, the xAPI application profile has been updated several times. In one of the earlier instantiations, for example, a MOOC's identifier was not stored as part of the xAPI statements, thus making it impossible to identify in which course an activity had taken place. Updating the xAPI application profile has no influence on the xAPI facts table as this component makes no assumption on the xAPI schema. However, the query table that stores a flat serialisation of the xAPI records has to be extended with a new column, i.e. course identifier in this case. Next, a new table with this data is created and all data in the xAPI facts table is synchronised with this new table. Upon completion, data visualisation queries are routed to the newly created table and the old table is deleted. A similar scenario is necessary when data is to be deleted from the xAPI facts table, e.g. in cases where a user wants data to be removed.

The advantage of a PaaS-based NoSQL and SQL database is that the project is scalable, yet also enables a cheap start, as no initial expensive servers have to be acquired. At the time of writing, the ECO facts table contains 2.3 M statements, which corresponds to a total of 2.5 GB of storage and thus accumulates to a monthly storage fee of \$0.50. The SQL query table of course contains the same amount of records, but uses less storage space (0.46 GB) as only values are stored. Storage of this data is cheaper and corresponds to \$0.01 per month. Queries, e.g. to gather input for a learning analytics dashboards, are, however, more expensive (\$5 per TB). Using query caches, though, the ECO dashboard falls within the free quota allocated by the

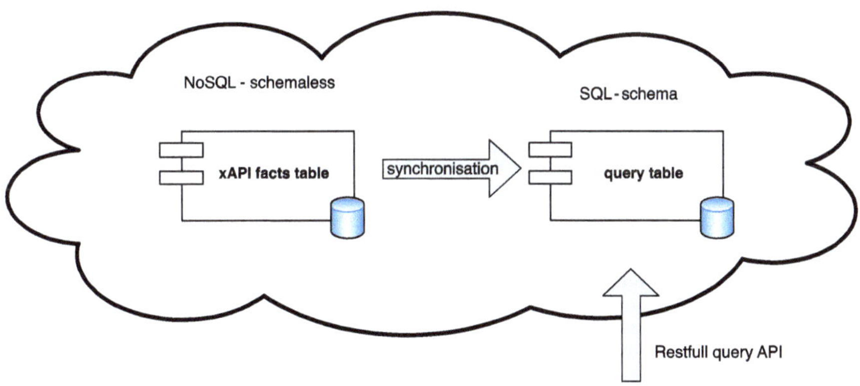

Fig. 3 Synchronisation from the facts table to a pre-stored SQL query table

cloud provider. This illustrates how a cloud-based learning analytics solutions can and should be set up in order to save costs. The cost of such a system scales very well with an increasing number of users.

3.2 Real-Time Feedback in ECO

The ECO cloud-based learning analytics infrastructure can thus offer services to various stakeholders. A researcher can connect analysis tools like SPSS, R or Tableau to the learning analytics backend, and by doing so can dissect and mine the data. Learners represent another important class of stakeholders. They can profit from real-time feedback about their learning process. Various indicators, e.g. a 'current performance' indicator, require real-time access to the data. Having to wait for the results of nightly or even weekly data mining jobs will render the visualisation of these indicators useless.

Big infrastructures such as Twitter rely on so-called lambda architectures. A lambda architecture defines a batch and speed layer. The batch layer is a—potentially slow—layer that processes incoming new data and makes it available for querying. In a real-time system, however, queries must yield recent data. A merged view thus combines the batch layer with the data delivered by the speed layer. The latter layer processes the stream of incoming data without the need for completeness. By doing so, the merge delivers both historic and recent data. The main criticism on this architecture is related to its complexity.

The ECO platform relies on a simple architecture that is a pure streaming approach. This solution comes with a small latency due to two aspects: the MOOC providers' submission latency to the facts table and the synchronisation latency between the facts table and the query table. While the first process, i.e. the time between a user's action in a course and the submission of the corresponding action to the fact table, depends on the MOOC providers and ranges anywhere between immediate and every 5 min, the latter process takes place every minute. It can thus take up to 6 min for data to be reflected in the query table, and thus in any tools that are built on querying this table, e.g. the learning analytics dashboard.

The ECO learning analytics platform has been extended with a query cache. Some queries are expensive, as they need to reflect all records in the database. However, visualisations that trigger these queries are often hardly influenced by new data. The learning analytics query services are therefore extended with a query cache expiration parameter. This parameter indicates how long the result of the query can be served from cache before it has to be recomputed from the query table.

3.3 The ECO Learning Analytics Dashboard

The ECO learning analytics dashboard visualises information at three different levels: micro, meso, and macro. The macro-level analytics provide cross-institutional information and can thus only be provided when all institutions agree on a common xAPI recipe to document learner experiences. Meso-level analytics operate at the level of an institution and typically provide insight on a specific course. Micro-level analytics zoom in on the level of a single learner and track data for individuals.

The ECO MOOC Monitor (see Fig. 4) is a typical example of a macro level widget that is available on the ECO dashboard. This widget visualises the number of activities in relation to the number of launches grouped by MOOC. The colour code displays the MOOC provider while the circle size corresponds to the number of users. ECO aggregates MOOCs that are hosted by different institutions. In addition, an institution can choose between four different MOOC platforms to host the MOOC.

The ECO Activity Widget (see Fig. 5) exemplifies a meso-level widget. It sorts all learners in a MOOC according to their level of activity. Active students are displayed on the right, passive students on the left. The widget displays the position of the logged in user in red, so that the learner knows how well he performs with respect to his peers.

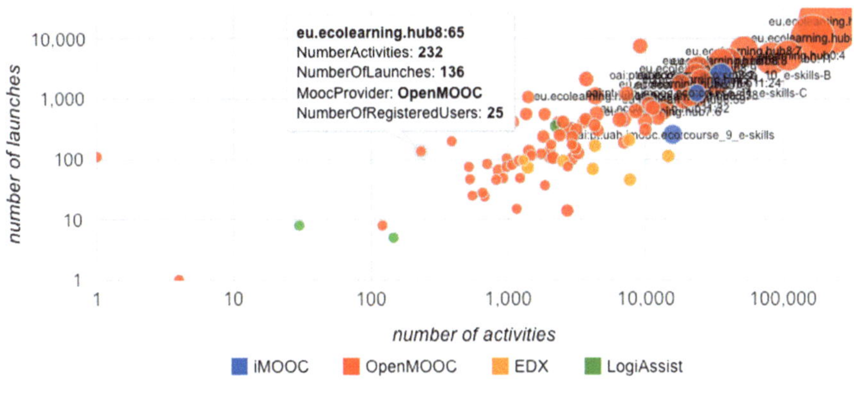

Fig. 4 The ECO MOOC monitor

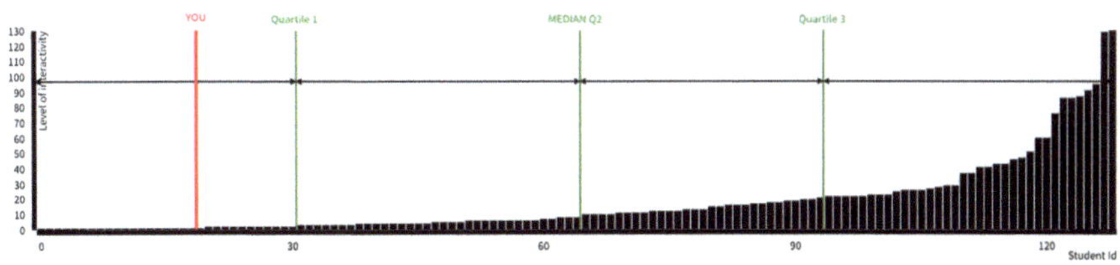

Fig. 5 The ECO activity widget

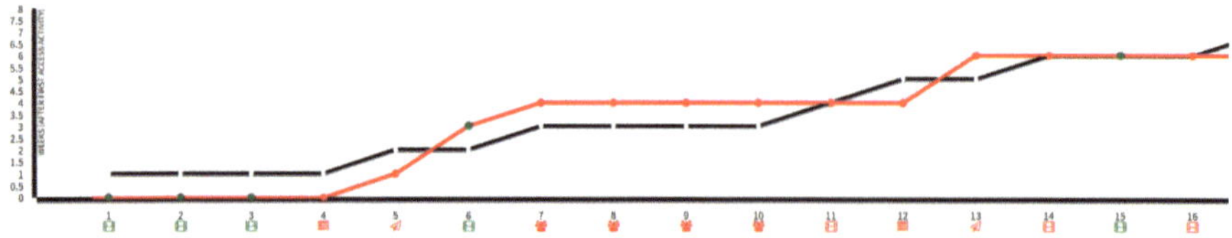

Fig. 6 The ECO progress widget

Finally, the dashboard also contains micro-level widgets that provide feedback on the performance of the individual learner, e.g. by showing a user's activity log indicating what they have done in the system or by providing feedback on progress. The ECO Progress Widget (see Fig. 6) provides feedback on course progress and indicates to what extend a course has been completed. User evaluations using the evaluation framework for learning analytics have been conducted for some of these widgets (Scheffel, Drachsler, Toisoul, Ternier, & Specht, 2017).

The ECO dashboard is an extensible component and can easily be complemented with new visualisations. So far, visualisations based on the Data-Driven Documents (D3) library[11] and on Google Charts[12] are supported. When creating a new widget, a developer must define the corresponding query on the server. Results are serialised into a tabular JSON-based format that is sent to the client. A developer must write a javascript component that binds the results to one of the supported visualisations.

When registering a query to the dashboard, a developer must specify a cache expiration time. This value indicates how long the result will stay cached. For the ECO MOOC Monitor this value is set to 24 h as very recent data will hardly influence the overall impression of the visualisation. For more detailed visualisations such as the ECO Progress Widget, this value was set to 10 min. Widget developers must be careful when defining a query. Ideally, a query must not deliver more than 100 rows of data at a time as this is transferred over the wire to the web-based client. Bigger volumes would result in widgets that take too long to load. Queries must aggregate data and should not expose single xAPI records to respect a user's privacy. For this reason, widget queries are to be registered on the server, to prevent users from altering queries and getting access to raw data.

4 Conclusions and Future Developments

Whether the learning data that is collected and analysed for learning analytics purposes in higher education institutions is to be seen as big data in the literal sense of volume when being compared to the vast amounts of data being processed by companies such as Google is certainly debatable. However, when looking at other

[11]https://d3js.org.

[12]https://developers.google.com/chart/.

data-related challenges than sheer size, learning analytics data is to be seen as big data. The xAPI specification as well as the learning analytics infrastructure presented in this chapter allows a smooth and affordable way of data collection, storage and analysis and in combination help to tackle the six big data challenges of volume, variety, velocity, veracity, validity and volatility.

The efforts that originated in the ECO project have since then been extended to other projects. For example, within the LACE project[13] the Open University of the Netherlands conducted further studies focused on advanced learning analytics tools that made use of the ECO learning analytics infrastructure. Making use of multimodal data sources (see Fig. 7), i.e. (1) desktop application logs collected with RescueTime,[14] (2) heart rate logs collected with FitBit[15] wristbands, (3) weather data collected with OpenWeatherMap,[16] and (4) contextual data such as noise level collected with feedback cubes (Börner et al., 2015), the Learning Pulse study (Di Mitri et al., 2017) explored conditions for productive and unproductive learning contexts. The ECO big data infrastructure was able to handle the heterogeneous data streams very efficiently. Any logged activities that had not been covered by the DSLA until those points were added to the xAPI recipe collection.

Although the data collected in Learning Pulse was quite different from the traditional course xAPI data collected in ECO so far—especially in terms of volume and velocity—, the ECO infrastructure managed to consume all the resources, e.g. the hear rate values that were updated every five seconds. Querying the multimodal data

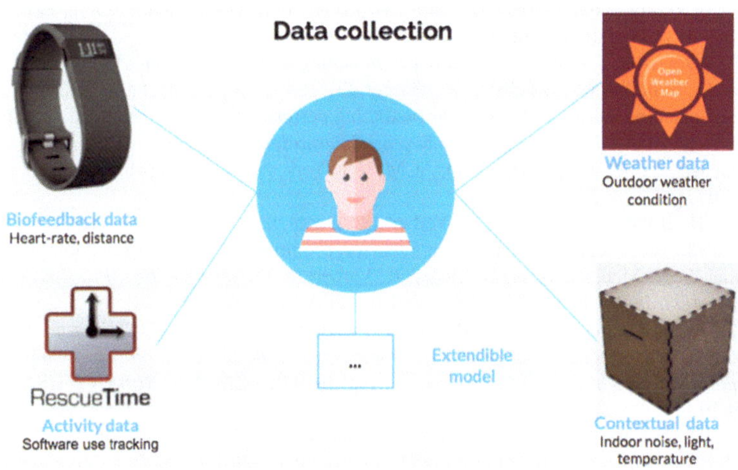

Fig. 7 Information sources collected for the learning pulse study

---

[13]http://www.laceproject.eu.

[14]https://www.rescuetime.com.

[15]https://www.fitbit.com.

[16]https://openweathermap.org.

and plotting it on a dedicated dashboard that predicted the learning progress was also easily executable.

These very positive experiences strengthen and support the approach developed in the ECO project. It will be further developed and extended within the Open University of the Netherlands as a general big data storage that can handle diverse data streams for various purposes.

References

Berg, A., Scheffel, M., Drachsler, H., Ternier, S., & Specht, M. (2016). Dutch cooking with xAPI recipes: The good, the bad and the consistent. In *Proceedings of the International Conference on Advanced Learning Technologies, ICALT '16* (pp. 234–236). https://doi.org/10.1109/icalt.2016.48.

Berland, M., Baker, R S Jd, & Bilkstein, P. (2014). Educational data mining and learning analytics: Applications to constructionist research. *Technology, Knowledge and Learning, 19*(1–2), 205–220. https://doi.org/10.1007/s10758-014-9223-7.

Börner, D., Tabuenca, B., Storm, J., Happe, S., & Specht, M. (2015). Tangible interactive ambient display prototypes to support learning scenarios. In *Proceedings of the Ninth International Conference on Tangible, Embedded, and Embodied Interaction (TEI '15)* (p. 721). New York, NY, USA: ACM.

Brouns, F., Mota, J., Morgado, L., Jansen, D., Fano, S., Silva, A., et al. (2014, October 27–28). A networked learning framework for effective MOOC design: The ECO project approach. In A. M. Teixeira & A. Szücs (Eds.), *Proceedings of the 8th EDEN Research Workshop—Challenges for Research into Open & Distance Learning: Doing Things Better: Doing Better Things* (pp. 161–171). Budapest, Hungary: EDEN.

Dasu, T., & Johnson, T. (2003). *Exploratory data mining and data cleaning*. Wiley.

Di Mitri, D., Scheffel, M., Drachsler, H., Börner, D., Ternier, S., & Specht, M. (2017). Learning pulse: A machine learning approach for predicting performance in self-regulated learning using multimodal data. In *Proceedings of the Seventh International Conference on Learning Analytics & Knowledge, LAK'17* (pp. 188–197), ACM: New York, NY, USA. https://doi.org/10.1145/3027385.3027447.

Drachsler, H., Bogers, T., Vuorikari, R., Verbert, K., Duval, E., Manouselis, N., et al. (2010). Issues and considerations regarding sharable data sets for recommender systems in technology enhanced learning. In N. Manouselis, H. Drachsler, K. Verbert, & O. Santos (Eds.), *Procedia Computer Science, 1*(2), 2849–2858. https://doi.org/10.1016/j.procs.2010.08.010.

Drachsler, H., & Greller, W. (2016). Privacy and analytics—It's a DELICATE issue. A checklist to establish trusted learning analytics. In *Proceedings of the Sixth International Conference on Learning Analytics and Knowledge, LAK '16* (pp. 89–98). ACM: New York, NY, USA. https://doi.org/10.1145/2883851.2883893.

Drachsler, H., & Kalz, M. (2016). The MOOC and learning analytics innovation cycle (MOLAC): A reflective summary of ongoing research and its challenges. *Journal of Computer Assisted Learning, 32*(3), 281–290. https://doi.org/10.1111/jcal.12135.

Greller, W., & Drachsler, H. (2012). Translating learning into numbers: A generic framework for learning analytics. *Educational Technology & Society, 15*(3), 42–57.

Jivet, I., Scheffel, M., Drachsler, H., & Specht, M. (2017). Awareness is not enough. Pitfalls of learning analytics dashboards in the educational practise. In É. Lavoué, H. Drachsler, K. Verbert, J. Broisin, & M. Pérez-Sanagustín (Eds.), *LNCS: Vol. 10474. Data driven approaches in digital education: Proceedings of the 12th European conference on technology enhanced learning (EC-*

TEL 2017) (pp. 82–96). Springer: Berlin, Heidelberg. https://doi.org/10.1007/978-3-319-66610-5_7.
Kitto, K., Cross, S., Waters, Z., & Lupton, M. (2015). Learning analytics beyond the LMS: The connected learning analytics toolkit. In *Proceedings of the Fifth International Conference on Learning Analytics and Knowledge, LAK'15* (pp. 11–15). ACM: New York, NY, USA. https://doi.org/10.1145/2723576.2723627.
Koper, R., & Olivier, B. (2004). Representing the learning design of units of learning. *Educational Technology & Society, 7*(3), 97–111.
Pijeira-Díaz, H. J., Drachsler, H., Järvelä, S., & Kirschner, P. A. (2016). Investigating collaborative learning success with physiological coupling indices based on electrodermal activity. In *Proceedings of the Sixth International Conference on Learning Analytics and Knowledge, LAK '16* (pp. 64–73), ACM: New York, NY, USA. https://doi.org/10.1145/2883851.2883897.
Qu, C., & Nejdl, W. (2002, September). Towards interoperability and reusability of learning resources: A SCORM-conformant courseware for computer science education. In *Proceedings of the 2nd IEEE International Conference on Advanced Learning Technologies (IEEE ICALT 2002)*, Kazan, Tatarstan, Russia.
Scheffel, M., Drachsler, H., Toisoul, C., Ternier, S., & Specht, M. (2017). The proof of the pudding: Examining validity and reliability of the evaluation framework for learning analytics. In É. Lavoué, H. Drachsler, K. Verbert, J. Broisin, M. Pérez-Sanagustín (Eds.), *LNCS: Vol. 10474. Data Driven Approaches in Digital Education: Proceedings of the 12th European Conference on Technology Enhanced Learning (EC-TEL 2017)* (pp. 194–208). Springer: Berlin, Heidelberg. https://doi.org/10.1007/978-3-319-66610-5_15.
Verbert, K., Duval, E., Klerkx, J., Govaerts, S., & Santos, J. (2013). Learning analytics dashboard applications. *American Behavioral Scientist, 57*(10), 1500–1509. https://doi.org/10.1177/0002764213479363.

Stefaan Ternier is an assistant professor at the Welten Institute of the Open University of the Netherlands. From 2000 until 2008, Stefaan was active as technical architect for the ARIADNE foundation. His current areas of research include mobile learning, metadata management, architectures for learning object repositories and learning analytics. Stefaan was a member of the CEN/ISSS Workshop on Learning Technologies (WS/LT). At this workshop, he coordinated the developments of the Simple Publishing Interface (SPI) and contributed to several other standardisation initiatives (including SQI). Stefaan is an Associate Editor of IEEE Transactions on Learning Technologies. Over the past few years, he was active in many European projects that had an impact on standardisation in TEL, including ProLearn, MELT, MACE, Share.TEC, OpenScout, weSPOT and ECO.

Maren Scheffel is an assistant professor at the Welten Institute (Research Centre for Learning, Teaching and Technology) of the Open University of the Netherlands. She holds an MA degree in Computational Linguistics and a Ph.D. degree in Educational Sciences. She previously worked at the Fraunhofer Institute for Applied Information Technology (FIT) focussing on aspects related to technology-enhanced learning and was also involved in managing the ROLE project. Since 2014, she has been working at the Welten Institute where she was involved in the management as well as the research for the LACE project and now contributes to the research for the SHEILA project and the SafePAT project while also being involved in the management of the CompetenSEA project. During her Ph.D. project, she developed the Evaluation Framework for Learning Analytics (EFLA) and now continues research related to the evaluation of learning analytics tools. She is the vice chair of SURF SIG Learning Analytics.

Hendrik Drachsler is professor of Educational Technologies and Learning Analytics at the Goethe University Frankfurt, the German Institute of International Educational Research (DIPF), and the Welten Institute of the Open University of the Netherlands. His research interests include learning analytics, personalisation technologies, recommender systems, educational data, and mobile devices. He is elected member of the Society of Learning Analytics Research (SoLAR). In the past, he has been principal investigator and scientific coordinator of various national and EU projects (e.g., laceproject.eu, patient-project.eu, LinkedUp-project.eu). He regularly chairs international scientific events and is Associate Editor of IEEE Transactions on Learning Technologies, and Special Issue Editor of the Journal of Computer Assisted Learning (JCAL).

Cloud Services in Collaborative Learning: Applications and Implications

Ding-Chau Wang and Yong-Ming Huang

Abstract Cloud services have been construed as powerful learning tools for students. Different from previous technologies, cloud services serve the function of synchronous collaboration, which is considered fairly helpful for students' collaborative learning. Based on this fact, this chapter is primarily dedicated to explaining the relations between cloud services and collaborative learning. Specifically speaking, this chapter firstly points out the merits of collaborative learning and reveals the difficulties in implementing this approach, and then explains why cloud services can be used to overcome these difficulties and thereby facilitate collaborative learning. This chapter also contains several case studies on cloud service-based collaborative learning. Analyzing the findings of these case studies, we found that facilitating conditions, social influence, and social presence are significant factors behind students' intention to use cloud services in collaborative learning. In sum, this chapter not only gives researchers and practitioners a deeper understanding of the relations between cloud services and collaborative learning, but also promotes the development and application of cloud service in the field of education.

Keywords Cloud services · Collaborative learning · Facilitating conditions
Social influence · Social presence

D.-C. Wang
Department of Information Management, Southern Taiwan University of Science and Technology, Tainan, Taiwan, R.O.C.
e-mail: dcwang@mail.stust.edu.tw

Y.-M. Huang (✉)
Department of Multimedia and Entertainment Science, Southern Taiwan University of Science and Technology, Tainan, Taiwan, R.O.C.
e-mail: ym.huang.tw@gmail.com

J. M. Spector et al. (eds.), *Frontiers of Cyberlearning*, Lecture Notes in Educational Technology, https://doi.org/10.1007/978-981-13-0650-1_11

1 Introduction

Collaborative learning has received considerable scholarly attention (McCarthy, Bligh, Jennings, & Tangney, 2005; Oxford, 1999; Wang & Huang, 2016; Wang, 2009), because it highlights that students should actively gain knowledge through collaboration rather than passively wait for teachers to impart knowledge. Originating from social constructivism, collaborative learning holds that the pursuit of knowledge actually proceeds through interpersonal interaction (Oxford, 1999), because human cognitive development per se is not so much an independent process as a product of social construction (Vygotsky, 1978). On a more specific basis, human beings were born and brought up in social communities where they gradually develop their cognitive faculty by interacting with the other community members. Accordingly, collaborative learning underscores that knowledge should be actively acquired by students rather than passively transferred from teachers (Schunk, 2012). For example, when a task falls to students, they should actively discuss, communicate and exchange their ideas in order to work out a solution instead of passively waiting for teachers to offer answers (Huang, 2015, 2017). It is exactly for this reason that collaborative learning sets great store not so much by the outcome (e.g. task accomplished) as by the process of learning (Oxford, 1999), because such an emphasis enables students to brainstorm ideas and gain knowledge through collaboration.

Despite the abovementioned advantages, it is by no means easy to implement collaborative learning, particularly with traditional technologies that usually do not support synchronous collaboration (Huang, 2015, 2017). Specifically speaking, collaborative learning features collaboration among students (Huang, 2015, 2017) in either synchronous or asynchronous way. The former way is more advantageous than the latter in terms of learning, because it provides students with a real-time learning environment that gives them a feeling of face-to-face interaction (Kang & Shin, 2015). More importantly, such real-time interaction not only kindles students' interest in learning but also facilitates their brainstorming (Kim, 2014), for they can put forward ideas or questions immediately during collaboration and their misunderstanding can be clarified right away (Murphy & Collins, 1998). In other words, students need not to spend time waiting for one another's responses; otherwise the ideas flashing through their mind would vanish in the course of time. However, most traditional technologies such as Microsoft Word do not serve the function of synchronous collaboration. This is because synchronous collaboration entails sophisticated technologies to allow multiple users to edit the same document simultaneously, hence traditional technologies support only asynchronous collaboration, namely one person at a time (Huang, Wang, & Liu, 2015; Wang& Huang, 2016). Applying traditional technologies to collaborative learning thus may be unfavorable for students, because they have to take turns editing the same document, which prevents them from fulfilling synchronous collaboration.

Fortunately, cloud services have made synchronous collaboration possible and collaborative learning easier. Originating from cloud computing, cloud services are Internet-based computing services that the hardware and software of all stripes are installed in a number of large-scale data centers through which services are provided (Huang, Chen, Hwang, & Huang, 2013a; Huang, Wang, Guo, Shih, & Chen, 2013b). For instance, Google Docs is a cloud computing-based office suite service which performs many functions such as word processing, spreadsheet, presentation, drawing, and so forth. One of its features is that its data are stored in the data center and can be shared through the Internet, which makes synchronous collaboration an easy task (Huang et al., 2015; Liu & Huang, 2015b). More specifically, with traditional technologies such as Microsoft Word, a user needs to edit and save a file in his/her own computer, which prevents other users from collaborating in editing that file simultaneously. On the contrary, with cloud services such as Google Docs, the edited file is saved at the data center, which allows the file to be shared through the Internet and other users to edit it simultaneously. Accordingly, the Internet-based cloud services are perfectly suitable for collaboration learning (González-Martínez, Bote-Lorenzo, Gómez-Sánchez, & Cano-Parra, 2015). For example, students using Google Docs to write their collaborative report can discuss their ideas through instant messaging as if they do it face-to-face. They can also communicate their respective ideas synchronously on the shared document. The emergence of cloud services has significantly transformed collaborative learning from an asynchronous process to a synchronous endeavor.

This chapter elaborately collocates and analyzes several case studies in which could services were applied to collaborative learning, thereby giving the readers a deeper understanding of such kind of application and its implications. These studies specifically investigated students' opinions about cloud service-based collaborative learning. These investigations are crucial especially from an educational perspective, because they contribute to the application of cloud services to collaborative learning, and students' view on cloud services can be employed as an indicator for assessing whether the services are successfully integrated into learning activities (Huang, Huang, Huang, & Lin, 2012; Liu & Huang, 2015a). By grasping students' opinions on this regard, we may also develop strategies to promote the application of cloud services to the field of education (Arpaci, 2016; Huang, 2015; Wang & Huang, 2016; Wu, Lan, & Lee, 2013). Besides, the findings of these studies may serve as feedbacks to designers, helping them grasp the user experience and bridging the user-designer gap, thereby improving the services insofar as to satisfy users' needs (Huang, 2016, in press). To sum up, these studies not only advanced our understanding of the application of cloud services to collaborative learning, but also carried some implications that facilitate the promotion of could services in the field of education.

2 Background

2.1 Collaborative Learning

Collaborative learning is distinct from cooperative learning. The former features the interaction and communication among members, while the latter gives prominence to their division of labor (Oxford, 1999). Collaborative learning treats "learning" as a social activity through which knowledge is socially constructed among the community members who exchange ideas, forge consensuses, and advance the body of knowledge shared by the community (Olsen & Kagan, 1992; Oxford, 1999). Cooperative learning regards "learning" as an organized group activity through which knowledge is acquired by the division of labor among the group members who are responsible for their respective assignments with the aim of accomplishing a collective task (Olsen & Kagan, 1992; Oxford, 1999). Both of them are pedagogic strategies that set great store by teamwork. However, the former is a less organized teamwork which emphasizes the acculturation among members, while the latter is a more organized teamwork that accentuates each member's own responsibility (Oxford, 1999; Springer, Stanne, & Donovan, 1999). Let's assume a learning task requiring students to complete it as a team. Those adopting collaborative learning will exchange their ideas based on their specialties and produce a solution to this task as a result. Students adopting cooperative learning will divide the task into several assignments and allocate them to different members who have to fulfill their own assignments as best as they can for the purpose of completing the task. It shows that both strategies lay great stress on teamwork and collective solution. Nonetheless, the most salient difference between collaborative learning and cooperative learning is that the former underlines mutual support among members while the latter highlights their division of labor. In the case when a student is unable to independently finish an assignment, cooperative learning exerts no positive effect on the student, while collaborative learning allows the student to be a team member and learn from more capable colleagues. In general, collaborative learning encourages idea exchange and mutual support, through which students can learn more by internalizing one another's knowledge in the process of collaboratively completing the common learning task.

There have been various tools used or designed for facilitating students' collaborative learning. For example, some researchers applied word processing software such as Microsoft Word in this regard (Noël & Robert, 2004; Sotillo, 2002). The functions of tracking changes and comments offered by Microsoft Word are helpful for students' collaborative writing. The former function enables students to see the changes made by their teammates, and the latter allows students to explain or suggest revisions. Accordingly, the two functions help students achieve collaborative writing on the one hand, and improve their writing efficiency and quality on the other. However, this tool provides only limited support for synchronous collaboration. Students can only check the revisions and explanations made by their teammates in a posterior manner, unless they gather in the same place. With the advancement of Web 2.0 technologies, many researchers noticed Wiki's potential for collaborative learning (Lo, 2009; Su & Beaumont, 2010). Wiki is a web application which enables users to collaborate through the Internet. It not only allows users to add, revise, or delete the content of entries quickly, but also performs the function similar to tracking changes. Therefore, users can compare the variations among different versions, and even return to edit previous versions. In addition to the function of traditional word processing, Wiki further transcends the rigid confines of location. In other words, it enables students to engage in collaborative learning outside the confines of time and space. Lo (2009) adopted instant messaging (IM) and Wiki to facilitate students' collaborative learning. Students can initiate synchronous discussion through IM and collaborate through Wiki. However, Wiki itself is unable to provide an environment of synchronous collaboration for students, even though it allows students to collaborate beyond the temporal and spatial limits.

Some researchers focused on designing their own tools for supporting students' collaborative learning. For example, Chiu, Huang, and Chang (2000) developed a collaborative concept-mapping tool to assist students in constructing a collective conceptual map. Specifically speaking, the tool not only provides students with a chat room (i.e., a synchronous communication), but also allows them to select, move and delete concepts through which they construct or modify the collective conceptual map. It is important to note that the map can be controlled by only one member of the team at a time. The other members can observe the changes made on the map shown on their own web browsers. Students can then discuss their views and establish a collective conceptual map through the Internet. McCarthy et al. (2005) developed a collaborative music composition tool for students to create a collective piece of music. The tool is based on the client-server model which brings students at different locations together into a shared virtual space where they can collaborate in composing the collective piece of music. Accordingly, the tool supports synchronous collaboration in two ways. The first is a chat room in which students can synchronously discuss the issues concerning their task. The second is a graphics-based shared virtual space which is more important than the first, because it serves the function of automatically informing all the members of the changes that any member made in the space by showing messages on their monitors. As a result, this tool enables students to collaborate synchronously in composing music.

In sum, the abovementioned studies have revealed that the implementation of collaborative learning, particularly with traditional technologies, is by no means easy, unless we adopt independently developed tools. However, it is almost impossible for teachers to develop their own tools due to their lack of R&D capability, which has prevented them from making full use of collaborative learning in classes. Fortunately, as cloud technology improves, cloud services of all stripes have gradually facilitated synchronous collaboration. To put it differently, synchronous collaborative learning is no longer confined to specific researchers. Teachers can introduce synchronous collaborative learning to their classes simply by using the cloud service applicable to their teaching contexts. The next section will elaborate on several cloud services that aid the implementation of synchronous collaboration.

2.2 Cloud Services

Cloud services are based on cloud computing, a technology provides many innovative services through a great deal of software and hardware placed large-scale data centers (Huang et al., 2013a; 2013b). Specifically speaking, cloud computing is comprised of three service models, including Infrastructure as a Service (IaaS), Platform as a Service (PaaS), and Software as a Service (SaaS) (Huang, et al. 2013b). IaaS provides hardware infrastructure such as computing resources and storage spaces. It directly leases the infrastructure to software developers and ergo saves their time and energy. More significantly, the service allows the scale of hardware infrastructure to be easily modified to meet the rapidly changing demands from the users. Amazon EC2 (Elastic Cloud Computing) that provides computing resources and Amazon S3 (Simple Storage Service) that offers storage spaces are two stellar examples of IaaS. PaaS provides a platform for software development. It enables software developers to design, program, debug, deploy, and run their pieces of software on the cloud platform. Different from IaaS, PaaS spares the users from additional procedures of hardware setting. Google App Engine and Microsoft Azure are two typical examples that allow the users to develop their own software on the cloud platform without having to deal with the setting of hardware. SaaS provides online software applications of all stripes. It allows the users to run the software directly through their web browsers without the need to install it on their computers. SaaS is distinct from PaaS in the way that the former provides full-fledged software applications only, while the latter serves as a platform for software development. G Suite for Education that provides educational software and Google Docs primarily used for word processing are two most frequently utilized services in this category.

Of all cloud services, collaboration service is the most useful for educational researchers owing to its great potential for materializing collaborative learning (Huang, 2015, 2016, 2017, in press; Huang et al., 2013b, 2015; Liu & Huang, 2015b; Wang & Huang, 2016). On a more specific basis, collaboration service not only offers the users software applications but also facilitates their synchronous collaboration. Google Docs is exactly a service of this kind that not only facilitates word processing but also allows multiple users to edit the same document synchronously. What is more important is that this kind of services is getting more common in terms of their application and mature in terms of their technologies. In the present era of information explosion, along with the ensuing increase of information exchange frequency, individuals are no longer able to process the massive pieces of information alone, and teamwork is a necessary commodity if we want to successfully accomplish our tasks, particularly in the business world. As a result, an increasing number of collaboration services have been developed to support companies in the collaboration among their employees or their partners. Besides, the advancement of cloud computing has essentially enhanced the utility of cloud services in synchronous collaboration. For instance, redundant works would be done if a member has completed his/her assignment yet the other members did not know it in a timely manner. Accordingly, the function of synchronization offered by cloud services may influence the effectiveness of collaboration among users, and such function is improved with the advancement of cloud computing. To sum up, cloud services have become a focus of educational researchers' attention and has been applied to their teaching activities dedicated to facilitating students' collaborative learning.

3 Applications

This section features several practical examples of cloud service-based collaborative learning. Table 1 shows the application contexts of cloud services regarding collaborative learning. Prezi, a cloud-based presentation service, is used for assisting students in collaboratively drafting the content of presentation slides (Huang, 2015). Google Slides, which is also a cloud-based presentation service, helps students collaboratively design the structure of a website (Wang & Huang, 2016). Google Docs, a cloud-based document service, is used by students to translate articles (Liu & Huang, 2015b) and write animation scripts (Huang, 2016) in a collaborative manner.

Huang (2015) applied Prezi to an Internet application course in which the subjects were required to create the content of presentation slides collaboratively. In that course, the subjects were divided into different groups and each group needed to introduce a novel Internet application. The members of each group must firstly agree on their subject matter, followed by collecting and organizing relevant pieces of information, and finally present the results with slides. Students used to discuss and decide their subject matter face-to-face, collect information separately with their own computers, and then send the gathered information to the member in charge of integrating the data into the presentation slides. However, it was not so much collaborative learning as simply the division of labor by assigning each member a specific task such as collecting or organizing information, because traditional technologies such as Microsoft PowerPoint do not support synchronous multi-user editing. In view of this deficiency, Huang (2015) examined the utility of Prezi in helping students edit their presentation slides collaboratively. In this case, the subjects decided their subject matter face-to-face and collected relevant information on their own computers. Then they used Prezi to add the collected data directly on their shared presentation slides. The members of each group could thus immediately see the information added and discuss whether it is appropriate or decide how to use it right away. With the

Table 1 Application contexts

Tool	Type	Activity
Prezi	Presentation service	Collaborative presentation slides making
Google Slides	Presentation service	Collaborative website design
Google Docs	Document service	Collaborative translation
Google Docs	Document service	Collaborative animation script writing

assistance of Prezi, the subjects could therefore edit a shared presentation slides in the way of synchronous collaboration.

Wang and Huang (2016) adopted Google Slides in a website design course to help students design a website collaboratively. Dividing the subjects into several groups, this course required each group to design its own website. Students used to discuss the framework of the website face-to-face, and tended to elect a member responsible for designing the website with computer according to the opinions and ideas the other members offered about the design. The reason why only one member of each group could play the role of a helmsman is that traditional technologies such as Microsoft Visio do not support synchronous multi-user designing. In this sense, this approach is unfavorable for students' collaboration because the members of each group would need to compete for using the same computer when they wanted to express (or materialize) their ideas at the same time. The students having no access to the computer might thus lose their interest in the discussion and opt out the collaboration over the course of time. As a result, Wang and Huang (2016) applied Google Slides to help students achieve collaborative and synchronous design. In this case, the subjects similarly discussed the website design face-to-face, but no sooner did they come up with an idea than they would use their own computers to modify the website framework on their shared slides, which was a perfect embodiment of synchronous collaboration.

Liu and Huang (2015b) and Huang (2016) respectively applied Google Docs to a translation course and an animation course. The former divided the subjects into several groups, and each group was required to translate an article. The latter also divided the subjects into different groups and demanded each group to write an animation script. Both courses entailed discussion and collaboration. Previously, students in these kinds of courses tended to be restricted by the limited functions that traditional technologies perform, which resulted in the situation that only one member can play the role of a helmsman responsible for translating the article or writing the animation script with computer according to the opinions and ideas the other members expressed during the discussion. To solve this problem, Liu and Huang (2015b) and Huang (2016) applied Google Docs to help students translate articles and write animation scripts through synchronous collaboration. Google Docs not only allowed the subjects in both cases to express their opinions or discuss their ideas synchronously, but also enabled them to add their ideas immediately and directly on their shared documents, immersing them in a congenial environment of synchronous collaboration.

In sum, the abovementioned applications clearly demonstrated that the real difference between traditional technologies and cloud services lies in whether they support synchronous multi-user editing. Figure 1 shows such a difference in terms of collaboration. Traditional technologies support only one-user editing and render the other collaborators play assistants to the editor. This approach tends to precipitate the assistants into bystanders because they have no way to use the computer to materialize their ideas, which may consequently reduce their motivation to remain in the collaboration. Being able to support synchronous multi-user editing, cloud services manage to turn each member of a group into an assistant as well as an executor. To

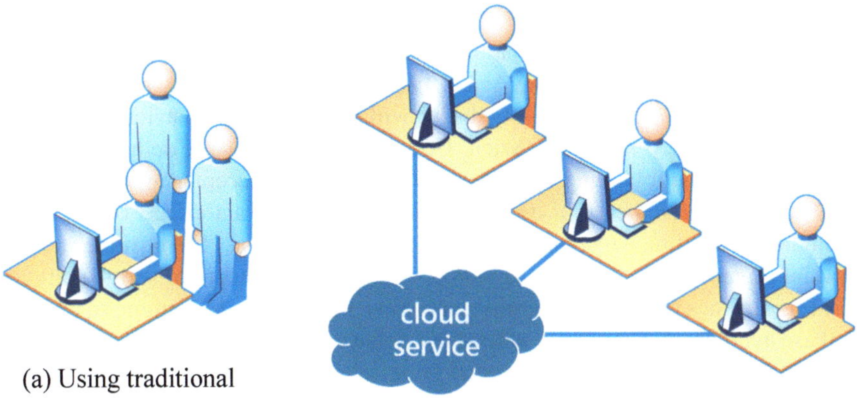

(a) Using traditional technologies

(b) Using cloud services

Fig. 1 The difference between traditional technologies and cloud services in terms of multi-user collaboration

put it another way, the members can substantially contribute to the collaboration in addition to voicing their opinions. Hence, each member has the opportunity to put his/her own ideas into practice, which is why this approach is more effective than the traditional one to facilitate students' collaborative learning.

4 Research Design

This section presents a systematic research design to investigate students' opinions about cloud service-based collaborative learning. This research design relies heavily on the case studies discussed in previous studies (Huang, 2015, 2016; Liu & Huang, 2015b; Wang & Huang, 2016).

4.1 Research Model

The technology acceptance model (TAM) has been widely viewed as an important theoretical basis in the studies of information development (Davis, 1989; Davis, Bagozzi, & Warshaw, 1989), because it can be used to investigate users' opinions on information systems. Developed by Davis et al. (Davis, 1989; Davis et al., 1989), the TAM contains four main constructs, including perceived ease of use, perceived usefulness, attitude toward using, and behavioral intention. Perceived ease of use means that "the degree to which a person believes that using a particular system would be free from effort" (Davis 1989: 320), while perceived usefulness means that "the degree to which a person believes that using a particular system would enhance his or her job performance" (Davis 1989: 320). Attitude toward using refers to "a person's general feeling of favorableness or unfavorableness toward some stimulus object [e.g. a particular system]" (Fishbein & Azjen, 1975: 216), and behavioral intention refers to "a person's subjective probability that he will perform some behavior [e.g. using a particular system]" (Fishbein & Azjen, 1975: 288). Based on these definitions, Davis et al. proposed the following hypotheses to predict users' acceptance of a particular system: (1) perceived ease of use has positive and significant effects on perceived usefulness and attitude toward using; (2) perceived usefulness has positive and significant effects on attitude toward using and behavioral intention; and (3) attitude toward using has positive and significant effects on behavioral intention. In addition to these hypotheses, Davis et al. argued that some external variables (e.g. facilitating conditions, social influence, and social presence) may directly or indirectly affect perceived ease of use, perceived usefulness, and behavioral intention. Accordingly, the TAM was used in previous studies (Huang, 2015, 2016; Liu & Huang, 2015b; Wang & Huang, 2016) to explore the factors behind students' intention to use cloud services.

4.2 Research Tools

The research tools consist mainly of cloud services and questionnaires. The cloud services comprise three collaboration services, namely Prezi, Google Slides, and Google Docs. The first service is used to facilitate students' collaboration in making presentation slides. The second service is offered to support students in collaborative website design. The third service is employed to help students translate and write animation scripts in a collaborative way. The four structured questionnaires were developed based on an extensive review of previous studies (Bhattacherjee, 2001; Davis et al., 1989; Davis, 1989; Kreijns, Kirschner, Jochems, & Van Buuren, 2004; Venkatesh, Morris, Davis, & Davis, 2003). The questionnaires involved nine constructs, including facilitating conditions, perceived ease of use, perceived usefulness, and attitude toward using, social influence, social presence, satisfaction, behavioral intention, and continuance intention. The final questionnaires were distributed to the subjects who were asked to indicate their level of agreement or disagreement with the items using a Likert scale, according to which their opinions on these cloud services can be collected and analyzed.

4.3 Data Collection and Data Analysis

Drawing on the experience gained from previous studies (Huang, 2015, 2016; Liu & Huang, 2015b; Wang & Huang, 2016), the data collection proceeded in three steps. First of all, the subjects took part in the learning activity through which they learned different subjects such as website or animation design. After the end of the learning activity, they were randomly divided into several groups and each group was required to produce a collaborative project with cloud services. Finally, no sooner did the subjects complete their collaborative projects, than they were asked to fill in the questionnaires for the purpose of collecting their opinions on cloud services.

The partial least squares approach (PLS) was adopted to analyze the data collected from the questionnaires. It is a multivariate analysis more suitable than structural equation modeling (SEM) for tackling non-normal distributed samples or a small sample size (Chin & Newsted, 1999). The SmartPLS software (Ringle, Wende, & Becker, 2015) was applied to perform the PLS, just like its usage in previous studies (Huang, 2015, 2016; Liu & Huang, 2015b; Wang & Huang, 2016).

5 Implications

Drawing on the case studies discussed in this chapter (Huang, 2015, 2016; Liu & Huang, 2015b; Wang & Huang, 2016), this section addresses the critical implications for the application of cloud services to collaborative learning. In addition to applying cloud services to help students in collaborative learning, these studies were accompanied by sophisticatedly designed questionnaires to investigate students' opinions on the applied could services and thereby identified the factors behind students' intention or continuance intention to use these cloud services. These case studies carry three major implications explained as follows.

First of all, adequate educational training determines students' acceptance of cloud services. Huang (2015) and Liu and Huang (2015b) revealed that facilitating conditions exert a significant influence on students' intention to use cloud services (shown in Table 2). Facilitating conditions are defined as "the degree to which an individual believes that an organizational and technical infrastructure exists to support use of the system" (Venkatesh et al., 2003: 453). In this chapter, the term refers to that schools or teachers offer supporting resources such as educational training to help students use cloud services. Cloud services support synchronous multi-user editing in a way that traditional technologies do not, and a large number of students have no such experience of using cloud services. Students' intention to use cloud services will definitely be enhanced if their teachers are able to offer them associated educational training such as how to set up the function of synchronous collaboration. To put it differently, teachers have to give students a full understanding of the collaboration functions before asking them to use the services in collaborative learning. Students do not have any intention to use cloud services until they know how to use them and ergo perceive their usefulness. Such a result echoes the findings of Wang and Huang (2016), illustrating that facilitating conditions greatly influenced the perceived usefulness of the given cloud service when the subjects used it to accomplish their task of synchronous collaboration. However, when the cloud service was applied to asynchronous collaboration, facilitating conditions failed to be a decisive factor behind the perceived usefulness of the service. This result suggests that students must be acquainted with the functions offered by cloud services before engaging in collab-

Table 2 The total effects on intention to use cloud services

Cloud services	Dependent variable	Independent variables	Total effects	Study
Prezi	Behavioral intention	Attitude toward using	0.62	Huang (2015)
		Perceived ease of use	0.21	
		Perceived usefulness	0.37	
		Facilitating conditions	0.39	
		Social influence	0.43	
Google Docs	Behavioral intention	Effort expectancy	0.20	Liu and Huang (2015b)
		Performance expectancy	Non-significant	
		Facilitating conditions	0.47	
		Social influence	0.26	

orative learning with them. Having a full understanding of the functions of cloud services, students will perceive its usefulness, especially when they need to set up and activate these functions by themselves.

Secondly, the influence from teachers and classmates is also a key factor behind students' intention to use cloud services. Huang (2015) and Liu and Huang (2015b) revealed that social influence also has a significant effect on students' intention to use cloud services (shown in Table 2). Social influence is defined as "the degree to which an individual perceives that important others believe he or she should use the new system" (Venkatesh et al., 2003: 451). In this chapter, social influence refers to the opinions from important people for students, such as their teachers or classmates, on the cloud service they are using. Huang (2015) and Liu and Huang (2015b) illustrated that students would use cloud services under the influence of important people. Such a finding is quite intriguing, for it confirmed that of Teo (2012) but contradicted that of Teo (2011). A possible explanation could be the difference in the age or experience of the subjects. That is, the subjects in Huang (2015), Liu and Huang (2015b), and Teo (2012) were students aged between 18 and 22, while the subjects in Teo (2011) were teachers with an average age of 35. In other words, younger users tend to have insufficient experience and are hence susceptible to others' influence, while older users usually have extensive experience and therefore dance to nobody's tune. This implies that, to apply a cloud service to teaching, teachers should not only encourage their students in using the service, but also ask those who are more familiar with the service to guide the other students, thereby influencing the latter's intention to use it. Wang and Huang (2016) presented similar findings that social influence plays a key role in students' intention to use cloud services when they engage in synchronous collaboration. However, social influence failed to be a key factor when the cloud service was applied to asynchronous collaboration. A possible explanation is that students are willing to use cloud services to achieve synchronous collaboration due to their classmates' influence. In the case of asynchronous collaboration, only one student is the executor, while the other students are assistants who are predisposed to be free-riders or lurkers because they have no sense of engagement and ergo lack the willingness to continue the collaboration. In the case of synchronous collaboration, contrarily, each student is both an assistant and an executor, which ensures all of them to be involved in the collaborative learning, through which students are required to discuss with their classmates in addition to contributing their respective efforts, which renders them more susceptible to the influence from their classmates and are therefore willing to stay in the collaborative venture.

Finally, social presence is the decisive factor behind students' continuance intention to use cloud services. Huang (2016) suggested that social presence not only plays the most important role in influencing students' continuance intention to use cloud services, but also significantly shapes students' attitude towards this kind of services. Social presence is defined as "the degree to which a person is perceived as a 'real person' in mediated communication" (Gunawardena & Zittle, 1997: 9). In this chapter, the term refers to students' feeling of personally collaborating with their classmates when they use cloud services to accomplish their collaborative tasks. This implies that, when students interact with one another through cloud services, the stronger presence of their classmates they detect, the firmer continuance intention they have to use cloud services. This finding is by no means surprising because previous studies have pointed out that the depth of interaction among students may influence their willingness to learn when they engage in online learning (Muirhead & Juwah, 2004; Muirhead, 2004). On a more specific basis, when students use cloud services to achieve synchronous collaboration, they can see in real-time not only their classmates' cursors but also the modifications they made such as adding a new paragraph. As far as students are concerned, this is a novel and important experience they have never had before. Previously with traditional technologies of word processing, only the one user can modify the working document. Nowadays when students use cloud services to edit the same document, the authorship is shared by all the collaborators, which allows the students to detect the substantial presence of their teammates. In other words, students will be less likely to confront free-riders or lurkers during their synchronous collaboration, because each member is substantially involved in the collaborative venture and can detect the others' presence, which renders themselves more willing to continue using cloud services to engage in their collaboration.

6 Conclusions

We have witnessed an increasing number of cases applying the burgeoning cloud services to collaborative learning. This chapter clarified this point by presenting the readers crucial applications of cloud services in collaborative learning as well as their practical implications. Four contributions can be recognized in this chapter. Firstly, this chapter familiarized the readers with collaborative learning, including its merits, its difference from cooperative learning, and the challenges facing its implementation. Secondly, this chapter helped the readers get a good grasp of cloud services, including their characteristics, types, and the advantages of applying them to collaborative learning. Thirdly, this chapter illustrated concrete examples that serve as a source of reference for instructors to incorporate cloud services into their teaching contexts. Finally, this chapter put forward constructive suggestions for further research, which has proved very useful for not only peer researchers but also educational practitioners.

Notwithstanding this chapter's contribution to the understanding of cloud services' applications to collaborative learning, it does have some limitations. First, cloud services cannot provide students with personal learning environment for the time being, particularly when students use them for collaborative learning. As a matter of fact, personalized learning assistance has undergone long-term development, yet related researches have focused primarily on learning activities at the individual level. For example, a personalized learning system may render different extent of assistance to students according to their respective knowledge about the given subject. To put it another way, such kind of personalized learning systems will offer various extent of assistance based on individual users' prior knowledge as well as their objectives, backgrounds and situations of learning, thereby fulfill the vision of adaptive learning. Accordingly, since personalized learning assistance may be helpful for students' collaborative learning, how to lend students this type of assistance when they engage in cloud service-based collaborative learning will become a major challenge for future research. Besides, as cloud service-based collaborative learning popularizes every day, students' learning portfolios have increased considerably because this type of learning is based on students' interaction. Therefore, another crucial topic for future research will be how to apply big data analytics to students' learning process, so as to effectively help students raise the level of their learning achievements. Finally, the applications of cloud services remain quite limited although they are conductive to collaborative learning. For example, most existing cloud services lack a useful evaluation mechanism for teachers. On a more specific basis, teachers can only complete the performance evaluation of each group rather than each student when using cloud services to facilitate students' collaborative learning, unless they specifically examine each student's learning process and make individual evaluation. As a result, it is also a topic in urgent need for comprehensive study on how cloud services manage to offer teachers useful evaluation mechanisms when they are widely applied to education; otherwise teachers would have no choice but to do taxing job in examining each student's learning process and perform evaluation on an individual basis.

Acknowledgements The authors would like to thank the Ministry of Science and Technology of the Republic of China, Taiwan, for financially supporting this research under Contract No. MOST 106-2511-S-218-006-MY3.

References

Arpaci, I. (2016). Understanding and predicting students' intention to use mobile cloud storage services. *Computers in Human Behavior, 58,* 150–157.

Bhattacherjee, A. (2001). Understanding information systems continuance: An expectation-confirmation model. *MIS Quarterly, 25*(3), 351–370.

Chin, W. W., & Newsted, P. R. (1999). Structural equation modeling analysis with small samples using partial least squares. In R. Hoyle (Ed.), *Statistical strategies for small sample research* (pp. 307–341). California: Sage Publications.

Chiu, C. H., Huang, C. C., & Chang, W. T. (2000). The evaluation and influence of interaction in network supported collaborative concept mapping. *Computers & Education, 34*(1), 17–25.

Davis, F. D. (1989). Perceived usefulness, perceived ease of use and user acceptance of information technology. *MIS Quarterly, 13*(3), 319–340.

Davis, F. D., Bagozzi, R. P., & Warshaw, P. R. (1989). User acceptance of computer technology: A comparison of two theoretical models. *Management Science, 35*(8), 982–1003.

Fishbein, M., & Ajzen, I. (1975). *Belief, attitude, intention, and behavior: An introduction to theory and research.* Reading, MA: Addison-Wesley.

González-Martínez, J. A., Bote-Lorenzo, M. L., Gómez-Sánchez, E., & Cano-Parra, R. (2015). Cloud computing and education: A state-of-the-art survey. *Computers & Education, 80,* 132–151.

Gunawardena, C., & Zittle, F. (1997). Social presence as a predictor of satisfaction within a computer-mediated conferencing environment. *The American Journal of Distance Education, 11*(3), 8–26.

Huang, Y. M. (2015). Exploring the factors that affect the intention to use collaborative technologies: The differing perspectives of sequential/global learners. *Australasian Journal of Educational Technology, 31*(3), 278–292.

Huang, Y. M. (2016). The factors that predispose students to continuously use cloud services: social and technological perspectives. *Computers & Education, 97,* 86–96.

Huang, Y. M. (2017). Exploring the intention to use cloud services in collaboration contexts among Taiwan's private vocational students. *Information Development, 33*(1), 29–42.

Huang, Y. M. (in press). Exploring students' acceptance of team messaging services: the roles of social presence and motivation. *British Journal of Educational Technology*, https://doi.org/10.1111/bjet.12468.

Huang, Y. M., Chen, H. C., Hwang, J. P., & Huang, Y. M. (2013a). Application of cloud technology, social networking sites and sensing technology to e-learning. In R.-H. Huang, Kinshuk, & J. M. Spector (Eds.), *Reshaping learning* (pp. 343–364). Berlin: Springer.

Huang, Y. M., Huang, Y. M., Huang, S. H., & Lin, Y. T. (2012). A ubiquitous English vocabulary learning system: Evidence of active/passive attitudes versus usefulness/ease-of-use. *Computers & Education, 58*(1), 273–282.

Huang, Y. M., Wang, C. S., Guo, J. Z., Shih, H. Y., & Chen, Y. S. (2013b). Advancing collaborative learning with cloud service. *Lecture Notes in Electrical Engineering, 253,* 717–722.

Huang, Y. M., Wang, C. S., & Liu, Y. C. (2015). A study of synchronous vs. asynchronous collaborative design in students' learning motivation. *International Journal of Information and Education Technology, 5*(5), 354–357.

Kang, M., & Shin, W. S. (2015). An empirical investigation of student acceptance of synchronous e-learning in an online university. *Journal of Educational Computing Research, 52*(4), 475–495.

Kim, I. H. (2014). Development of reasoning skills through participation in collaborative synchronous online discussions. *Interactive Learning Environments, 22*(4), 467–484.

Kreijns, K., Kirschner, P. A., Jochems, W., & Van Buuren, H. (2004). Determining sociability, social space, and social presence in (a)synchronous collaborative groups. *CyberPsychology & Behavior, 7*(2), 155–172.

Liu, C. H., & Huang, Y. M. (2015a). An empirical investigation of computer simulation technology acceptance to explore the factors that affect user intention. *Universal Access in the Information Society, 14*(3), 449–457.

Liu, Y. C., & Huang, Y. M. (2015b). Using the UTAUT model to examine the acceptance behavior of synchronous collaboration to support peer translation. *JALT CALL, 11*(1), 77–91.
Lo, H. C. (2009). Utilizing computer-mediated communication tools for problem-based learning. *Educational Technology & Society, 12*(1), 205–213.
McCarthy, C., Bligh, J., Jennings, K., & Tangney, B. (2005). Virtual collaborative learning environments for music: networked drumsteps. *Computers & Education, 44*(2), 173–195.
Muirhead, B. (2004). Encouraging interaction in online classes. *International Journal of Instructional Technology and Distance Learning, 1*(6), 45–50.
Muirhead, B., & Juwah, C. (2004). Interactivity in computer-mediated college and university education: a recent review of the literature. *Educational Technology & Society, 7*(1), 12–20.
Murphy, K. L., & Collins, M. P. (1998). Development of communication conventions in instructional electronic chats. *Journal of Distance Education, 12,* 177–200.
Noël, S., & Robert, J. M. (2004). Empirical study on collaborative writing: what do co-authors do, use, and like? *Computer Supported Cooperative Work, 13*(1), 63–89.
Olsen, R. E. W. B., & Kagan, S. (1992). About cooperative learning. In C. Kessler (Ed.), *Cooperative language learning: a teacher's resource book* (pp. 1–30). Englewood Cliffs, NJ: Prentice Hall.
Oxford, R. L. (1999). Cooperative learning, collaborative learning, and interaction: Three communicative strands in the language classroom. *The Modern Language Journal, 81*(4), 443–456.
Ringle, C. M., Wende, S., & Becker, J. M. (2015). *SmartPLS 3*. Bönningstedt: SmartPLS. Retrieved October from http://www.smartpls.com.
Schunk, D. H. (2012). *Learning theories: An educational perspective* (6th ed.). Boston: Pearson Education Inc.
Sotillo, S. M. (2002). Constructivist and collaborative learning in a wireless environment. *TESOL Journal, 11*(3), 16–20.
Springer, L., Stanne, M. E., & Donovan, S. S. (1999). Effects of small-group learning on undergraduates in science, mathematics, engineering, and technology: A meta-analysis. *Review of Educational Research, 69*(1), 21–51.
Su, F., & Beaumont, C. (2010). Evaluating the use of a wiki for collaborative learning. *Innovations in Education and Teaching International, 47*(4), 417–431.
Teo, T. (2011). Factors influencing teachers' intention to use technology: model development and test. *Computers & Education, 57*(4), 2432–2440.
Teo, T. (2012). Examining the intention to use technology among pre-service teachers: An integration of the technology acceptance model and theory of planned behavior. *Interactive Learning Environments, 20*(1), 3–18.
Venkatesh, V., Morris, M. G., Davis, G. B., & Davis, F. D. (2003). User acceptance of information technology: Toward a unified view. *MIS Quarterly, 27*(3), 425–478.
Vygotsky, L. (1978). *Mind in society: The development of higher psychological processes*. Cambridge, MA: Harvard University Press.
Wang, Q. (2009). Design and evaluation of a collaborative learning environment. *Computers & Education, 53*(4), 1138–1146.
Wang, C. S., & Huang, Y. M. (2016). Acceptance of cloud services in face-to-face computer supported collaborative learning: a comparison between single-user mode and multi-user mode. *Innovations in Education and Teaching International, 53*(6), 637–648.
Wu, W. W., Lan, L. W., & Lee, Y. T. (2013). Factors hindering acceptance of using cloud services in university: a case study. *The Electronic Library, 31*(1), 84–98.

Cloud Computing Environment in Big Data for Education

Dharmpal Singh

Abstract The term 'cloud computing' has rapidly spread in the framework of Big Data and Business Intelligence for better performance of the analysis result. This new word used in big data scenario to overcome those problems that cannot be effectively or efficiently solved using current standard computing resources. This chapter emphasizes the used of cloud computing in Big Data along with necessity of cloud computing in the education. Nowadays cloud computing paradigm has gained popularity over the others due to the number of benefits it offers. The main features of cloud computing to stress its elasticity in the use of computing resources and space in less management effort and flexible costs. In this article, an overview on the topic of Big Data, cloud computing usage of cloud computing education has addressed from the perspective of Cloud Computing and its programming frameworks. In particular, the chapter focuses on cloud data management and big data processing mechanisms, key issues of big data processing, including cloud computing platform, cloud architecture, cloud database and data storage scheme. Several architectures, problems, and technology of the cloud computing in Big data has been identified and a solution has been furnished henceforth. Finally, open issues and challenges, and deeply explore the research directions in the future of cloud computing in education environments.

1 Introduction

The education system is changing from the classroom environment to open environment and students are serious about the study but not the exams. Now a day's situation is changed, in many schools and colleges, the internet facility is available and even teachers' use power-point presentation for teaching that improves easy understanding. At the same time, education institutions are under increasing pressure to deliver more for less, and they need to find ways to offer rich, affordable services and tools. Those educators who can deliver these sophisticated communications environments,

D. Singh (✉)
JIS College of Engineering, Block 'A' Phase III, 741235 Kalyani, Nadia, West Bengal, India
e-mail: dharmpal.singh@jiscollege.ac.in

J. M. Spector et al. (eds.), *Frontiers of Cyberlearning*, Lecture Notes in Educational Technology, https://doi.org/10.1007/978-981-13-0650-1_12

including the desktop applications that employers use today, will be helping their students find better jobs and greater opportunities in the future.

Cloud computing can be proved the boon in this scenario. Using Cloud Computing, anyone can access any file or any document or even videos from any corner of the world. It also helps students to get the basic lessons and creative learning experience to their problems to make the country more educated.

Cloud computing is a network of computing resources located just about anywhere that can be shared. Thus, by implementing cloud computing technology, we can overcome all these short comes and maintain a centralized system where all the authorities can check the education system for each and every aspect and continue monitoring and guide the system. They aren't not only checking the needs of the institutions but also ensure that quality education is provided to every student and also his attendance, class performances etc. can be effectively maintained without worrying for the infrastructure issue. The cloud helps ensure that students, teachers, faculty, parents, and staff have on-demand access to critical information using any device from anywhere. Both public and private institutions can use the cloud to deliver better services, even as they work with fewer resources. The modes of the delivery of cloud service and several big data cloud platform need to compare to take the decision to choose the cloud environment for organization need.

The data collected from the different areas of the world may be larger and huge storage will require to perfume the benefits of cloud computing. Therefore, big data is a methodology to analysis the huge amount of the data based on the recent advanced technologies and architecture of cloud computing which further enhance the education system benefits in the country.

The data collected from the different areas of the world may be the large and huge storage will required to perfume the benefits of cloud computing. Therefore, Big data is a methodology to analysis the huge amount of the data based on the recent advanced technologies and architecture of cloud computing which further enhance the education system benefits in country.

1.1 Introduction of Big Data

Big data (Vesset et al. 2012) is a so large or complex that traditional data processing application software is inadequate to deal with the challenges which includes capture, storage, analysis, data duration, search, sharing, transfer, visualization, querying, updating and information privacy of data set. The term "big data" simple to use for predictive analytics, user behavior analytics, or certain other advanced data analytics methods that extract value from data, and seldom to a particular size of the data set.

Scientists, business executives, practitioners of medicine, advertising and governments alike regularly meet difficulties with large data-sets in areas including Internet search, finance, urban informatics, and business informatics due to limitation of e-Science work, including meteorology, complex physics simulations, biological and environmental research.

The data can be gathered from cheap and numerous information-sensing mobile devices, aerial (remote sensing), software logs, cameras, microphones, radio-frequency identification (RFID) readers and wireless sensor networks and due to this reason, per-capita capacity to store information has roughly doubled every 40 months since the 1980s; as of 2012, every day 2.5 Exabytes (2.5 × 1018) of data are generated. One question for large enterprises is to determine initiatives that affect the storage of the big data.

The work of Big data required massively parallel software running on tens, hundreds or even thousands of servers to produce the desired result which is not possible by relational database management systems and desktop statistics and visualization-packages, processing system The term "big data" varies on the capabilities of the users and their tools, and expanding capabilities make big data a moving target. Most definitions of big data focus on the size of data in storage. Size matters, but there are other important attributes of big data, namely data variety and data velocity. The three Vs of big data (volume, variety, and velocity) constitute a comprehensive definition, and they bust the myth that big data is only about data volume. In addition, each of the three Vs has its own ramifications for analytics. (https://www.sas.com/content/dam/SAS/en_us/doc/research2/big-data-analytics-105425.pdf).

1.1.1 Problem in Big Data

The big data are used to preserve the number of relevant, disparate datasets for analyzed of new patterns, trends, and insights in the dataset. Government agencies, along with cyber expert are also required to understand linking and analysis for preserving privacy rights of the individual. The big data faced the following furnished problem to adhere the aforesaid right of the individual.

Meeting the need for speed
In today's business competitive environment, companies not only find and analyze the relevant data, but they have to also think about how quick find the value in the data. Visualization helps to organizations to the performed analysis and makes decisions much more quickly, but the challenge is going through the complete volumes of data and accessing the level of detail needed at a high speed. The one possible solution is to use cloud computing for powerful parallel processing to crunch large volumes of data extremely quickly.

Understanding the data
It takes a lot of understanding to know the user of the data received from social media, education, organization and business organization for general sense, such as a customer using a particular set of products and understand what it is you're trying to visualize out of the data. Without some sort of context, visualization tools are likely to be of less value to the user.

Addressing data quality
The concept of decision-making purposes will be jeopardized to the consumer if the data is not analyzed accurate or timely. This is a challenge with any data analysis,

but when considering the volumes of information involved in big data projects, it becomes even more pronounced to clean the data in proper format for further used for processing. To address the aforesaid issue, companies need to have data governance or an information management process in place to ensure the data is clean or not. It's always best to have a proactive method to address data quality issues so problems won't arise later.

Displaying meaningful results
Displaying meaningful result in the form of a graph becomes difficult when dealing with extremely large amounts of information or a variety of categories of information. One way to resolve these issues to create clusters of smaller groups of data become and used "binning," for more effectively visualize of data.

Dealing with outliers
The graphical representations of data made possible by visualization can communicate trends and outliers much faster than tables containing numbers and text. Users can easily spot issues that need attention simply by glancing at a chart of outliers which is typically represented about 1–5% of data, but when you're working with massive amounts of data, viewing 1–5% of the data is rather difficult. Thereafter, how is possible to represent those points without getting into plotting issues? Therefore, the possible solutions is to remove the outliers from the data (and therefore from the chart) or to create a separate chart for the outliers.

2 Market and Business Drivers for Big Data Analytics

Big data is everywhere these days. Marketing materials are bursting with references to how products have been enhanced to handle big data. Consultants and analysts are busy writing new articles and creating elegant presentations. But the sad reality is that big data remains one of the most ill-defined terms, we've seen in many a year.

The problem is that data volume is a metric that tells us little about the data characteristics that allow us to understand its sources, its uses in business and the ways we need to handle it in practice. Even the emerging approach of talking about big data in terms of volume, velocity, and variety leaves a lot to be desired in terms of clarity about what big data really are.

The concept of the Big data can be applied to every area of the life for better understanding the data value and use of the resource for futuristic performance.

2.1 Separating the Big Data Reality from Hype

The origins of big data as a concept and phrase can be traced back to the scientific community. Researchers in astronomy, physics, biology, and other fields have long been at the forefront of collecting vast quantities of data from ever more sophisticated sensors. By the early 2000s, they encountered significant problems in processing and storing these volumes and coined the term *big data* probably as a synonym for big headaches. We see here the beginnings of the business driver mentioned above, as science today is founded largely on statistical analysis of collected data. What begins with pure science moves inexorably to engineering and finally emerges in business and, especially, marketing.

The second class, also machine-sourced, consists of computer event logs tracking everything from processor usage and database transactions to click streams and instant message distribution. While machine-generated, data in both of these classes are proxies for events in the real world. In business terms, those that record the results of human actions are of particular interest. For example, measurements of speed, acceleration, and braking forces from an automobile can be used to make inferences about driver behavior and thus insurance risk. In classes three and four, we have social media information directly created by humans, divided into the more highly structured textual information and the less structured multimedia audio, image and video categories. Statistical analysis of such information, gives direct access to people's opinions and reactions, allowing new methods of individual marketing and direct response to emerging opportunities or problems. Much of the current hype around big data comes from the insights into customer behavior that Web giants like Google and eBay and mega-retailers such as Walmart can obtain by analyzing data in these classes especially the textual class, so far. However, in the longer term, machine-generated data, particularly from the metrics and measures class, is likely to be the biggest game-changer simply because of the number of events recorded and communicated.

2.2 Understanding the Business Drivers

By now, you've probably noticed that there are many different options that you can select for your big data analytics program. Options include vendor tool types and tool features, users' techniques and methodologies, and team or organizational structures. The list is long and complex, and it includes a few items you probably haven't considered seriously. Regardless of what project stage you're in with big data analytics, knowing the available options is foundational to making good decisions about approaches to take and software or hardware products to evaluate.

To quantify these and other issues, TDWI presented survey respondents with a long list of options for big data analytics. The list includes options that arrived fairly recently (clouds, Map Reduce, complex event processing), have been around for a few years, but are just now experiencing broad adoption (data visualization, predictive analytics), or have been around for years and are firmly established (statistical analysis, hand-coded SQL). The list is a catalog of available options for big data analytics and responses to survey questions indicated what combinations of analytic functions, platforms, and tool types users are employing today, as well as which they anticipate using in a few years. From this information, we can deduce priorities that can guide users in planning. We can also quantify trends and project future directions for advanced analytics and big data. (https://www.sas.com/content/dam/SAS/en_us/doc/research2/big-data-analytics-105425.pdf).

Business driver also used the following furnished points to understand the data of business driver.

The quest for Business agility, Increased data volumes being captured and stored, increased data volumes pushed into the network, Growing variation in types of data assets for analysis, alternate and unsynchronized methods for facilitating data delivery rising demand for real-time integration of analytical results, Technology Trends Lowering Barriers to Entry.

3 Cloud Computing

Cloud computing used the capability of high-speed processing and high storage computer over the Internet instead of physical computer's hard drive. It goes back to the days of flowcharts and presentations that would represent the gigantic server-farm infrastructure of the Internet as nothing but a puffy, white cumulus cloud, accepting connections and doling out information as it floats.

What cloud computing is not about is your hard drive. When you store data on or run programs from the hard drive, that's called local storage and computing. Everything you need is physically close to you, which means accessing your data is fast and easy, for that one computer, or others on the local network. Working off your hard drive is how the computer industry functioned for decades; some would argue it's still superior to cloud computing, for reasons I'll explain shortly. The cloud is also not about having dedicated network-attached storage (NAS) hardware or server in residence. Storing data on a home or office network does not count as utilizing the cloud as shown in Fig. 1. However, some NAS will let you remotely access things over the Internet, and there's at least one brand from Western Digital named "My Cloud," just to keep things confusing.

For it to be considered "cloud computing," you need to access your data or your programs over the Internet, or at the very least, have that data synced with other information over the Web. In a big business, you may know all there is to know about what's on the other side of the connection; as an individual user, you may never have any idea what kind of massive data processing is happening on the other end. The end result is the same: with an online connection, cloud computing can be done anywhere, anytime.

3.1 Definition of Cloud Computing

Cloud computing have the different types of the definition from the difference expert, but the prominent definition from the reliable source has been furnished as follows:

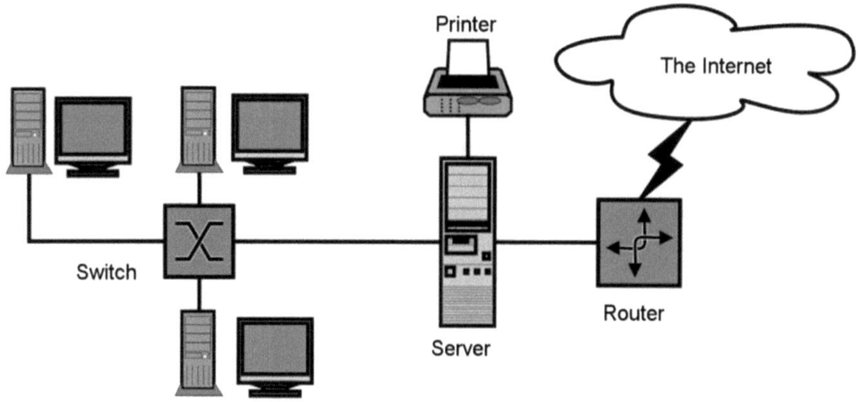

Fig. 1 Connection of Internet with Local Network (http://in.pcmag.com/networking-communications-software/38970/feature/what-is-cloud-computing)

Cloud computing is a type of computing that relies on sharing computing resources rather than having local servers or personal devices to handle applications. Cloud computing is comparable to grid computing, a type of computing where unused processing cycles of all computers in a network are harnesses to solve problems too intensive for any stand-alone machine (http://www.webopedia.com/TERM/C/cloud_computing.html).

Cloud computing is a type of Internet-based computing that provides shared computer processing resources and data to computers and other devices on demand. It is a model for enabling ubiquitous, on-demand access to a shared pool of configurable computing resources (e.g., computer networks, servers, storage, applications and services) (https://en.wikipedia.org/wiki/Cloud_computing).

3.1.1 Introduction of Cloud Computing

Cloud computing is a buzzword that has a different meaning to different people. For some, it's just another way of describing IT (information technology) "outsourcing"; others use it to mean any computing service provided over the Internet or a similar network.

History of Cloud Computing surprisingly began almost 50 years ago. The father of this idea is considered John McCarthy, a professor at MIT University in US, who first in 1961 presented the idea of sharing the same computer technology as being the same as for example sharing electricity. Electrical power needs many households/firms that possess a variety of electrical appliances, but do not possess power plant. One power plant serves many customers and using the electricity example, power plant service provider, distribution network internet and the households/firms' computers (Hoffman & Fodor, 2010).

Since that time, Cloud computing has evolved through a number of phases which include grid and utility computing, application service provision (ASP), and Software as a Service (SaaS). One of the first milestones was the arrival of Salesforce.com in 1999, which pioneered the concept of delivering enterprise applications via a simple website. The next development was Amazon Web Services in 2002, which provided a suite of cloud-based services including storage, computation, and even human intelligence. Another big milestone came in 2009 as Google and others started to offer browser-based enterprise applications, though services such as Google Apps (Schaefer, 2012).

3.1.2 Cloud Computing Characteristics

This cloud model promotes availability and is composed of five essential characteristics, three service models, and four deployment models (Discussed in later section).

On-demand self-service: A consumer can unilaterally obtain computing capabilities, such as server time and network storage, as needed automatically without requiring human interaction with each service provider.

Broad network access: Cloud capabilities are available over a network and can be accessed through standard mechanisms that promote use by (multiple) client platforms [e.g., mobile phones, laptops, and personal digital assistants (PDAs)].

Resource pooling: One of the great strengths of cloud computing is that the provider is able to pool the computing resources, such as storage, processing, memory, network bandwidth, and virtual machines, to serve multiple consumers with different physical and virtual resources dynamically assigned and reassigned according to the consumer demand. The subscriber generally has knowledge of the exact location of the provided resources.

Rapid elasticity: IT capabilities can be rapidly and elastically provisioned, in some cases automatically, according to the scale required. To the consumer, the capabilities available often appear to be unlimited and can be purchased in any quantity at any time.

Measured service: Cloud systems automatically control and optimize resource use by filtering service appropriately by its type. Resource use is monitored, controlled, and reported, providing transparency for both the provider and consumer of the service.

3.2 Role of the Cloud Computing in Education

The benefits of cloud computing are being seen in associations and foundations, regardless of how you look like on it, with pretty much 90% of associations starting now using some kind of cloud-based application.

In the course of the most recent decade, the education business in the country has become crucial. In India, the education space is by a long shot the biggest industry promoted with government spending, up to 30 billion USD and private sector spending to 50 billion USD3. One of the biggest challenges that the government faces in providing education is the lack of infrastructure and if available, then maintenance of that infrastructure and other issues are Procuring and maintaining a wide range of hardware and software require ample, ongoing investment and the skills to support them.

A solution to all this issue can be Cloud computing. It's a set-up of computing resources located just about anywhere that can be shared. Accordingly, by implementing cloud computing innovation, we can defeat all these short comes and keep up a unified framework where every one of the powers can check the education framework from every single angle and proceed with screen and guide the framework. They check the requirements of the institutes as well as guarantee that quality training is given to each student after his participation, class exhibitions and so on can be adequately kept up without stressing for the framework issue.

The cloud guarantees that students, instructors, personal, guardians, and staff have access to basic data utilizing any gadget from anywhere. Both open and private foundations can utilize the cloud to convey better administrations, even as they work with fewer assets.

Why store in the cloud? The followings are the reasons for the implementation of the clouds.

76% of the institutes have reduced the cost of the applications by moving to the cloud.

35% of the institutes have uploaded at least 1 Tb of data to the cloud.

If stats are to be believed 43% of the higher education institutes have opted for the cloud or planning for cloud computing solutions.

Beside the above statistics, following furnished point is the also reasons for the implementation of the cloud.

3.2.1 Diminished Costs

Cloud-based administrations can help institutes decrease costs and quicken the utilization of innovations to meet developing educational needs. Students can utilize office applications without purchasing, install, and stay up with the latest on their PCs. It likewise gives the instructors of Pay per use for a few applications.

3.2.2 Easy Access

Lesson arranges labs, grades, notes, and PowerPoint slides—pretty much anything computerized that you use in training is effectively transferred.

3.2.3 Security

Your information, content, data, pictures anything you store in the cloud normally requires verification (ID and secret word, for instance) so it is not effectively available for anybody.

3.2.4 Share Ability

Cloud computing opens up a universe of new conceivable outcomes for students, particularly the individuals who are not served well by customary training frameworks. With cloud computing, one can reach more and more diverse, students.

Source: http://www.ijircce.com/upload/2014/february/21_Role.pdf.

3.2.5 No Costly Programming Required

One of the greatest focal points of cloud-based, registering is the software-as-an-Service (SaaS) model. Numerous product projects are presently accessible either free or on an ease membership premise, which considerably brings down the expense of key applications for students.

3.2.6 Easy Update

Roll out improvements to a lesson and need to change it back? Don't worry about it. Cloud computing will spare various corrections and variants of a record with the goal that you can sequentially follow back the development of a thing.

In these and different ways, cloud computing is lessening costs, as well as making a situation where all students can have admittance to amazing instruction and assets. Whether you are a chairman, an instructor, a student, or the guardian of a student, now is an incredible time to investigate how cloud-based applications can advantage you, your youngsters, and your school.

See more at: https://www.esds.co.in/blog/importance-of-cloud-computing-in-education-sector/#sthash.x8h26i1X.dpuf, https://www.esds.co.in/blog/importance-of-cloud-computing-in-education-sector/.

3.2.7 Roles and Boundaries

Organizations and humans can assume different types of predefined roles depending on how they relate to and/or interact with a cloud and its hosted IT resources. Each of the upcoming roles participates and carries out responsibilities in relation to cloud-based activity. The following sections define these roles and identify their main interactions.

Cloud computing act as the Cloud Provider, Cloud Consumer, Cloud Service Owner, and Cloud Resource Administrator with Additional Resources but it also has the boundary like Organizational Boundaries and Trust Boundaries. The details of aforesaid topics is available on (http://whatiscloud.com/roles_and_boundaries/index).

3.3 *Cloud Delivery Models*

A cloud delivery model used a specific, pre-packaged combination of IT resources offered by a cloud provider. Following furnished cloud delivery models widely established and formalized in IT industry:

(1) Infrastructure-as-a-Service (IaaS)
(2) Platform-as-a-Service (PaaS)
(3) Software-as-a-Service (SaaS).

These three models are interrelated in how the scope of one can encompass that of another, as explored in the Combining Cloud Delivery Models section later in this chapter.

Cloud computing technology can provide solutions for the above-mentioned problems in education system. Cloud computing enables users to control and access data via the Internet. The main users of a typical higher education cloud include students, Faculty, administrative staff, Examination Branch and Admission Branch as shown in Fig. 2. All the main users of the institution are connected to the cloud. Separate login is provided for all the users for their respective work. Teachers can upload their class Tutorials, assignments, and tests on the cloud server which students will be able to access all the teaching material provided by the teachers via Internet using computers and other electronic devices both at home and college and 24 × 7. The education system will make it possible for teachers to identify problem areas in which students tend to make mistakes, by analyzing students' study records. In doing so, it will also allow teachers to improve teaching materials.

This will not only make it possible for students to use online teaching materials during class but they will also be able to access these materials at home, using them to prepare for and review lessons. Utilization of cloud computing systems will reduce the cost of operation because servers and learning materials are shared with other colleges.

In the traditional deployment model, all Information Technology resources are housed and managed in-house. Many aspects of these services and tools may be migrated to the cloud and consumed directly over the Internet as either fully functional applications (SaaS), development platforms (PaaS) or raw computing resources (IaaS). Fig. 3 shows how the different categories of university users may consume cloud services.

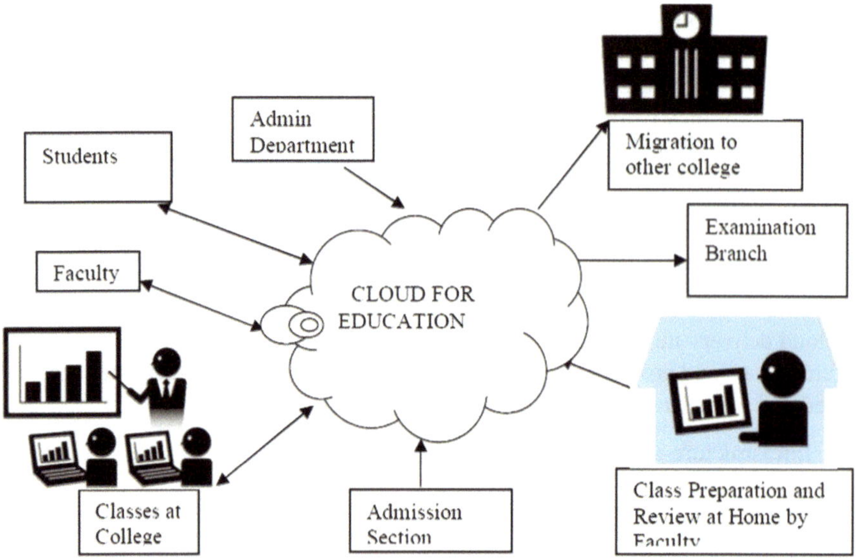

Fig. 2 Services attached to education cloud

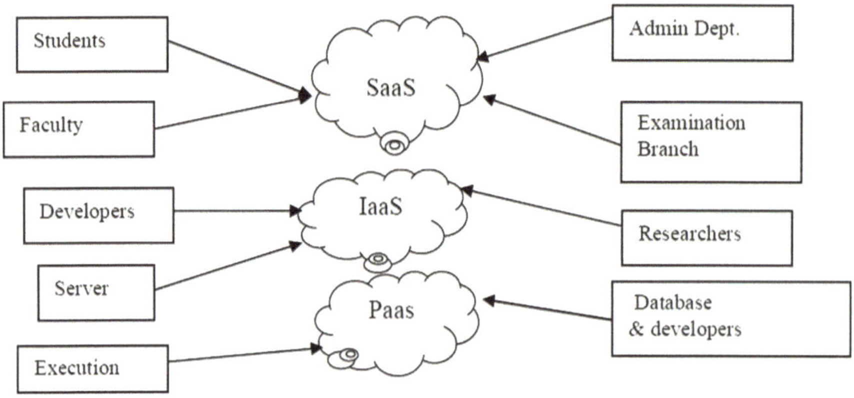

Fig. 3 Users of an education cloud computing system

3.4 Cloud Deployment Models

A cloud deployment model primarily distinguished by ownership, size, and access needs.

Private cloud: Operated solely for an organization, a private cloud may be managed by the organization or a third party and may exist on or off the premises.

Public cloud: The infrastructure is made available to the general public or a large industry group and owned by an organization selling cloud services.

Community cloud: A community cloud is shared by several organizations and supports a specific community that has shared concerns (e.g., mission, security requirements, policy, and compliance considerations). It may be managed by the organizations or a third party and may exist on or off premises. For example, a state government may set-up a community cloud infrastructure for all its separate organizations to pool resources.

Hybrid cloud: This infrastructure combines two or more clouds (private, community, or public) that remain unique entities but are bound together by standardized or proprietary technology that enables data and application portability (eg, cloud bursting, or a dynamic redistribution of resources between clouds to handle the demand surge and balance loads).

As more companies consider the use of clouds, one of their first decisions is whether to use a private or a public cloud or a hybrid. Many companies are favoring private over public cloud. Twenty-six percent companies worldwide are presently investing in public cloud applications, 20% in public cloud, and 38% in private cloud infrastructure.

One of the major advantages of a private cloud is its greater security via dedicated resources under the control of one user. Private clouds also offer the highest level of customization as per the company's needs. However, the downside is increased cost over public cloud options. Its greatest advantage includes scalability and lower costs. However, because it is a form of shared assets, public cloud providers are able to offer minimal customization. In addition, security of the public cloud depends on the provider. Hence, it is advisable that the reliability of any public cloud provider must be evaluated thoroughly.

4 Broadband Networks and Internet Architecture in Cloud Computing

Grouping Cloud computing resources in close proximity with one another, rather than having them geographically dispersed, allows for power sharing, higher efficiency in shared IT resource usage, and improved accessibility for IT personnel. These are the advantages that naturally popularized the data center concept. Modern data centers exist as specialized IT infrastructure used to house centralized IT resources, such as servers, databases, networking and telecommunication devices, and software systems.

4.1 Data Center Technology

Data centers are typically comprised of the following technologies and components:

- Virtualization
- Standardization and Modularity

- Automation
- Remote Operation and Management
- High Availability
- Security-Aware Design, Operation, and Management
- Facilities
- Computing Hardware
- Storage Hardware
- Network Hardware
- Technical and Business Considerations.

4.2 Virtualization Technology

Virtualization is the process of converting a physical IT resource into a virtual IT resource.

Most types of IT resources can be virtualized, including:

- *Servers*—A physical server can be abstracted into a virtual server.
- *Storage*—A physical storage device can be abstracted into a virtual storage device or a virtual disk.
- *Network*—Physical routers and switches can be abstracted into logical network fabrics, such as VLANs.
- *Power*—A physical UPS and power distribution units can be abstracted into what are commonly referred to as virtual UPSs.

This section focuses on the creation and deployment of virtual servers through server virtualization technology.

The first step in creating a new virtual server through virtualization software is the allocation of physical IT resources, followed by the installation of an operating system. Virtual servers use their own guest operating systems, which are independent of the operating system in which they were created.

Both the guest operating system and the application software running on the virtual server are unaware of the virtualization process, meaning these virtualized IT resources are installed and executed as if they were running on a separate physical server. This uniformity of execution that allows programs to run on physical systems as they would on virtual systems is a vital characteristic of virtualization. Guest operating systems typically require seamless usage of software products and applications that do not need to be customized, configured, or patched in order to run in a virtualized environment.

Virtualization software runs on a physical server called a *host* or *physical host*, whose underlying hardware is made accessible by the virtualization software. The virtualization software functionality encompasses system services that are specifically related to virtual machine management and not normally found on standard operating systems. This is why this software is sometimes referred to as a virtual machine manager or a virtual machine monitor (VMM), but most commonly known as a *hypervisor*.

4.3 Web Technology

Due to cloud computing fundamental reliance on internetworking, Web browser universality, and the ease of Web-based service development, Web technology is generally used as both the implementation medium and the management interface for cloud services.

This section introduces the primary Web technologies and their relationship to cloud services.

Artifacts accessible via the World Wide Web are referred to as *resources* or *Web resources*. This is a more generic term than IT resources. IT resource, within the context of cloud computing, represents a physical or virtual IT-related artifact that can be software or hardware-based. A resource on the Web, however, can represent a wide range of artifacts accessible via the World Wide Web. For example, a JPG image file accessed via a Web browser is considered a resource. For examples of common IT resources, see the *IT Resource* section.

Furthermore, the term resource may be used in a broader sense to refer to general types of process able artifacts that may not exist as standalone IT resources. For example, CPUs and RAM memory are types of resources that are grouped into resource pools and can be allocated to actual IT resources.

4.4 Multitenant Technology

The multitenant application design was created to enable multiple users (tenants) to access the same application logic simultaneously. Each tenant has its own view of the application that it uses, administers, and customizes as a dedicated instance of the software while remaining unaware of other tenants that are using the same application.

Multitenant applications ensure that tenants do not have access to data and configuration information that is not their own. Tenants can individually customize features of the application, such as:

- *User Interface*—Tenants can define a specialized "look and feel" for their application interface.
- *Business Process*—Tenants can customize the rules, logic, and workflows of the business processes that are implemented in the application.
- *Data Model*—Tenants can extend the data schema of the application to include, exclude, or rename fields in the application data structures.

- *Access Control*—Tenants can independently control the access rights for users and groups.

Multitenant application architecture is often significantly more complex than that of single-tenant applications. Multitenant applications need to support the sharing of various artifacts by multiple users (including portals, data schemas, middleware, and databases), while maintaining security levels that segregate individual tenant operational environments.

4.5 Service Technology

The field of service technology is a keystone foundation of cloud computing that formed the basis of the "as-a-service" cloud delivery models. Several prominent service technologies that are used to realize and build upon cloud-based environments are described in this section.

Reliant on the use of standardized protocols, *Web-based services* are self-contained units of logic that support interoperable machine-to-machine interaction over a network. These services are generally designed to communicate via non-proprietary technologies in accordance with industry standards and conventions. Because their sole function is to process data between computers, these services expose APIs and do not have user interfaces. Web services and REST services represent two common forms of Web-based services.

4.6 Case Study Example

Cloud Computing in education in the Czech Republic
Introduction

Not much has been written about Cloud Computing in the Czech Republic. Articles speak about its use in education, but not focused on its use in vocational education, thus ignoring the use of cloud storage and online office suites, such as processing and storage of measurement reports online in Czech Republic.

With the process of informatics technology is very important to monitor new trends. A lot of schools are fighting with the lack of money and it is difficult for them to buy new technologies. To buy new hardware and software is an expensive investment that the schools are not able to afford.

One solution how to reduce the investment costs is to maximize the effectiveness of ICT by using Cloud Computing. Then you can ensure superior education without the huge investment to the expensive software applications.

What is the case study about?

This case study is about Cloud computing implementation in Czech Republic in general and about iTřída—e-learning tool for Czech Elementary schools.

Some more detail

Cloud computing allows practical use of ICT and access to information practically anywhere, where you have WI-FI, regardless school, class, state or continent. This is the way how to share, update, and back up data, application, and services. The schools can use their applications, operation systems and are able to meet requirements of student.

Cloud services separation
IAAS—Infrastructure as a service. Is it a supply of hardware or connectivity?
PAAS—Platform as a service. The provider offers support for the whole cycle of creation process and provides web applications. All programs are realized in the web setting.
SAAS—Software as a service. It is a service, which is realized by remote server. It is an access to application, not application as itself. The most common uses are: Google Apps (Gmail, Calender, Docs,.) Zoho Office,Drop Box and so on.

Why yes and why not? The biggest reason why the schools are afraid of Cloud tools is safety and the distrust in external server. On the contrary, the schools that are already using Cloud tools mention exactly the safety of the deposited data as the best advantage of this solution. The next advantage is flexibility and the availability of application and files everywhere.

Czech Republic and Europe: The statisticians found out that in 2014, 1.3 million people in the Czech Republic were using an Internet clearance site for files, this means 15% of the population, men (19%) used the Cloud more than women (11%). This use is definitely the domain of young people. The most part of users are in the age group 20–24 years and 25-29 years, and especially sharing files between students from the point of view of the international comparison the Czech Republic is above the EU average, where there are about 21% of individual users in ages 16–74. Denmark is the first followed by Great Britain, where the Cloud is used by 40% of people.

If schools and teachers want to "be in" the Cloud, they should find more information about this topic. Today many educational institutions offer courses in using Cloud Computing. Some elementary and high schools are using Cloud Computing. All universities are using it.

iTřída—e-learning tool for Czech Elementary schools
The Czech educational system offers Cloud-based classroom e-learning tools designed for teachers, pupils and their parents to direct and indirect teaching. The teacher can use modules from iTřída, students can enter teaching materials, assignments or tests. Students can also write messages, news and information, provoke discussion and brainstorming. The ITřída environment is linked to the portal DUMy.cz where users have access to more than 130,000 educational materials.

I learning, i teaching: Cloud services have proved to be very simple and effective assistant in school management and teaching. It can be argued both from a global perspective on the functioning of schools and in terms of individual teachers who have these services can lead and organize the teaching of their own subjects, or collaborate with colleagues. Currently, however, the Cloud is facing major obstacles due to the unwillingness on the part of users who would need to learn how to use new applications. This is despite the fact that they know that it would help their work and make other activities easier, which has been confirmed by two surveys, in which users have stated that despite the initial negative opinions they are now happy using the Cloud for teaching and learning.
http://www.statistikaamy.cz/2015/01/byt-mlady-a-nemit-cloud-je-out/
http://www.nidv.cz/cs/projekty/projekty-esf/icdv/podrobne-o-projektu.ep/
http://clanky.rvp.cz/clanek/c/g/14721/CLOUD-COMPUTING—NEJEN-TEMA-ALE-I-NASTROJ.html/
https://theses.cz/id/odrhowhttp://www.itveskole.cz/itrida-2.

5 Cloud Computing Usage in Big Data and Education

The rise of cloud computing and cloud data stores has been a precursor and facilitator to the emergence of big data. Cloud computing is the co modification of computing time and data storage by means of standardized technologies.

It has significant advantages over traditional physical deployments. However, cloud platforms come in several forms and sometimes have to be integrated with traditional architectures.

This leads to a dilemma for decision makers in charge of big data projects. How and which cloud computing is the optimal choice for their computing needs, especially if it is a big data project? These projects regularly exhibit unpredictable, bursting, or immense computing power and storage needs. At the same time, business stakeholders expect swift, inexpensive, and dependable products and project outcomes. This article introduces cloud computing and cloud storage, the core cloud architectures, and discusses what to look for and how to get started with cloud computing https://www.qubole.com/resources/article/big-data-cloud-database-computing/#sthash.CVzGDRgJ.dpuf, https://www.qubole.com/resources/article/big-data-cloud-database-computing/).

1. **No more expensive textbooks**.

It's no secret that university-level textbooks are expensive. The cost of textbooks has outpaced the cost of virtually everything else in education, including tuition. As a result, many students are simply refusing to buy them. Cloud-based textbooks can solve this problem as digital content is significantly less expensive than printed content. This levels the playing field so that low-income students can have the same access to quality learning materials as their higher-income counterparts. Currently, higher education institutions across the United States are piloting an e-textbook program involving 50 publishers and close to 30,000 textbooks.

2. **No More Outdated Learning Materials**

In the K-12 arena, the problem of expensive textbooks means that many of the materials students are using are outdated. The average social studies book in elementary and junior high schools are seven to eleven years old, which means that the world maps in these books are no longer correct. With cutbacks in school budgets, many districts, especially in less affluent areas, simply can't afford to replace these outdated resources. Cloud-based materials are easy to update in real time so that students always have access to the most current learning resources.

3. **No Expensive Hardware Required**

Cloud-based applications can be run on Internet browsers, but most are compatible with mobile devices as well. This means that schools and students do not necessarily need to own expensive computers-a $50 smart phone can access these applications just as well as a $500 laptop. Students also don't need to purchase external storage devices as there are plenty of companies, like Google, that offer free cloud-based storage.

4. **No Expensive Software Required**

One of the biggest advantages of cloud-based computing is the software-as-a-service (SaaS) model. Many software programs are now available either free or on a low-cost subscription basis, which substantially lowers the cost of essential applications for students. For example, instead of purchasing a single Microsoft Office student license for $140, students and their families can purchase a cloud-based subscription for five computers and five mobile devices for only $10 per month. Even better, they can use Google Docs for free. Institutions can also save big by using SaaS applications-traditional learning management systems can cost upwards of $50,000 or more, but cloud-based learning management systems like ProProfs' Training Maker are available starting at $60 a month with no per-user fee.

5. **Reaching More, and More Diverse, Students**

The cloud computing opens up a world of new possibilities for students, especially those who are not served well by traditional education systems. For example, until education moved online, the options for adult students who didn't finish high school were very limited-now these students can earn their diploma or GED online. There are many other types of students for whom a traditional school environment simply doesn't work, and these students now have many options for pursuing alternative forms of education.

In these and other ways, cloud computing is not only reducing costs, but also creating an environment where all students can have access to high-quality education and resources. Whether you are an administrator, a teacher, a student, or the parent of a student, now is a great time to explore how cloud-based applications can benefit you, your children, and your school.

5.1 Comparison of Several Big Data Cloud Platform

Cloud Dataproc and Amazon EMR have very similar service models. Each is a scalable platform for filtering and aggregating data, and each is tightly integrated with Apache's big data tools and services, including Apache Hadoop, Apache Spark, Apache Hive, and Apache Pig.

In both services, a user creates a cluster that comprises a number of nodes. The service creates a single master node and a variable number of worker nodes. Amazon EMR further classifies worker nodes into core nodes and task nodes.

Once a cluster has been provisioned, the user submits an application-called a job in Cloud Dataproc and a stepin Amazon EMR-for execution by the cluster. Application dependencies are typically added to the cluster nodes using custom Bash scripts called initialization actions in Cloud DataProc and bootstrap actions in Amazon EMR. Applications typically read data from stable storage, such as Amazon S3, Cloud Storage, or HDFS, and then process the data using an Apache data processing tool or service. After the data has been processed, the resulting data can be further processed or pushed back to stable storage.

Amazon EMR, Cloud Dataproc, and Cloud Dataflow compare (Fig. 4) to each other as follows:

5.2 Limitation of Cloud Computing in Education

Cloud computing; undoubtedly continue to play an increasingly major role for non-profits, charities, and libraries as well as in their IT. But the organization in the dilemma to decide which elements of IT infrastructure should move into the cloud.

Technology is changing constantly and issues related to cloud computing difficulties may be resolved in later on. Therefore, if any, organization not quite ready for the cloud may find a good cloud solution later.

	Hortonworks	Cloudera	HDInsight	Altiscale	TreasureData	Databricks	AmazonEMR	Qubole
Product Summary	100% open Source Hadoop	Open Source Hadoop with proprietary management	Big Data Infrastructure as a Service in the Azure Cloud	Big Data in Dedicated Cloud Service	Cloud-based data warehousing	Standalone Spark Service	Big Data Infrastructure as a Service in the AWS Cloud	Cross-platform Big Data Service with Unified Metadata
Must Migrate Data To Platform	**YES**	**YES**	**NO***	**YES**	**YES**	**NO****	**NO****	**NO*****
Out-of-the-box Data Processing Engines	Installation required	Installation required	MapReduce, Hive, Pig, Spark, HBase, Storm	MapReduce, Hive, Pig, Spark	Hive, Presto	Spark	MapReduce, Hive, Pig, HBase, Cascading, Impala, Spark, Presto	MapReduce, Hive, Pig, HBase, Cascading, Spark, Presto
Deployment Model	On-Premises/I	On-Premises	Cloud	Cloud	Cloud	Cloud	Cloud	Cloud
Data Store	On-Premises	On-Premises	Azure	Alitscale Data Cloud	TreasureData Cloud	AWS	AWS	AWS, GCP, Azure
Setup	Manual	Manua	Automat	Automat	Automat	Automat	**** Automat	Automat
Management	Support and 3rd Party Consulting	Support and 3rd Party Consulting	No Big Data-specific Support	Full Management and Support	Full Management and Support	Full Management and Support	No Big Data-specific Support	Full Management and Support
Economic Structure	Software License and Support, Infrastructure Purchase and Personnel	Software License and Support, Infrastructure Purchase and Personnel	Elastic compute pricing	Fixed Rate	Pay-per-use	Elastic compute pricing	Elastic compute pricing	Elastic compute pricing
Scalability	Fixed Cluster	Fixed Cluster	Manual scaling, elastic, on-demand, no graceful downscaling	Manual scaling, elastic, on-demand	Manual scaling, elastic, on-demand	Manual scaling, elastic, on-demand, no graceful downscaling	Manual scaling, elastic, on-demand	Automatic, elastic, on-demand

Fig. 4 Comparison of vender of big data. See more at: https://www.qubole.com/resources/solution/big-data-vendors-comparison/#sthash.HZHvhUHV.dpuf

5.2.1 Confidentiality

Cloud suppliers have developed numerous protocols to maintain confidentiality and safety of the data for their clients on their servers, with additional safekeeping of information, warranties, and services.

Therefore, it is opined that the cloud's internal security is good, but a particular computer terminal might not have the same safety protocols. Thereafter, a person might be reluctant to enter into confidential information with fears about the safe-keeping of confidential information on foreign-based servers where data protection regulation is not available.

UNESCO is aware of these concerns, and states that several cloud suppliers have contracts that guarantee personal data is only stored in determined countries with safe legal systems.

5.2.2 Lack of Control

Many organization manger their information in one given cloud software using centralizes system. This system also integrated into an intricate network of services that may be shut down overnight without further notice. Therefore, institutions must diversify the number of software suppliers to minimize risks.

5.2.3 Dependence of Network Performance

The institute manages the high volume of information managed through the cloud, depends heavily on the use of broadband or fiber optics of the network. Therefore, it may be complex to work in a scenario where the institute is suddenly offline and its software is overly dependent on an online internet connection.

Cloud have the other problem related to the maintenance cost of the system, low internet and load shading major issue in the rural areas.

Though the cloud computing has the limitation, it is a quickly changing area that will undoubtedly continue to play an increasingly major role for nonprofits, charities, and libraries as well as their IT systems. But the concerned issue is to choose IT infrastructure to move in the cloud and you should way from the cloud.

Finally, because technology is changing constantly, you can't just evaluate cloud solutions once. An issue that may make cloud computing difficult or impossible for you today may be resolved six months from now. And more cloud tools are being developed all the time. So even if you're not quite ready for the cloud right now, you may find a good cloud solution at a later time.

6 Conclusion

This paper presented a description of a systematic flow of survey of the cloud computing environment in education using Big data. We discussed about the applications, advantages and challenges faced by education when used over a cloud computing environment.

In future, the challenges are need to be overcome and make way for the even more efficient use of the cloud computing in education environment. It is very much needed that the computer scholars and IT professionals to cooperate and make a successful and long term use of cloud computing and explores new ideas for the usage of the cloud computing in big data and education environment.

References

Hoffman, D. L., & Fodor, M. (2010). Can you measure the ROI of your social media marketing? *MIT Sloan Management Review, 52*(1), 41–49.

Schaefer, M. W. (2012). *Return on influence* (pp. 5–6). McGraw-Hill.

Vesset, D., Morris, H. D., Little, G., Borovick, L., Feldman, S., Eastwood, M., … Yezhkova, N. (2012). IDC market analysis: Worldwide big data technology and services.

http://www.statistikaamy.cz/2015/01/byt-mlady-a-nemit-cloud-je-out/.

http://www.nidv.cz/cs/projekty/projekty-esf/icdv/podrobne-o-projektu.ep/.

http://clanky.rvp.cz/clanek/c/g/14721/CLOUD-COMPUTING—NEJEN-TEMA-ALE-I-NASTROJ.html/https://theses.cz/id/odrhowhttp://www.itveskole.cz/itrida-2.

Head in the Clouds: Some of the Possible Issues with Cloud Computing in Education

Richard A. W. Tortorella, Kinshuk and Nian-Shing Chen

1 Introduction

Not all that glitters is gold, not all who wander are lost, and equally as true, cloud computing is not the ultimate solution to educational computing problems. Although the possibility of utilizing cloud computing can appear to be a heaven-sent solution for educational applications, a more down to earth review of the possible drawbacks and limitations needs to be conducted.

These limitations range from possibly benign problems such as bandwidth connectivity issues for mobile devices (Dinh, Lee, Niyato, & Wang, 2013), to more deal-breaking aspects of security and privacy (Hashizume, Rosado, Fernández-Medina, & Fernandez, 2013). The safeguarding of sensitive data is of key importance to the educational domain (González-Martínez, Bote-Lorenzo, Gómez-Sánchez, & Cano-Parra, 2015), and must be addressed both in terms of cloud management and secure software as a cloud service provider (Almorsy, Grundy, & Müller, 2016).

Security and access to data residing within cloud computing are of importance to educational usage, as the data can be student records, student accounts, or student learning data. Therefore, understanding security policy concerns and potential gaps in current laws and regulations is vital to the educational domain (Jaeger, Lin, & Grimes, 2008).

R. A. W. Tortorella (✉)
School of Computing, University of Eastern Finland, Joensuu, Finland
e-mail: tortorella@ieee.org

Kinshuk
College of Information, University of North Texas, Denton, TX 76203-5017, USA
e-mail: kinshuk@ieee.org

N.-S. Chen
Department of Information Management, National Sun Yat-Sen University, Kaohsiung, Taiwan
e-mail: nschen@mis.nsysu.edu.tw

J. M. Spector et al. (eds.), *Frontiers of Cyberlearning*, Lecture Notes in Educational Technology, https://doi.org/10.1007/978-981-13-0650-1_13

In a 2015 survey of Tunisian universities (Chihi, Chainbi, and Ghdira), 97% of the respondents indicated that security concerns are important within the cloud. Indeed, according to a 2017 survey (Weins, 2017), security challenges rated as the top challenge for IT professionals adopting cloud infrastructure. However, security does not pose the only potential setback to cloud computing as it appertains to education. Infrastructure limitations and concerns affecting educational cloud computing, specifically in aspects of collaboration and interactivity, can be negatively affected by network performance and latency (González-Martínez et al., 2015).

The goal of this chapter is not to downplay the enormous potential that cloud computing can and will have on education. Rather, the aim is to provide a balanced and holistic perspective on the subject matter of cloud computing within education.

2 *Educational Cloud Computing*: Security Concerns

Implementing any form of new technology usually generates questions about its usage and overall functionality. In the case of the new technology of cloud computing, one of the questions that arise is that of security concerns relating to its use. In recent news, it has been revealed that intelligence agencies are able to employ a myriad of common everyday devices to suit their investigative needs. Although this may not be the case in our daily lives for an educator, we do have to ensure that safeguards are in place when it comes to educational activity and usage of any technology, and this applies to cloud computing. Any type of security concerns one may have are further increased when we are forced to contend with potentially sensitive student data and privacy.

Although the topic of data security would require several times to fully cover, this chapter will focus on the general overview of this topic. There are several main aspects of any type of computing technology in terms of security. One such aspect is that of hardware infrastructure security, or the safety of the physical devices and connections themselves. Another is that of data security, where the ability of the data to remain safe and secure is addressed. A third, and perhaps less obvious security concern, is that of third-party outsourcing and the security issues it exposes.

The first two topics are relatively self-descriptive in their meaning, and are likely familiar to most readers—at least conceptually. The last of the three, third-party outsourcing, revolves around the central question of who exactly is performing the work of hosting and managing the computers that make up the cloud computing infrastructure. For example, it is one thing to hire a firm to do X, but is that firm really the one doing X or outsourcing it to another provider? As an educator, do we know if our computing information is being handled by the firms we think are doing the work? These questions are critical, since these outsourced companies may have diminished the ability to adequately safeguard sensitive educational data. Are third-party resources adequately vetted for security before being employed? Are they under the same legal protection and requirements as the originally contracted firm? Are issues regarding the loss of data governance, the handling of security concerns, security audits and compliance, and general legal risks all disclosed when using third-party resources?

These various issues are addressed in detail in the rest of this chapter.

3 Hardware/Infrastructure Security

Although often overlooked, the issue regarding some of the possible ramifications with security concerning the physical server hardware and infrastructure is a source for potential security concern for any educator considering using cloud computing. Hardware and infrastructure concerns address the safety and integrity of the physical computing devices, and the various means by which the varying systems are interconnected (such as networks).

One of the ever-present online threats to computer security is that of a cyberattack or digital attack. A cyberattack or digital attack can be defined as an action targeting computer infrastructure, networks, or devices in a negative manner in order to steal, remove, or alter information. Cyberattacks come in numerous guises such as malware, man-in-the-middle, cross-site scripting, or denial-of-service, to name a few (Shabut, Lwin, & Hossain, 2016). Yet, out of the many types of cyberattacks present, few have proven more effective than simple social engineering attacks: attacks, which cause victims to provide confidential information or perform actions that would compromise security (Švehla, Sedinić, & Pauk, 2016). A common form of social engineering attack is email phishing attack or impersonation. These are attacks where the perpetrators of the attack attempt to gain sensitive user information (such as ID, passwords, and banking information) by impersonating or disguising themselves as a trustworthy source, typically via email. Under normal circumstances, this type of threat is usually directed toward the end user. However, it is certainly a possibility that this type of attack could be directed toward the hosting services for the cloud computing hardware, and thus potentially placing educational data at risk. As is often the case, when large multinational companies report the loss of people's confidential information—it is as a result of an attack on their online cloud resources. From nude photographs of celebrities to sensitive student data, everything is a potential target.

Another concern about the hardware and infrastructure security, more specifically the hardware level, is the physical security of the devices themselves. The means by which physical access is limited to personnel or the safety in preventing unauthorized computer access is of concern to the administration and safety of cloud computing facilities. This further becomes a problem when systems are being outsourced to third parties, as additional security problems due to the interconnecting of systems increase potential security vulnerabilities.

Security consideration relating to hardware can be something as apparently trivial as outsourcing offsite storage backups and procedures. The question that arises is who will be keeping the backups secure, and how are the outsourced bodies achieving the appropriate level of security. These questions raise the idea of data security to the forefront of the discussion.

4 Data Security

The security, safety, and privacy of student data are always of high importance, especially when students are of the age of minority. This section will address the possible issues pertaining to the usage of cloud computing on the security of sensitive student and educational data.

Although the security of the hardware itself, as mentioned previously, is a concern, in the event of a physical security breach, even if the security of the hardware and infrastructure is compromised, the security of the data itself should provide an additional layer of protection. This securing of the data is handled via encryption, a means by which the data is stored in a manner that requires a special key or passcode to decode into a usable format.

However, encryption may not be a straightforward solution, as given enough access and resources, even encryption could be overcome. In order to break (via brute force) encryption protocols, vast amounts of computational power are required. In fact, this is the largest obstacle facing anyone wishing to break encryption protocols: raw mathematical computational power. In the past, large-scale advanced cryptography (or the use of ciphers to protect information) has been limited to mostly large government entities with access to vast computational resources. However, the advent of cloud computing has provided a suitable alternative in terms of access to free computational power as public cloud services become available (Jaber & Zolkipli, 2013).

Additionally, the decoding of encrypted data can be facilitated if the attacker has direct access to the data itself: a potential problem for cloud computing storage. Having cloud access to storage increases the chances for direct access by unauthorized people. Although this is still a concern for local storage, the central location of cloud storage provides a veritable treasure trove of information.

Generally speaking, cloud computing services, which provide infrastructure as a service (IaaS), are heavily reliant on virtualization technology. Virtualization technology is the ability of larger computer systems to behave as a multitude of smaller independent systems. In the same way as a large housing complex can be subdivided into smaller self-contained living areas, a large computer system can behave as many smaller interconnected systems. The drawback of such technology is that although customers appear to have their own dedicated hardware, they are in reality multi-tenant systems (Mishra, Mathur, Jain, & Rathore, 2013). Multi-tenant systems are systems where multiple users have their systems created virtually (through virtual machines) onto a larger system. Thus, much like apartment tenants who share the aforementioned large housing complex, multi-tenant systems have users coexist in the same server hardware. This situation creates a means by which other tenants of the server hardware are able to share resources. This sharing of resources, although a core idea being cloud computing, also provides a potential beachhead from which to launch security attacks on other systems, and thus possibly compromising sensitive data.

The transmission and storage of data, as well as associated security risks, are also a concern when reviewing the possibility of utilizing cloud computing for educational reasons. Data can be transmitted from the device to the cloud (the details of which fall upon application programming and not cloud computing itself), and from cloud computing servers to other cloud computing servers. Interconnectivity between servers is one of the major advantages and benefits of cloud computing, allowing cloud computing servers to talk among themselves. This interconnectivity can provide worldwide access to courses without perceivable latency. This is accomplished by having data residing on several servers worldwide, providing almost immediate access to course repositories. However, it also poses a risk when reviewing issues of data security: if data is being shared, it can also be intercepted and potentially stolen.

Within the education realm, this transmission of data could be sensitive student data moved between servers, or perhaps grades and coursework. But, is data security a real issue? In a recent study conducted by Maghrabi (2014), 50 university students were asked, and half of the surveyed students were not sure their data was safe within the cloud. However, although a large percentage of the respondents valued their privacy, a staggering 62.5% of respondents who utilized the cloud computer services did not read the terms and conditions provided by the cloud storage provider (Maghrabi, 2014). The consequences of not reading the terms and conditions may mean that the students were not aware of the potential of third-party outsourcing and the risks they agreed upon.

5 Third-Party Outsourcing

Often, third parties are contracted to handle various aspects of cloud computing. This can result in security concerns for educators when these third parties reside in regions with different laws governing data storage, data retention, and data information privacy.

Many countries in the world possess different levels of regulation and enforcement (see Fig. 1).

Traditionally, access control techniques (selective restrictions of data access and resources) assume that the data owner and the various data storage servers are present on the same domain (Bhukya, Pabboju, & Sharma, 2016). However, with cloud computing, this is not always the case, and the question of the data's actual location becomes a very important issue.

Cloud computing service providers may opt to store their data offsite at a location different from the main computational servers. This allows for the usage of less expensive third-party contractors to handle certain aspects of a user's cloud computing system. From a financial standpoint, third-party contractors may be ideal. As third-party contractors often operate on foreign soil, significantly reduced electrical power costs and diminished computer cooling (air conditioning) costs in certain regions allow for a cheaper overall infrastructure cost, enabling third parties to offer services at a reduced cost. Additionally, labor costs on foreign soil may be cheaper, with different labor laws, allowing for less expensive 24/365 support. So, although

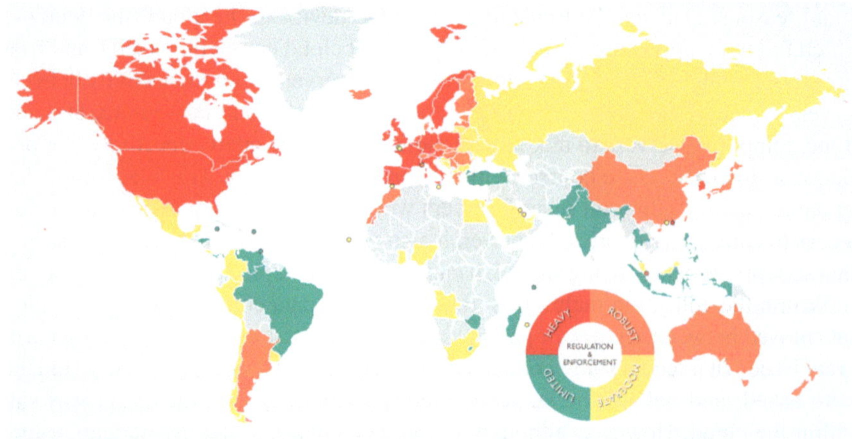

Fig. 1 Data protection laws of the world (DLA-Paper, 2017)

operationally they may be ideal, as an educator concerned with student data safety and privacy the specter of data security is always present.

Although outsourced work or data storage may fall under direct service-level agreements, agreed upon with the initial provider, it can be difficult to ensure that all possible security measures are in place. A few considerations are as follows: Do the various third-party contracts have adequate security audits? Do they ensure that security compliance and general legal risks are all addressed? Typically, the educator and their organization using these services are not privy to any such information. Many cloud computing services do not specify which services are being outsourced or to whom. This can result in decision-makers being unaware that secure student data is being stored in distant countries, under unknown security conditions with a myriad of different laws governing the data's usage.

Outsourcing is not the only concern for educators and decision-makers when it comes to cloud computing within education; a potentially overlooked issue is that of infrastructure concerns. As all communication with cloud computing services require an Internet connection, how will this affect an educational institution's networking resources? The following section will address some of these concerns.

6 *Educational Cloud Computing*: Infrastructure Concerns

Although data security and privacy are likely the most commonly addressed concern involving any student data, when discussing cloud computing technology for educational usage, operational and quality issues of cloud computing as a resource also need to be investigated, as the daily operation and implementation of cloud computing is always dependant on the available infrastructure.

In terms of the cloud computing setup, cloud computing is merely a fancy way of describing what has been around in one form or another since the 1960s: centralized computing. As the name suggests, centralized computing is computing performed at a central location, using terminals to communicate with the main computing system. Although the speed and systems involved with cloud computing are much more advanced than its 1960s counterparts, it is still simply an advanced version of a client/server infrastructure. As such, it is susceptible to many of the infrastructure issues that have plagued client/server infrastructure in the past: connection speed and latency, as well as connection reliability. These problems can have considerable negative impact on different aspects of educational computing, such as student collaboration and interactivity. Therefore, although it is ever changing, the infrastructure on which cloud computing is utilized both from the server and client side needs to be reviewed for potential issues. The three subareas dealing with infrastructure issues of cloud computing, which are important for education, include hardware connectivity, access speed for mobile learning device, and local versus remote resources.

7 Hardware Connectivity

Connectivity to any type of cloud computing service, by definition, requires some type of network connectivity. This type of connectivity can be a wired solution for desktop applications, but for mobile learning systems, it is most often some type of wireless communication.

The problem with wireless communication is that of speed: when wireless and wired networks converge, data bottlenecks may arise (Sanaei, Abolfazli, Gani, & Buyya, 2014). As such, this may result in varying levels of communication issues, and cloud computing resources could become unavailable. This lack of availability is indeed more of a concern for wireless network connected devices than devices employing only wired connection (Dinh et al., 2013). Yet, from an educational standpoint, the result of having a severe lag or intermittent access can be detrimental to student collaboration and real-time interactivity.

Network availability, or the ability to always access resources located across a network, is also a potentially overlooked issue. Without access to a wireless network or mobile data service, it is not possible to utilize the services of cloud computing. Although the percentage of the world's population covered by 3G mobile cellular signals is increasing, and the overall affordability is improving in non-first world areas (Littman-Quinn et al., 2011), connectivity still remains a significant issue. Even taking into consideration planned and unplanned network outages, the infrastructure supporting the communication between devices and the cloud needs to be as reliable and fast as possible. Improved network reliability will permit educators to shift their concern from the reliability of the technology to focus on the education of their students.

8 Access Speed for Mobile Learning Devices

Even if the network connection between a mobile device and cloud servers is present, the speed of the connection can have a great effect on the usability of the device as it connects to the cloud servers. Even though network speeds are ever increasing, the availability of additional bandwidth is being utilized by software developers. Some common examples of this heightened usage are Netflix and YouTube. Both applications will take advantage of every available bit of bandwidth made available to them in order to provide better video quality to the end user. Similarly, with wireless connections, the increase in wireless network speeds permits the usage of more network-intensive applications such as video, streaming, and high bandwidth content. So, although higher network speeds have resulted in better real-time live interactions, the availability of additional bandwidth resources is not always present to allow for additional services such as cloud computing.

Be it streaming recorded video, performing video-based cooperative learning or participating in a Massive Open Online Course (MOOC), the bandwidth requirements of a device are always a concern. Of similar concern is the density of student devices accessing cloud computing resources. Although a solitary device may not create, nor encounter, any bottlenecks in wireless data flow, a classroom full of devices, all connected to a cloud computing resource, may pose data flow problems.

Of concern in a classroom scenario is not only the local classroom's Wi-Fi bandwidth limitation but the overall bandwidth limit of the school itself. This is of concern in a classroom scenario where students potentially all share a common Wi-Fi access point (AP). Depending on the network topology, upward of 50 to 100 students (with a maximum of 255 connections) could share the same AP or wireless connection. All the APs in a given location then usually share a common Internet connection. Therefore, a classroom of students accessing some type of cloud computing-based education resources may easily create more bandwidth demand than what the infrastructure can support. Although this is, of course, dependent on the facilities present in each and every classroom (and certainly cannot be generalized), it is nonetheless something to consider when reviewing educational use of cloud computing.

A final type of issue involving access speed, which may arise even if the entire infrastructure is capable of handling the bandwidth, is a flooding attack. A flooding attack is where attackers send large amount of random data to services, creating a bottleneck (Jensen, Schwenk, Gruschka, & Iacono, 2009), which can result in a direct denial-of-service (DDOS). This is a security concern and risk for the cloud computing service provider but also affects the end user, resulting in a reduction or cessation of resource availability.

9 Remote Versus Local Resources

A question that arises from the possible connectivity issues and access speeds involving cloud computing is that of comparing remote resources with local resources. Remote resources are resources that are not on the user's device itself, whereas local resources are resources that are onboard the device. Each of the two resources types has its own advantages and disadvantages. However, the fundamental question when reviewing the possibility of utilizing cloud computing (remote) resources is simple, whether it is necessary to use cloud computing.

There are countless benefits to using cloud computing, as can be seen in the remainder of this book. However, there are a few simple questions which could be asked to determine if an educator requires cloud computing. Do students need to have their resources located on a remote server? Is the processing power available on the various local devices not sufficient and requires the additional processing power provided by cloud computing? Will students require the centralized system offered by a cloud computing resource?

Certainly, local resources have fewer security issues and are very quick to access and always available. However, they do lack the ability to exist outside the silo created by the local hardware and resources. When resourced are self-contained and isolated, they lack the ability to communicate with other similar resources. Aristotle's phrase holds true when looking at resources, "The whole is greater than the sum of its parts". When resources are interconnected, it allows for novel applications involving user interaction and systems interoperability. So, local resources do not promote many aspects of education found within this book and force a focus shift to be primarily on the individual student rather than the learning community.

Although cloud computing can bring forward amazing opportunities for both teaching and learning, educators must be aware that if any of the above infrastructure concerns are realized, the implications could be counterproductive to the student. This is where the best of intentions for utilizing cloud computing can backfire and negatively affect student learning and general teacher productivity. However, none can be as damaging as the potential implications of having private information fall into the wrong hands.

10 *Educational Cloud Computing*: Licensing/Ownership Concerns

Cloud computing allows for the potential remote data storage, and along with it, the issues emerge related to foreign access to data and information. This is certainly a grave concern for educators concerned with educational data rights and student data privacy. As this involves information that may be potentially confidential/private involving minors (students), additional care must be taken to understand the issues at hand.

When utilizing cloud computing within an educational environment, it is imperative to consider the fact that the data may not be stored on servers owned by one's educational institution. On the contrary, the data stored in the cloud may be kept on one or more servers owned by companies from varying countries. These countries may have significantly different laws regarding the usage and ownership of data on servers. Is the data owned by the individual who placed it there, or is the data property of the cloud hosting service?

Additionally, allowing sensitive student data to be hosted on servers on foreign soil is illegal in some countries. For example, in Canada, public bodies must adhere to the law stating that personal information data cannot be stored or accessed outside of Canada. Members of the European Union (EU) prohibit the transfer of personal information to any foreign soil that has not met the EUs definition of adequacy for privacy protection standard. Similarly, Australia only permits cross-border transfers of information to other groups with similar legal protection of the data as itself ("Where in the World May Personal Information Be Stored?" 2015).

The main reason is that the data on those servers is then subject to foreign laws, from which the source country has no legal protection or involvement. Assuming the above problems do not materialize, what happens to the student data when one closes the contract with the cloud service provider? A commonly overlooked issue is that of archival or backups, and the ultimate destruction of the data (Chen & Zhao, 2012). Once an educational institution is no longer a paying customer of the cloud services, what legal rights does it have to ensure its data is removed from all preexisting sources and offsite backups?

This section indeed raises more questions than providing answers, as the answers differ from country to country. However, it is of vital importance for the educators to consider both foreign and domestic legal implications when using cloud computing for their educational uses.

Although the argument is potentially a worst-case scenario, the potential future implications of leaked student information can be disastrous. Ultimately, the student's safety can be at risk, from potential future implications of leaked grades and scores (in terms of job loss), to the darker aspect of student information dissemination such as photographs and home addresses. Safety should always be a concern.

11 Not All Doom and Gloom

As demonstrated, there are many issues to consider before jumping with both feet into cloud computing. From privacy to security, to overall functionality of the system, it can negatively affect the student's experience, and in a worst-case scenario divulge sensitive student data.

Privacy and security issues are not necessarily new to computing. In some form or another, all the abovementioned points have been raised before under different guises. They all, however, have several things in common: safety, security, and productivity. On the contrary, the purpose is to inform and educate educators of the potential risks associated with cloud computing—in order to help alleviate fears of some and mitigate the effects of others.

Here is a brief set of questions for educators to ponder based on the above findings presented in this chapter:

- Consider the need for cloud computing services—does the task at hand warrant the increased processing capabilities, or storage provided by cloud services?
- Does the interconnectivity of cloud computing provide services beyond that of a standard standalone device?
- Who is providing the cloud computing services? Where are they located? Are they using third-party outsourcing for data processing or data storage?
- Does the cloud computing service provider offer adequate security for the student data?
- What are the legal implications in one's particular country, given the storage of sensitive student data?
- Can the local network infrastructure support the increased strain on connectivity and bandwidth brought on by utilizing cloud computing resources?

While there are indeed various issues to be addressed when reviewing cloud computing both by itself, and more specifically as it is involved within education, the forecast does not call for inclement weather. Ultimately, there is a silver lining of cloud computing within education. Although any new technology is like a double-edged sword, the benefits and potential educational used within the field show that the future is indeed very bright for cloud computing within an educational setting. However, it is the duty of educators and the decision-makers to remain vigilant to the potential problems that may arise, like all technology that has come before, we will use it and grow along with it.

References

Almorsy, M., Grundy, J., & Müller, I. (2016). *An analysis of the cloud computing security problem*. arXiv preprint arXiv:1609.01107.

Bhukya, S., Pabboju, S., & Sharma, K. V. (2016). *Data security in cloud computing and outsourced databases*. Paper presented at the International Conference on Electrical, Electronics, and Optimization Techniques (ICEEOT).

Chen, D., & Zhao, H. (2012). *Data security and privacy protection issues in cloud computing*. Paper presented at the International Conference on Computer Science and Electronics Engineering (ICCSEE), 2012.

Chihi, H., Chainbi, W., & Ghdira, K. (2015). *Cloud computing architecture and migration strategy for universities and higher education*. Paper presented at the 2015 IEEE/ACS 12th International Conference of Computer Systems and Applications (AICCSA).

Dinh, H. T., Lee, C., Niyato, D., & Wang, P. (2013). A survey of mobile cloud computing: architecture, applications, and approaches. *Wireless Communications and Mobile Computing, 13*(18), 1587–1611.

DLA-Paper. (2017). *Compare data protection laws around the world*. Retrieved May 30, 2017, from https://www.dlapiperdataprotection.com/index.html.

González-Martínez, J. A., Bote-Lorenzo, M. L., Gómez-Sánchez, E., & Cano-Parra, R. (2015). Cloud computing and education: A state-of-the-art survey. *Computers & Education, 80,* 132–151.
Hashizume, K., Rosado, D. G., Fernández-Medina, E., & Fernandez, E. B. (2013). An analysis of security issues for cloud computing. *Journal of Internet Services and Applications, 4*(1), 5.
Jaber, A. N., & Zolkipli, M. F. B. (2013). *Use of cryptography in cloud computing.* Paper presented at the 2013 IEEE International Conference on Control System, Computing and Engineering (ICCSCE).
Jaeger, P. T., Lin, J., & Grimes, J. M. (2008). Cloud computing and information policy: Computing in a policy cloud? *Journal of Information Technology & Politics, 5*(3), 269–283.
Jensen, M., Schwenk, J., Gruschka, N., & Iacono, L. L. (2009). *On technical security issues in cloud computing.* Paper presented at the IEEE International Conference on Cloud Computing, CLOUD'09, 2009.
Littman-Quinn, R., Chandra, A., Schwartz, A., Fadlelmola, F. M., Ghose, S., Luberti, A. A., … Steenhoff, A. (2011). *mHealth applications for telemedicine and public health intervention in Botswana.* Paper presented at the IST-Africa Conference Proceedings, 2011.
Maghrabi, L. A. (2014). *The threats of data security over the cloud as perceived by experts and university students.* Paper presented at the 2014 World Symposium on Computer Applications & Research (WSCAR).
Mishra, A., Mathur, R., Jain, S., & Rathore, J. S. (2013). Cloud computing security. *International Journal on Recent and Innovation Trends in Computing and Communication, 1*(1), 36–39.
Sanaei, Z., Abolfazli, S., Gani, A., & Buyya, R. (2014). Heterogeneity in mobile cloud computing: Taxonomy and open challenges. *IEEE Communications Surveys & Tutorials, 16*(1), 369–392.
Shabut, A. M., Lwin, K., & Hossain, M. (2016). *Cyber attacks, countermeasures, and protection schemes—A state of the art survey.* Paper presented at the 2016 10th International Conference on Software, Knowledge, Information Management & Applications (SKIMA).
Švehla, Z. L., Sedinić, I., & Pauk, L. (2016). *Going white hat: Security check by hacking employees using social engineering techniques.* Paper presented at the 2016 39th International Convention on Information and Communication Technology, Electronics and Microelectronics (MIPRO).
Weins, K. (2017, February 15). *Cloud computing trends: 2017 State of the cloud survey* from http://www.rightscale.com/blog/cloud-industry-insights/cloud-computing-trends-2017-state-cloud-survey.
Where in the World May Personal Information Be Stored? (2015). Retrieved from CoreHealth Technologies website: https://corehealth.global/docs/default-source/default-document-library/corehealthwhitepaper-whereintheworldmaypersonalinfobestored.pdf.

MIX
Papier aus verantwortungsvollen Quellen
Paper from responsible sources
FSC® C105338

If you have any concerns about our products,
you can contact us on
ProductSafety@springernature.com

In case Publisher is established outside the EU,
the EU authorized representative is:
Springer Nature Customer Service Center GmbH
Europaplatz 3, 69115 Heidelberg, Germany

Printed by Libri Plureos GmbH
in Hamburg, Germany